Book 5: Portfolio Management and Ethical and Professional Standards

SchweserNotes™ 2022

Level I CFA®

KAPLAN® SCHWESER

SCHWESERNOTES™ 2022 LEVEL I CFA® BOOK 5: PORTFOLIO MANAGEMENT AND ETHICAL AND PROFESSIONAL STANDARDS

Published in 2021 by Kaplan, Inc.

10 9 8 7 6 5 4 3 2

ISBN: 978-1-0788-1606-9

CONTENTS

LEARNING OUTCOME STATEMENTS (LOS)

STUDY SESSION 17

The topical coverage corresponds with the following CFA Institute assigned reading:
48. Portfolio Management: An Overview
The candidate should be able to:
a. describe the portfolio approach to investing. (page 1)
b. describe the steps in the portfolio management process. (page 2)
c. describe types of investors and distinctive characteristics and needs of each. (page 3)
d. describe defined contribution and defined benefit pension plans. (page 4)
e. describe aspects of the asset management industry. (page 6)
f. describe mutual funds and compare them with other pooled investment products. (page 7)

The topical coverage corresponds with the following CFA Institute assigned reading:
49. Portfolio Risk and Return: Part I
The candidate should be able to:
a. calculate and interpret major return measures and describe their appropriate uses. (page 15)
b. compare the money-weighted and time-weighted rates of return and evaluate the performance of portfolios based on these measures. (page 17)
c. describe characteristics of the major asset classes that investors consider in forming portfolios. (page 20)
d. calculate and interpret the mean, variance, and covariance (or correlation) of asset returns based on historical data. (page 22)
e. explain risk aversion and its implications for portfolio selection. (page 24)
f. calculate and interpret portfolio standard deviation. (page 26)
g. describe the effect on a portfolio's risk of investing in assets that are less than perfectly correlated. (page 27)
h. describe and interpret the minimum-variance and efficient frontiers of risky assets and the global minimum-variance portfolio. (page 29)
i. explain the selection of an optimal portfolio, given an investor's utility (or risk aversion) and the capital allocation line. (page 30)

The topical coverage corresponds with the following CFA Institute assigned reading:
50. Portfolio Risk and Return: Part II
The candidate should be able to:
a. describe the implications of combining a risk-free asset with a portfolio of risky assets. (page 41)
b. explain the capital allocation line (CAL) and the capital market line (CML). (page 42)
c. explain systematic and nonsystematic risk, including why an investor should not expect to receive additional return for bearing nonsystematic risk. (page 45)
d. explain return generating models (including the market model) and their uses. (page 47)
e. calculate and interpret beta. (page 49)

f. explain the capital asset pricing model (CAPM), including its assumptions, and the security market line (SML). (page 51)
g. calculate and interpret the expected return of an asset using the CAPM. (page 51)
h. describe and demonstrate applications of the CAPM and the SML. (page 55)
i. calculate and interpret the Sharpe ratio, Treynor ratio, M^2, and Jensen's alpha. (page 57)

STUDY SESSION 18

The topical coverage corresponds with the following CFA Institute assigned reading:

51. Basics of Portfolio Planning and Construction

The candidate should be able to:

a. describe the reasons for a written investment policy statement (IPS). (page 67)
b. describe the major components of an IPS. (page 68)
c. describe risk and return objectives and how they may be developed for a client. (page 68)
d. explain the difference between the willingness and the ability (capacity) to take risk in analyzing an investor's financial risk tolerance. (page 69)
e. describe the investment constraints of liquidity, time horizon, tax concerns, legal and regulatory factors, and unique circumstances and their implications for the choice of portfolio assets. (page 70)
f. explain the specification of asset classes in relation to asset allocation. (page 71)
g. describe the principles of portfolio construction and the role of asset allocation in relation to the IPS. (page 73)
h. describe how environmental, social, and governance (ESG) considerations may be integrated into portfolio planning and construction. (page 74)

The topical coverage corresponds with the following CFA Institute assigned reading:

52. The Behavioral Biases of Individuals

The candidate should be able to:

a. compare and contrast cognitive errors and emotional biases. (page 82)
b. discuss commonly recognized behavioral biases and their implications for financial decision making. (page 82)
c. describe how behavioral biases of investors can lead to market characteristics that may not be explained by traditional finance. (page 91)

The topical coverage corresponds with the following CFA Institute assigned reading:

53. Introduction to Risk Management

The candidate should be able to:

a. define risk management. (page 97)
b. describe features of a risk management framework. (page 98)
c. define risk governance and describe elements of effective risk governance. (page 98)
d. explain how risk tolerance affects risk management. (page 99)
e. describe risk budgeting and its role in risk governance. (page 99)

f. identify financial and non-financial sources of risk and describe how they may interact. (page 99)
g. describe methods for measuring and modifying risk exposures and factors to consider in choosing among the methods. (page 101)

The topical coverage corresponds with the following CFA Institute assigned reading:

54. Technical Analysis

The candidate should be able to:

a. explain principles and assumptions of technical analysis. (page 109)
b. describe potential links between technical analysis and behavioral finance. (page 110)
c. compare principles of technical analysis and fundamental analysis. (page 110)
d. describe and interpret different types of technical analysis charts. (page 111)
e. explain uses of trend, support, and resistance lines. (page 113)
f. explain common chart patterns. (page 114)
g. explain common technical indicators. (page 116)
h. describe principles of intermarket analysis. (page 120)
i. explain technical analysis applications to portfolio management. (page 122)

The topical coverage corresponds with the following CFA Institute assigned reading:

55. Fintech in Investment Management

The candidate should be able to:

a. describe "fintech." (page 127)
b. describe Big Data, artificial intelligence, and machine learning. (page 128)
c. describe fintech applications to investment management. (page 129)
d. describe financial applications of distributed ledger technology. (page 131)

STUDY SESSION 19

The topical coverage corresponds with the following CFA Institute assigned reading:

56. Ethics and Trust in the Investment Profession

The candidate should be able to:

a. explain ethics. (page 137)
b. describe the role of a code of ethics in defining a profession. (page 138)
c. describe professions and how they establish trust. (page 138)
d. describe the need for high ethical standards in investment management. (page 139)
e. explain professionalism in investment management. (page 139)
f. identify challenges to ethical behavior. (page 140)
g. compare and contrast ethical standards with legal standards. (page 140)
h. describe a framework for ethical decision making. (page 141)

The topical coverage corresponds with the following CFA Institute assigned reading:

57. Code of Ethics and Standards of Professional Conduct

The candidate should be able to:

a. describe the structure of the CFA Institute Professional Conduct Program and the process for the enforcement of the Code and Standards. (page 145)

b. identify the six components of the Code of Ethics and the seven Standards of Professional Conduct. (page 146)
c. explain the ethical responsibilities required by the Code and Standards, including the sub-sections of each Standard. (page 147)

The topical coverage corresponds with the following CFA Institute assigned reading:

58. Guidance for Standards I–VII

The candidate should be able to:

a. demonstrate the application of the Code of Ethics and Standards of Professional Conduct to situations involving issues of professional integrity. (page 153)
b. identify conduct that conforms to the Code and Standards and conduct that violates the Code and Standards. (page 153)
c. recommend practices and procedures designed to prevent violations of the Code of Ethics and Standards of Professional Conduct. (page 153)

The topical coverage corresponds with the following CFA Institute assigned reading:

59. Introduction to the Global Investment Performance Standards (GIPS)

The candidate should be able to:

a. explain why the GIPS standards were created, what parties the GIPS standards apply to, and who is benefitted by the standards. (page 183)
b. describe the key concepts of the GIPS standards for firms. (page 184)
c. explain the purpose of composites in performance reporting. (page 185)
d. describe the fundamentals of compliance, including the recommendations of the GIPS Standards with respect to the definition of the firm and the firm's definition of discretion. (page 185)
e. describe the concept of independent verification. (page 185)

The topical coverage corresponds with the following CFA Institute assigned reading:

60. Ethics Application

The candidate should be able to:

a. evaluate practices, policies, and conduct relative to the CFA Institute Code of Ethics and Standards of Professional Conduct. (page 189)
b. explain how the practices, policies, and conduct do or do not violate the CFA Institute Code of Ethics and Standards of Professional Conduct. (page 189)

The following is a review of the Portfolio Management (1) principles designed to address the learning outcome statements set forth by CFA Institute. Cross-Reference to CFA Institute Assigned Reading #48.

READING 48

Portfolio Management: An Overview

Study Session 17

EXAM FOCUS

Here, we introduce the portfolio management process and the investment policy statement. In this topic review, you will learn the investment needs of different types of investors, as well as the different kinds of pooled investments. Later, our topic review of "Basics of Portfolio Planning and Construction" will provide more detail on investment policy statements and investor objectives and constraints.

MODULE 48.1: PORTFOLIO MANAGEMENT PROCESS

Video covering this content is available online.

LOS 48.a: Describe the portfolio approach to investing.

CFA® Program Curriculum, Volume 5, page 406

The **portfolio perspective** refers to evaluating individual investments by their contribution to the risk and return of an investor's portfolio. The alternative to taking a portfolio perspective is to examine the risk and return of individual investments in isolation. An investor who holds all his wealth in a single stock because he believes it to be the best stock available is not taking the portfolio perspective—his portfolio is very risky compared to holding a diversified portfolio of stocks. Modern portfolio theory concludes that the extra risk from holding only a single security is not rewarded with higher expected investment returns. Conversely, diversification allows an investor to reduce portfolio risk without necessarily reducing the portfolio's expected return.

In the early 1950s, the research of Professor Harry Markowitz provided a framework for measuring the risk-reduction benefits of diversification. Using the standard deviation of returns as the measure of investment risk, he investigated how combining risky securities into a portfolio affected the portfolio's risk and expected return. One important conclusion of his model is that unless the returns of the risky assets are perfectly positively correlated, risk is reduced by diversifying across assets.

In the 1960s, professors Treynor, Sharpe, Mossin, and Lintner independently extended this work into what has become known as modern portfolio theory (MPT). MPT results in equilibrium expected returns for securities and portfolios that are a linear function of each security's or portfolio's market risk (the risk that cannot be reduced by diversification).

One measure of the benefits of diversification is the **diversification ratio**. It is calculated as the ratio of the risk of an equally weighted portfolio of *n* securities (measured by its standard deviation of returns) to the risk of a single security selected at random from the *n* securities. If the average standard deviation of returns for the *n* stocks is 25%, and the standard deviation of returns for an equally weighted portfolio of the *n* stocks is 18%, the diversification ratio is 18 / 25 = 0.72. If the standard deviation of returns for an equally weighted portfolio is 25%, there are no diversification benefits and the diversification ratio equals one. A *lower* diversification ratio indicates a *greater* risk-reduction benefit from diversification.

While the diversification ratio provides a quick measure of the potential benefits of diversification, an equal-weighted portfolio is not necessarily the portfolio that provides the greatest reduction in risk. Computer optimization can calculate the portfolio weights that will produce the lowest portfolio risk (standard deviation of returns) for a given group of securities.

Portfolio diversification works best when financial markets are operating normally; diversification provides less reduction of risk during market turmoil, such as the credit contagion of 2008. During periods of financial crisis, correlations tend to increase, which reduces the benefits of diversification.

LOS 48.b: Describe the steps in the portfolio management process.

CFA® Program Curriculum, Volume 5, page 415

There are three major steps in the portfolio management process:

Step 1: The **planning step** begins with an analysis of the investor's risk tolerance, return objectives, time horizon, tax exposure, liquidity needs, income needs, and any unique circumstances or investor preferences.

This analysis results in an **investment policy statement** (IPS) that details the investor's investment objectives and constraints. It should also specify an objective benchmark (such as an index return) against which the success of the portfolio management process will be measured. The IPS should be updated at least every few years and any time the investor's objectives or constraints change significantly.

Step 2: The **execution step** involves an analysis of the risk and return characteristics of various asset classes to determine how funds will be allocated to the various asset types. Often, in what is referred to as a *top-down* analysis, a portfolio manager will examine current economic conditions and forecasts of such macroeconomic variables as GDP growth, inflation, and interest rates, in order to identify the asset classes that are most attractive. The resulting portfolio is typically diversified across such asset classes as cash, fixed-income securities, publicly traded equities, hedge funds, private equity, and real estate, as well as commodities and other real assets.

Once the asset class allocations are determined, portfolio managers may attempt to identify the most attractive securities within the asset class. Security analysts use model valuations for securities to identify those that appear undervalued in what is termed *bottom-up* security analysis.

Step 3: The **feedback step** is the final step. Over time, investor circumstances will change, risk and return characteristics of asset classes will change, and the actual weights of the assets in the portfolio will change with asset prices. The portfolio manager must monitor these changes and **rebalance** the portfolio periodically in response, adjusting the allocations to the various asset classes back to their desired percentages. The manager must also measure portfolio performance and evaluate it relative to the return on the benchmark portfolio identified in the IPS.

LOS 48.c: Describe types of investors and distinctive characteristics and needs of each.

CFA® Program Curriculum, Volume 5, page 419

Individual investors save and invest for a variety of reasons, including purchasing a house or educating their children. In many countries, special accounts allow citizens to invest for retirement and to defer any taxes on investment income and gains until the funds are withdrawn. Defined contribution pension plans are popular vehicles for these investments. Pension plans are described later in this topic review.

Many types of **institutions** have large investment portfolios. An **endowment** is a fund that is dedicated to providing financial support on an ongoing basis for a specific purpose. For example, in the United States, many universities have large endowment funds to support their programs. A **foundation** is a fund established for charitable purposes to support specific types of activities or to fund research related to a particular disease. A typical foundation's investment objective is to fund the activity or research on a continuing basis without decreasing the real (inflation adjusted) value of the portfolio assets. Foundations and endowments typically have long investment horizons, high risk tolerance, and, aside from their planned spending needs, little need for additional liquidity.

The investment objective of a **bank**, simply put, is to earn more on the bank's loans and investments than the bank pays for deposits of various types. Banks seek to keep risk low and need adequate liquidity to meet investor withdrawals as they occur.

Insurance companies invest customer premiums with the objective of funding customer claims as they occur. Life insurance companies have a relatively long-term investment horizon, while property and casualty (P&C) insurers have a shorter investment horizon because claims are expected to arise sooner than for life insurers.

Investment companies manage the pooled funds of many investors. **Mutual funds** manage these pooled funds in particular styles (e.g., index investing, growth investing, bond investing) and restrict their investments to particular subcategories of investments (e.g., large-firm stocks, energy stocks, speculative bonds) or particular regions (emerging market stocks, international bonds, Asian-firm stocks).

Sovereign wealth funds refer to pools of assets owned by a government. For example, the Abu Dhabi Investment Authority, a sovereign wealth fund in the United Arab Emirates funded by Abu Dhabi government surpluses, has approximately USD 700 billion in assets.[1]

Figure 48.1 provides a summary of the risk tolerance, investment horizon, liquidity needs, and income objectives for different types of investors.

Figure 48.1: Characteristics of Different Types of Investors

Investor	Risk Tolerance	Investment Horizon	Liquidity Needs	Income Needs
Individuals	Depends on individual	Depends on individual	Depends on individual	Depends on individual
Banks	Low	Short	High	Pay interest
Endowments	High	Long	Low	Spending level
Insurance	Low	Long—life Short—P&C	High	Low
Mutual funds	Depends on fund	Depends on fund	High	Depends on fund
Defined benefit pensions	High	Long	Low	Depends on age

LOS 48.d: Describe defined contribution and defined benefit pension plans.

CFA® Program Curriculum, Volume 5, page 419

A **defined contribution pension plan** is a retirement plan in which the firm contributes a sum each period to the employee's retirement account. The firm's contribution can be based on any number of factors, including years of service, the employee's age, compensation, profitability, or even a percentage of the employee's contribution. In any event, the firm makes no promise to the employee regarding the future value of the plan assets. The investment decisions are left to the employee, who assumes all of the investment risk.

In a **defined benefit pension plan**, the firm promises to make periodic payments to employees after retirement. The benefit is usually based on the employee's years of service and the employee's compensation at, or near, retirement. For example, an employee might earn a retirement benefit of 2% of her final salary for each year of service. Consequently, an employee with 20 years of service and a final salary of $100,000, would receive $40,000 ($100,000 final salary × 2% × 20 years of service) each year upon retirement until death. Because the employee's future benefit is defined, the employer assumes the investment risk. The employer

1. Source: SWF Institute (https://www.swfinstitute.org/.

makes contributions to a fund established to provide the promised future benefits. Poor investment performance will increase the amount of required employer contributions to the fund.

MODULE QUIZ 48.1

To best evaluate your performance, enter your quiz answers online.

1. Compared to investing in a single security, diversification provides investors a way to:
   A. increase the expected rate of return.
   B. decrease the volatility of returns.
   C. increase the probability of high returns.
2. Which of the following is *least likely* to be considered an appropriate schedule for reviewing and updating an investment policy statement?
   A. At regular intervals (e.g., every year).
   B. When there is a major change in the client's constraints.
   C. Frequently, based on the recent performance of the portfolio.
3. A top-down security analysis begins by:
   A. analyzing a firm's business prospects and quality of management.
   B. identifying the most attractive companies within each industry.
   C. examining economic conditions.
4. Portfolio diversification is *least likely* to protect against losses:
   A. during severe market turmoil.
   B. when markets are operating normally.
   C. when the portfolio securities have low return correlation.
5. Low risk tolerance and high liquidity requirements *best* describe the typical investment needs of:
   A. a defined-benefit pension plan.
   B. a foundation.
   C. an insurance company.
6. A long time horizon and low liquidity requirements *best* describe the investment needs of:
   A. an endowment.
   B. an insurance company.
   C. a bank.
7. In a defined contribution pension plan:
   A. the employee accepts the investment risk.
   B. the plan sponsor promises a predetermined retirement income to participants.
   C. the plan manager attempts to match the fund's assets to its liabilities.
8. In a defined benefit pension plan:
   A. the employee assumes the investment risk.
   B. the employer contributes to the employee's retirement account each period.
   C. the plan sponsor promises a predetermined retirement income to participants.

Video covering this content is available online.

MODULE 48.2: ASSET MANAGEMENT AND POOLED INVESTMENTS

LOS 48.e: Describe aspects of the asset management industry.

CFA® Program Curriculum, Volume 5, page 425

The asset management industry comprises firms that manage investments for clients. Asset management firms include both independent managers and divisions of larger financial services companies. They are referred to as **buy-side firms**, in contrast with **sell-side firms** such as broker-dealers and investment banks.

Full-service asset managers are those that offer a variety of investment styles and asset classes. **Specialist asset managers** may focus on a particular investment style or a particular asset class. A **multi-boutique firm** is a holding company that includes a number of different specialist asset managers.

A key distinction is between firms that use active management and those that use passive management. **Active management** attempts to outperform a chosen benchmark through manager skill, for example by using fundamental or technical analysis. **Passive management** attempts to replicate the performance of a chosen benchmark index. This may include traditional broad market index tracking or a **smart beta** approach that focuses on exposure to a particular market risk factor.

Passive management represents about one-fifth of assets under management. Its share of industry revenue is even smaller because fees for passive management are lower than fees for active management.

Asset management firms may also be classified as traditional or alternative, based on the asset classes they manage. Traditional asset managers focus on equities and fixed-income securities. Alternative asset managers focus on asset classes such as private equity, hedge funds, real estate, or commodities. Profit margins tend to be higher for the alternative asset classes. As a result, many traditional asset managers have been moving into this area, somewhat blurring the distinction between these types of firms.

Some trends in the asset management industry are worth noting:

- The market share for passive management has been growing over time. This is due in part to the lower fees passive managers charge investors, and in part to questions about whether active managers are actually able to add value over time on a risk-adjusted basis, especially in developed markets that are believed to be relatively efficient.
- The amount of data available to asset managers has grown exponentially in recent years. This has encouraged them to invest in information technology and third-party services to process these data, attempting to capitalize on information quickly to make investment decisions.
- **Robo-advisors** are a technology that can offer investors advice and recommendations based on their investment requirements and constraints, using a computer algorithm. These advisors increasingly appeal to younger investors and those with smaller portfolios than have typically been served by asset

management firms. They have also lowered the barriers to entry into the asset management industry for firms such as insurance companies.

PROFESSOR'S NOTE

Robo-advisors and issues related to Big Data are discussed further in our topic review of Fintech in Investment Management.

LOS 48.f: Describe mutual funds and compare them with other pooled investment products.

CFA® Program Curriculum, Volume 5, page 430

Mutual funds are one form of **pooled investments** (i.e., a single portfolio that contains investment funds from multiple investors). Each investor owns shares representing ownership of a portion of the overall portfolio. The total net value of the assets in the fund (pool) divided by the number of such shares issued is referred to as the **net asset value** (NAV) of each share.

With an **open-end fund**, investors can buy newly issued shares at the NAV. Newly invested cash is invested by the mutual fund managers in additional portfolio securities. Investors can **redeem** their shares (sell them back to the fund) at NAV as well. All mutual funds charge a fee for the ongoing management of the portfolio assets, which is expressed as a percentage of the net asset value of the fund. **No-load funds** do not charge additional fees for purchasing shares (up-front fees) or for redeeming shares (redemption fees). **Load funds** charge either up-front fees, redemption fees, or both.

Closed-end funds are professionally managed pools of investor money that do not take new investments into the fund or redeem investor shares. The shares of a closed-end fund trade like equity shares (on exchanges or over-the-counter). As with open-end funds, the portfolio management firm charges ongoing management fees.

Types of Mutual Funds

Money market funds invest in short-term debt securities and provide interest income with very low risk of changes in share value. Fund NAVs are typically set to one currency unit, but there have been instances over recent years in which the NAV of some funds declined when the securities they held dropped dramatically in value. Funds are differentiated by the types of money market securities they purchase and their average maturities.

Bond mutual funds invest in fixed-income securities. They are differentiated by bond maturities, credit ratings, issuers, and types. Examples include government bond funds, tax-exempt bond funds, high-yield (lower rated corporate) bond funds, and global bond funds.

A great variety of **stock mutual funds** are available to investors. **Index funds** are **passively managed**; that is, the portfolio is constructed to match the performance of a particular index, such as the Standard & Poor's 500 Index. **Actively managed** funds refer to funds where the management selects individual securities with the goal of producing returns greater than those of their benchmark indexes. Annual management fees are higher for actively managed funds, and actively managed funds have higher turnover of portfolio securities (the percentage of investments that are changed during the year). This leads to greater tax liabilities compared to passively managed index funds.

Other Forms of Pooled Investments

Exchange-traded funds (ETFs) are similar to closed-end funds in that purchases and sales are made in the market rather than with the fund itself. There are important differences, however. While closed-end funds are often actively managed, ETFs are most often invested to match a particular index (passively managed). With closed-end funds, the market price of shares can differ significantly from their NAV due to imbalances between investor supply and demand for shares at any point in time. Special redemption provisions for ETFs are designed to keep their market prices very close to their NAVs.

ETFs can be sold short, purchased on margin, and traded at intraday prices, whereas open-end funds are typically sold and redeemed only daily, based on the share NAV calculated with closing asset prices. Investors in ETFs must pay brokerage commissions when they trade, and there is a spread between the bid price at which market makers will buy shares and the ask price at which market makers will sell shares. With most ETFs, investors receive any dividend income on portfolio stocks in cash, while open-end funds offer the alternative of reinvesting dividends in additional fund shares. One final difference is that ETFs may produce less capital gains liability compared to open-end index funds. This is because investor sales of ETF shares do not require the fund to sell any securities. If an open-end fund has significant redemptions that cause it to sell appreciated portfolio shares, shareholders incur a capital gains tax liability.

A **separately managed account** is a portfolio that is owned by a single investor and managed according to that investor's needs and preferences. No shares are issued, as the single investor owns the entire account.

Hedge funds are pools of investor funds that are not regulated to the extent that mutual funds are. Hedge funds are limited in the number of investors who can invest in the fund and are often sold only to qualified investors who have a minimum amount of overall portfolio wealth. Minimum investments can be quite high, often between $250,000 and $1 million.

Private equity and **venture capital** funds invest in portfolios of companies, often with the intention to sell them later in public offerings. Managers of funds may take active roles in managing the companies in which they invest.

PROFESSOR'S NOTE

Hedge funds, private equity, and venture capital are addressed in the study session on Alternative Investments.

MODULE QUIZ 48.2

To best evaluate your performance, enter your quiz answers online.

1. Compared to exchange-traded funds (ETFs), open-end mutual funds are typically associated with lower:
   A. brokerage costs.
   B. minimum investment amounts.
   C. management fees.
2. Private equity and venture capital funds:
   A. expect that only a small percentage of investments will pay off.
   B. play an active role in the management of companies.
   C. restructure companies to increase cash flow.
3. Hedge funds *most likely*:
   A. have stricter reporting requirements than a typical investment firm because of their use of leverage and derivatives.
   B. hold equal values of long and short securities.
   C. are not offered for sale to the general public.

KEY CONCEPTS

LOS 48.a

A diversified portfolio produces reduced risk for a given level of expected return, compared to investing in an individual security. Modern portfolio theory concludes that investors that do not take a portfolio perspective bear risk that is not rewarded with greater expected return.

LOS 48.b

The three steps in the portfolio management process are:

1. **Planning:** Determine client needs and circumstances, including the client's return objectives, risk tolerance, constraints, and preferences. Create, and then periodically review and update, an investment policy statement (IPS) that spells out these needs and circumstances.
2. **Execution:** Construct the client portfolio by determining suitable allocations to various asset classes based on the IPS and on expectations about macroeconomic variables such as inflation, interest rates, and GDP growth (top-down analysis). Identify attractively priced securities within an asset class for client portfolios based on valuation estimates from security analysts (bottom-up analysis).
3. **Feedback:** Monitor and rebalance the portfolio to adjust asset class allocations and securities holdings in response to market performance. Measure and report performance relative to the performance benchmark specified in the IPS.

LOS 48.c

Types of investment management clients and their characteristics:

Investor Type	Risk Tolerance	Investment Horizon	Liquidity Needs	Income Needs
Individuals	Depends on individual	Depends on individual	Depends on individual	Depends on individual
Banks	Low	Short	High	Pay interest
Endowments	High	Long	Low	Spending level
Insurance	Low	Long—life Short—P&C	High	Low
Mutual funds	Depends on fund	Depends on fund	High	Depends on fund
Defined benefit pension	High	Long	Low	Depends on age

LOS 48.d

In a defined contribution plan, the employer contributes a certain sum each period to the employee's retirement account. The employer makes no promise regarding the future value of the plan assets; thus, the employee assumes all of the investment risk.

In a defined benefit plan, the employer promises to make periodic payments to the employee after retirement. Because the employee's future benefit is defined, the employer assumes the investment risk.

LOS 48.e

The asset management industry comprises buy-side firms that manage investments for clients. Asset management firms include both independent managers and divisions of larger financial services companies and may be full-service or specialist firms offering investments in traditional or alternative asset classes.

Active management attempts to outperform a chosen benchmark through manager skill. Passive management attempts to replicate the performance of a chosen benchmark index. Most assets under management are actively managed, but the market share for passive management has been increasing.

LOS 48.f

Mutual funds combine funds from many investors into a single portfolio that is invested in a specified class of securities or to match a specific index. Many varieties exist, including money market funds, bond funds, stock funds, and balanced (hybrid) funds. Open-ended shares can be bought or sold at the net asset value. Closed-ended funds have a fixed number of shares that trade at a price determined by the market.

Exchange-traded funds are similar to mutual funds, but investors can buy and sell ETF shares in the same way as shares of stock. Management fees are generally low, though trading ETFs results in brokerage costs.

Separately managed accounts are portfolios managed for individual investors who have substantial assets. In return for an annual fee based on assets, the investor receives personalized investment advice.

Hedge funds are available only to accredited investors and are exempt from most reporting requirements. Many different hedge fund strategies exist. A typical annual fee structure is 20% of excess performance plus 2% of assets under management.

Buyout funds involve taking a company private by buying all available shares, usually funded by issuing debt. The company is then restructured to increase cash flow. Investors typically exit the investment within three to five years.

Venture capital funds are similar to buyout funds, except that the companies purchased are in the start-up phase. Venture capital funds, like buyout funds, also provide advice and expertise to the start-ups.

ANSWER KEY FOR MODULE QUIZZES

Module Quiz 48.1

1. **B** Diversification provides an investor reduced risk. However, the expected return is generally similar or less than that expected from investing in a single risky security. Very high or very low returns become less likely. (LOS 48.a)

2. **C** An IPS should be updated at regular intervals and whenever there is a major change in the client's objectives or constraints. Updating an IPS based on portfolio performance is not recommended. (LOS 48.b)

3. **C** A top-down analysis begins with an analysis of broad economic trends. After an industry that is expected to perform well is chosen, the most attractive companies within that industry are identified. A bottom-up analysis begins with criteria such as firms' business prospects and quality of management. (LOS 48.b)

4. **A** Portfolio diversification has been shown to be relatively ineffective during severe market turmoil. Portfolio diversification is most effective when the securities have low correlation and the markets are operating normally. (LOS 48.a)

5. **C** Insurance companies need to be able to pay claims as they arise, which leads to insurance firms having low risk tolerance and high liquidity needs. Defined benefit pension plans and foundations both typically have high risk tolerance and low liquidity needs. (LOS 48.c)

6. **A** An endowment has a long time horizon and low liquidity needs, as an endowment generally intends to fund its causes perpetually. Both insurance companies and banks require high liquidity. (LOS 48.c)

7. **A** In a defined contribution pension plan, the employee accepts the investment risk. The plan sponsor and manager neither promise a specific level of retirement income to participants nor make investment decisions. These are features of a defined benefit plan. (LOS 48.d)

8. **C** In a defined benefit plan, the employer promises a specific level of benefits to employees when they retire. Thus, the employer bears the investment risk. (LOS 48.d)

Module Quiz 48.2

1. **A** Open-end mutual funds do not have brokerage costs, as the shares are purchased from and redeemed with the fund company. Minimum investment amounts and management fees are typically higher for mutual funds. (LOS 48.f)

2. **B** Private equity and venture capital funds play an active role in the management of companies. Private equity funds other than venture capital expect that the majority of investments will pay off. Venture capital funds do not typically restructure companies. (LOS 48.f)

3. **C** Hedge funds may not be offered for sale to the general public; they can be sold only to qualified investors who meet certain criteria. Hedge funds that hold equal values of long and short securities today make up only a small percentage of funds; many other kinds of hedge funds exist that make no attempt to be market neutral. Hedge funds have reporting requirements that are less strict than those of a typical investment firm. (LOS 48.f)

The following is a review of the Portfolio Management (1) principles designed to address the learning outcome statements set forth by CFA Institute. Cross-Reference to CFA Institute Assigned Reading #49.

READING 49

Portfolio Risk and Return: Part I

Study Session 17

EXAM FOCUS

This topic review makes use of many of the statistical and returns measures we covered in Quantitative Methods. You should understand the historical return and risk rankings of the major asset classes and how the correlation (covariance) of returns between assets and between various asset classes affects the risk of portfolios. Risk aversion describes an investor's preferences related to the tradeoff between risk and return. These preferences, along with the risk and return characteristics of available portfolios, can be used to illustrate the selection of an optimal portfolio for a given investor, that is, the portfolio that maximizes the investor's expected utility.

MODULE 49.1: RETURNS MEASURES

Video covering this content is available online.

LOS 49.a: Calculate and interpret major return measures and describe their appropriate uses.

CFA® Program Curriculum, Volume 5, page 442

Holding period return (HPR) is simply the percentage increase in the value of an investment over a given time period:

$$\text{holding period return} = \frac{\text{end-of-period value}}{\text{beginning-of-period value}} - 1 = \frac{P_t + Div_t}{P_0} - 1$$

$$= \frac{P_t - P_0 + Div_t}{P_0}$$

If a stock is valued at €20 at the beginning of the period, pays €1 in dividends over the period, and at the end of the period is valued at €22, the HPR is:

HPR = (22 + 1) / 20 – 1 = 0.15 = 15%

Average Returns

The **arithmetic mean return** is the simple average of a series of periodic returns. It has the statistical property of being an unbiased estimator of the true mean of the underlying distribution of returns:

$$\text{arithmetic mean return} = \frac{(R_1 + R_2 + R_3 + \ldots + R_n)}{n}$$

The **geometric mean return** is a compound annual rate. When periodic rates of return vary from period to period, the geometric mean return will have a value less than the arithmetic mean return:

$$\text{geometric mean return} = \sqrt[n]{(1+R_1) \times (1+R_2) \times (1+R_3) \times \ldots \times (1+R_n)} - 1$$

For example, for returns R_t over three annual periods, the geometric mean return is calculated as follows:

EXAMPLE: Return measures

An investor purchased $1,000 of a mutual fund's shares. The fund had the following total returns over a 3-year period: +5%, –8%, +12%. Calculate the value at the end of the 3-year period, the holding period return, the mean annual return, and the geometric mean annual return.

Answer:

ending value = (1,000)(1.05)(0.92)(1.12) = $1,081.92

holding period return = (1.05)(0.92)(1.12) – 1 = 0.08192 = 8.192%, which can also be calculated as 1,081.92 / 1,000 – 1 = 8.192%

arithmetic mean return = (5% – 8% + 12%) / 3 = 3%

geometric mean return = $\sqrt[3]{(1.05)(0.92)(1.12)} - 1 = 0.02659 = 2.66\%$, which can also be calculated as geometric mean return = $\sqrt[3]{1 + \text{HPR}} - 1 = \sqrt[3]{1.08192} - 1 = 2.66\%$.

Other Return Measures

Gross return refers to the total return on a security portfolio before deducting fees for the management and administration of the investment account. **Net return** refers to the return after these fees have been deducted. Note that commissions on trades and other costs that are necessary to generate the investment returns are deducted in both gross and net return measures.

Pretax nominal return refers to the return prior to paying taxes. Dividend income, interest income, short-term capital gains, and long-term capital gains may all be taxed at different rates.

After-tax nominal return refers to the return after the tax liability is deducted.

Real return is nominal return adjusted for inflation. Consider an investor who earns a nominal return of 7% over a year when inflation is 2%. The investor's approximate real return is simply 7 – 2 = 5%. The investor's exact real return is slightly lower, 1.07 / 1.02 – 1 = 0.049 = 4.9%.

Real return measures the increase in an investor's purchasing power: how much more goods she can purchase at the end of one year due to the increase in the value of her investments. If she invests $1,000 and earns a nominal return of 7%, she will have $1,070 at the end of the year. If the price of the goods she consumes has gone up 2%, from $1.00 to $1.02, she will be able to consume 1,070 / 1.02 = 1,049 units. She has given up consuming 1,000 units today but instead is able to purchase 1,049 units at the end of one year. Her purchasing power has gone up 4.9%; this is her real return.

A **leveraged return** refers to a return to an investor that is a multiple of the return on the underlying asset. The leveraged return is calculated as the gain or loss on the investment as a percentage of an investor's cash investment. An investment in a derivative security, such as a futures contract, produces a leveraged return because the cash deposited is only a fraction of the value of the assets underlying the futures contract. Leveraged investments in real estate are very common: investors pay for only part of the cost of the property with their own cash, and the rest of the amount is paid for with borrowed money.

PROFESSOR'S NOTE

An example of calculating the leveraged return from buying a stock using margin appears in Equity Investments.

LOS 49.b: Compare the money-weighted and time-weighted rates of return and evaluate the performance of portfolios based on these measures.

CFA® Program Curriculum, Volume 5, page 445

The **money-weighted return** applies the concept of IRR to investment portfolios. The money-weighted rate of return is defined as the internal rate of return on a portfolio, taking into account all cash inflows and outflows. The beginning value of the account is an inflow, as are all deposits into the account. All withdrawals from the account are outflows, as is the ending value.

EXAMPLE: Money-weighted rate of return

Assume an investor buys a share of stock for $100 at t = 0 and at the end of the year (t = 1), she buys an additional share for $120. At the end of Year 2, the investor sells both shares for $130 each. At the end of each year in the holding period, the stock paid a $2.00 per share dividend. What is the money-weighted rate of return?

Step 1: Determine the timing of each cash flow and whether the cash flow is an inflow (+), into the account, or an outflow (–), available from the account.

t = 0:	purchase of first share	=	+$100.00	inflow to account
t = 1:	purchase of second share	=	+$120.00	
	dividend from first share	=	–$2.00	
	Subtotal, t = 1		+$118.00	inflow to account
t = 2:	dividend from two shares	=	–$4.00	
	proceeds from selling shares	=	–$260.00	
	Subtotal, t = 2		–$264.00	outflow from account

Step 2: Net the cash flows for each time period and set the PV of cash inflows equal to the present value of cash outflows.

$$PV_{inflows} = PV_{outflows}$$

$$\$100 + \frac{\$118}{(1 + r)} = \frac{\$264}{(1 + r)^2}$$

Step 3: Solve for *r* to find the money-weighted rate of return. This can be done using trial and error or by using the IRR function on a financial calculator or spreadsheet.

The intuition here is that we deposited $100 into the account at t = 0, then added $118 to the account at t = 1 (which, with the $2 dividend, funded the purchase of one more share at $120), and ended with a total value of $264.

To compute this value with a financial calculator, use these net cash flows and follow the procedure(s) described to calculate the IRR.

Net cash flows: CF_0 = +100; CF_1 = +120 – 2 = +118; CF_2 = –260 + –4 = –264

Calculating money-weighted return with the TI Business Analyst II Plus®

Note that the values for F01, F02, etc., are all equal to one.

Key Strokes	Explanation	Display
[CF] [2nd][CLR WORK]	Clear Cash Flow Registers	CF0 = 0.00000
100 [ENTER]	Initial Cash Outlay	CF0 = +100.00000
[↓] 118 [ENTER]	Period 1 Cash Flow	C01 = +118.00000
[↓] [↓] 264 [+/–] [ENTER]	Period 2 Cash Flow	C02 = –264.00000
[IRR] [CPT]	Calculate IRR	IRR = 13.86122

The money-weighted rate of return for this problem is 13.86%.

PROFESSOR'S NOTE

In the preceding example, we entered the flows into the account as positive and the ending value as a negative (the investor could withdraw this amount from the account). Note that there is no difference in the solution if we enter the cash flows into the account as negative values (out of the investor's pocket) and the ending value as a positive value (into the investor's pocket). As long as payments into the account and payments out of the account (including the ending value) are entered with opposite signs, the computed IRR will be correct.

Time-weighted rate of return measures compound growth. It is the rate at which \$1 compounds over a specified performance horizon. Time-weighting is the process of averaging a set of values over time. The *annual* time-weighted return for an investment may be computed by performing the following steps:

Step 1: Value the portfolio immediately preceding significant additions or withdrawals. Form subperiods over the evaluation period that correspond to the dates of deposits and withdrawals.

Step 2: Compute the holding period return (HPR) of the portfolio for each subperiod.

Step 3: Compute the product of (1 + HPR) for each subperiod to obtain a total return for the entire measurement period [i.e., $(1 + HPR_1) \times (1 + HPR_2) \ldots (1 + HPR_n)] - 1$. If the total investment period is greater than one year, you must take the geometric mean of the measurement period return to find the annual time-weighted rate of return.

EXAMPLE: Time-weighted rate of return

An investor purchases a share of stock at t = 0 for \$100. At the end of the year, t = 1, the investor buys another share of the same stock for \$120. At the end of Year 2, the investor sells both shares for \$130 each. At the end of both years 1 and 2, the stock paid a \$2 per share dividend. What is the annual time-weighted rate of return for this investment? (This is the same investment as the preceding example.)

Answer:

Step 1: Break the evaluation period into two subperiods based on timing of cash flows.

Holding period 1:	Beginning value	= \$100
	Dividends paid	= \$2
	Ending value	= \$120
Holding period 2:	Beginning value	= \$240 (2 shares)
	Dividends paid	= \$4 (\$2 per share)
	Ending value	= \$260 (2 shares)

Reading 49

Step 2: Calculate the HPR for each holding period.

$$HPR_1 = [(\$120 + 2) / \$100] - 1 = 22\%$$

$$HPR_2 = [(\$260 + 4) / \$240] - 1 = 10\%$$

Step 3: Find the compound annual rate that would have produced a total return equal to the return on the account over the 2-year period.

$$(1 + \text{time-weighted rate of return})^2 = (1.22)(1.10)$$

$$\text{time-weighted rate of return} = [(1.22)(1.10)]^{0.5} - 1 = 15.84\%$$

In the investment management industry, *the time-weighted rate of return is the preferred method of performance measurement, because it is not affected by the timing of cash inflows and outflows.*

In the preceding examples, the time-weighted rate of return for the portfolio was 15.84%, while the money-weighted rate of return for the same portfolio was 13.86%. The results are different because the money-weighted rate of return gave a larger weight to the Year 2 HPR, which was 10%, versus the 22% HPR for Year 1. This is because there was more money in the account at the beginning of the second period.

If funds are contributed to an investment portfolio just before a period of relatively poor portfolio performance, the money-weighted rate of return will tend to be lower than the time-weighted rate of return. On the other hand, if funds are contributed to a portfolio at a favorable time (just prior to a period of relatively high returns), the money-weighted rate of return will be higher than the time-weighted rate of return. The use of the time-weighted return removes these distortions and thus provides a better measure of a manager's ability to select investments over the period. If the manager has complete control over money flows into and out of an account, the money-weighted rate of return would be the more appropriate performance measure.

LOS 49.c: Describe characteristics of the major asset classes that investors consider in forming portfolios.

CFA® Program Curriculum, Volume 5, page 459

An examination of the returns and standard deviation of returns for the major investable asset classes supports the idea of a tradeoff between risk and return. Using U.S. data over the period 1926–2017 as an example, shown in Figure 49.1, small-capitalization stocks have had the greatest average returns and greatest risk over the period. T-bills had the lowest average returns and the lowest standard deviation of returns.

Figure 49.1: Risk and Return of Major Asset Classes in the United States (1926–2017)[1]

Assets Class	Average Annual Return (Geometric Mean)	Standard Deviation (Annualized Monthly)
Small-cap stocks	12.1%	31.7%
Large-cap stocks	10.2%	19.8%
Long-term corporate bonds	6.1%	8.3%
Long-term government bonds	5.5%	9.9%
Treasury bills	3.4%	3.1%
Inflation	2.9%	4.0%

Results for other markets around the world are similar: asset classes with the greatest average returns also have the highest standard deviations of returns.

The annual nominal return on U.S. equities has varied greatly from year to year, ranging from losses greater than 40% to gains of more than 50%. We can approximate the real returns over the period by subtracting inflation. The asset class with the least risk, T-bills, had a real return of only approximately 0.5% over the period, while the approximate real return on U.S. large-cap stocks was 7.3%. Because annual inflation fluctuated greatly over the period, real returns have been much more stable than nominal returns.

Evaluating investments using expected return and variance of returns is a simplification because returns do not follow a normal distribution; distributions are negatively skewed, with greater kurtosis (fatter tails) than a normal distribution. The negative skew reflects a tendency towards large downside deviations, while the positive excess kurtosis reflects frequent extreme deviations on both the upside and downside. These non-normal characteristics of skewness ($\neq 0$) and kurtosis ($\neq 3$) should be taken into account when analyzing investments.

Liquidity is an additional characteristic to consider when choosing investments because liquidity can affect the price and, therefore, the expected return of a security. Liquidity can be a major concern in emerging markets and for securities that trade infrequently, such as low-quality corporate bonds.

1. 2018 SBBI Yearbook.

Video covering this content is available online.

MODULE 49.2: COVARIANCE AND CORRELATION

LOS 49.d: Calculate and interpret the mean, variance, and covariance (or correlation) of asset returns based on historical data.

CFA® Program Curriculum, Volume 5, page 476

Variance (Standard Deviation) of Returns for an Individual Security

In finance, the variance and standard deviation of returns are common measures of investment risk. Both of these are measures of the variability of a distribution of returns about its mean or expected value.

We can calculate the population variance, σ^2, when we know the return R_t for each period, the total number periods (T), and the mean or expected value of the population's distribution (μ), as follows:

$$\sigma^2 = \frac{\sum_{t=1}^{T}(R_t - \mu)^2}{T}$$

In the world of finance, we are typically analyzing only a sample of returns data, rather than the entire population. To calculate sample variance, s^2, using a sample of T historical returns and the mean, $\overline{R}$, of the observations, we use the following formula:

$$s^2 = \frac{\sum_{t=1}^{T}(R_t - \overline{R})^2}{T - 1}$$

Covariance and Correlation of Returns for Two Securities

Covariance measures the extent to which two variables move together over time. A positive covariance means that the variables (e.g., rates of return on two stocks) tend to move together. Negative covariance means that the two variables tend to move in opposite directions. A covariance of zero means there is no linear relationship between the two variables. To put it another way, if the covariance of returns between two assets is zero, knowing the return for the next period on one of the assets tells you nothing about the return of the other asset for the period.

Here we will focus on the calculation of the covariance between two assets' returns using **historical data**. The calculation of the sample covariance is based on the following formula:

$$\text{Cov}_{1,2} = \frac{\sum_{t=1}^{n}\left\{\left[R_{t,1} - \overline{R}_1\right]\left[R_{t,2} - \overline{R}_2\right]\right\}}{n-1}$$

where:
$R_{t,1}$ = return on Asset 1 in period *t*
$R_{t,2}$ = return on Asset 2 in period *t*
$\overline{R}_1$ = mean return on Asset 1
$\overline{R}_2$ = mean return on Asset 2
n = number of periods

The magnitude of the covariance depends on the magnitude of the individual stocks' standard deviations and the relationship between their co-movements. Covariance is an absolute measure and is measured in return units squared.

The covariance of the returns of two securities can be standardized by dividing by the product of the standard deviations of the two securities. This standardized measure of co-movement is called **correlation** and is computed as:

$$\rho_{1,2} = \frac{\text{Cov}_{1,2}}{\sigma_1 \sigma_2}$$

The relation can also be written as:

$$\text{Cov}_{1,2} = \rho_{1,2}\sigma_1\sigma_2$$

The term $\rho_{1,2}$ is called the *correlation coefficient* between the returns of securities 1 and 2. The correlation coefficient has no units. It is a pure measure of the co-movement of the two stocks' returns and is bounded by –1 and +1.

How should you interpret the correlation coefficient?

- A correlation coefficient of +1 means that deviations from the mean or expected return are always proportional in the same direction. That is, they are perfectly positively correlated.
- A correlation coefficient of –1 means that deviations from the mean or expected return are always proportional in opposite directions. That is, they are perfectly negatively correlated.
- A correlation coefficient of zero means that there is no linear relationship between the two stocks' returns. They are uncorrelated. One way to interpret a correlation (or covariance) of zero is that, in any period, knowing the actual value of one variable tells you nothing about the value of the other.

EXAMPLE: Calculating mean return, returns variance, returns covariance, and correlation

Given three years of percentage returns for assets A and B in the following table, calculate the mean return and sample standard deviation for each asset, the sample covariance, and the correlation of returns.

Year	Asset A	Asset B
1	5%	7%
2	–2%	–4%
3	12%	18%

Answer:

mean return for asset A = (5% – 2% + 12%) / 3 = 5%

mean return for asset B = (7% – 4% + 18%) / 3 = 7%

$$\text{sample variance of returns for asset A} = \frac{(5-5)^2 + (-2-5)^2 + (12-5)^2}{3-1}$$

$$= 49$$

sample standard deviation for asset A = $\sqrt{49}$ = 7%

$$\text{sample variance of returns for asset B} = \frac{(7-7)^2 + (-4-7)^2 + (18-7)^2}{3-1}$$

$$= 121$$

sample standard deviation for asset B = $\sqrt{121}$ = 11%

sample covariance of returns for assets A and B

$$= \frac{(5-5)(7-7) + (-2-5)(-4-7) + (12-5)(18-7)}{3-1} = 77$$

$$\text{correlation of returns for assets A and B} = \frac{77}{7 \times 11} = 1$$

In this example, the returns on assets A and B are perfectly positively correlated.

LOS 49.e: Explain risk aversion and its implications for portfolio selection.

CFA® Program Curriculum, Volume 5, page 473

A **risk-averse** investor is simply one that dislikes risk (i.e., prefers less risk to more risk). Given two investments that have equal expected returns, a risk-averse investor will choose the one with less risk (standard deviation, σ).

A **risk-seeking** (risk-loving) investor actually prefers more risk to less and, given equal expected returns, will choose the more risky investment. A **risk-neutral** investor has no preference regarding risk and would be indifferent between two such investments.

Consider this gamble: A coin will be flipped; if it comes up heads, you receive $100; if it comes up tails, you receive nothing. The expected payoff is 0.5($100) + 0.5($0) = $50. A risk-averse investor would choose a payment of $50 (a certain outcome) over the gamble. A risk-seeking investor would prefer the gamble to a certain payment of $50. A risk-neutral investor would be indifferent between the gamble and a certain payment of $50.

If expected returns are identical, a risk-averse investor will always choose the investment with the least risk. However, an investor may select a very risky portfolio despite being risk averse; a risk-averse investor will hold very risky assets if he feels that the extra return he expects to earn is adequate compensation for the additional risk.

MODULE QUIZ 49.1, 49.2

To best evaluate your performance, enter your quiz answers online.

1. An investor buys a share of stock for $40 at time t = 0, buys another share of the same stock for $50 at t = 1, and sells both shares for $60 each at t = 2. The stock paid a dividend of $1 per share at t = 1 and at t = 2. The periodic money-weighted rate of return on the investment is *closest* to:
   A. 22.2%.
   B. 23.0%.
   C. 23.8%.
2. Which of the following asset classes has historically had the highest returns and standard deviation?
   A. Small-cap stocks.
   B. Large-cap stocks.
   C. Long-term corporate bonds.
3. In a five-year period, the annual returns on an investment are 5%, –3%, –4%, 2%, and 6%. The standard deviation of annual returns on this investment is *closest* to:
   A. 4.0%.
   B. 4.5%.
   C. 20.7%.
4. A measure of how the returns of two risky assets move in relation to each other is:
   A. the range.
   B. the covariance.
   C. the standard deviation.
5. Which of the following statements about correlation is *least accurate*?
   A. Diversification reduces risk when correlation is less than +1.
   B. If the correlation coefficient is 0, a zero-variance portfolio can be constructed.
   C. The lower the correlation coefficient, the greater the potential benefits from diversification.

6. The variance of returns is 0.09 for Stock A and 0.04 for Stock B. The covariance between the returns of A and B is 0.006. The correlation of returns between A and B is:
   A. 0.10.
   B. 0.20.
   C. 0.30.
7. Which of the following statements about risk-averse investors is *most accurate*? A risk-averse investor:
   A. seeks out the investment with minimum risk, while return is not a major consideration.
   B. will take additional investment risk if sufficiently compensated for this risk.
   C. avoids participating in global equity markets.

Video covering this content is available online.

MODULE 49.3: THE EFFICIENT FRONTIER

LOS 49.f: Calculate and interpret portfolio standard deviation.

CFA® Program Curriculum, Volume 5, page 476

The variance of returns for a portfolio of two risky assets is calculated as follows:

$$\text{Var}_{\text{portfolio}} = w_1^2\sigma_1^2 + w_2^2\sigma_2^2 + 2w_1w_2\text{Cov}_{12}$$

where w_1 is the proportion of the portfolio invested in Asset 1, and w_2 is the proportion of the portfolio invested in Asset 2. w_2 must equal $(1 - w_1)$.

Previously, we established that the correlation of returns for two assets is calculated as:

$$\rho_{12} = \frac{\text{Cov}_{12}}{\sigma_1\sigma_2}, \text{ so that we can also write } \text{Cov}_{12} = \rho_{12}\sigma_1\sigma_2.$$

Substituting this term for Cov_{12} in the formula for the variance of returns for a portfolio of two risky assets, we have the following:

$$\text{Var}_{\text{portfolio}} = w_1^2\sigma_1^2 + w_2^2\sigma_2^2 + 2w_1w_2\rho_{12}\sigma_1\sigma_2$$

Because $\text{Var}_{\text{portfolio}} = \sigma^2_{\text{portfolio}}$, this can also be written as:

$$\sigma_{\text{portfolio}} = \sqrt{w_1^2\sigma_1^2 + w_2^2\sigma_2^2 + 2w_1w_2\rho_{12}\sigma_1\sigma_2}$$

Writing the formula in this form allows us to easily see the effect of the correlation of returns between the two assets on portfolio risk.

EXAMPLE: Calculating portfolio standard deviation

A portfolio is 30% invested in stocks that have a standard deviation of returns of 20% and is 70% invested in bonds that have a standard deviation of returns of 12%. The correlation of bond returns with stock returns is 0.60. What is the standard deviation of portfolio returns? What would it be if stock and bond returns were perfectly positively correlated?

Answer:

portfolio standard deviation

$$= \sqrt{(0.3^2)(0.2^2) + (0.7^2)(0.12^2) + 2(0.3)(0.7)(0.6)(0.2)(0.12)}$$

$$= 12.9\%$$

If stock and bond returns were perfectly positively correlated, portfolio standard deviation would simply be the weighted average of the assets' standard deviations: 0.3(20%) + 0.7(12%) = 14.4%.

LOS 49.g: Describe the effect on a portfolio's risk of investing in assets that are less than perfectly correlated.

CFA® Program Curriculum, Volume 5, page 476

If two risky asset returns are perfectly positively correlated, $\rho_{12} = +1$, then the square root of portfolio variance (the portfolio standard deviation of returns) is equal to:

$$\sigma_{portfolio} = \sqrt{Var_{portfolio}} = \sqrt{w_1^2\sigma_1^2 + w_2^2\sigma_2^2 + 2w_1w_2\sigma_1\sigma_2(1)} = w_1\sigma_1 + w_2\sigma_2$$

PROFESSOR'S NOTE

This might be easier to see by examining the algebra in reverse. If $w_1\sigma_1 + w_2\sigma_2$ equals the square root of the term under the radical in this special case, then $(w_1\sigma_1 + w_2\sigma_2)^2$ should equal the term under the radical. If we expand $(w_1\sigma_1 + w_2\sigma_2)^2$, we get:

$$(w_1\sigma_1 + w_2\sigma_2)^2 = (w_1\sigma_1)^2 + (w_1\sigma_1)(w_2\sigma_2) + (w_2\sigma_2)(w_1\sigma_1) + (w_2\sigma_2)^2$$

$$= (w_1\sigma_1)^2 + (w_2\sigma_2)^2 + 2(w_1\sigma_1)(w_2\sigma_2)$$

$$= w_1^2\sigma_1^2 + w_2^2\sigma_2^2 + 2w_1\sigma_1w_2\sigma_2$$

In this unique case, with $\rho_{12} = 1$, the portfolio standard deviation is simply a weighted average of the standard deviations of the individual asset returns. A portfolio 25% invested in Asset 1 and 75% invested in Asset 2 will have a standard deviation of returns equal to 25% of the standard deviation (σ_1) of Asset 1's return, plus 75% of the standard deviation (σ_2) of Asset 2's return.

Focusing on returns correlation, we can see that the greatest portfolio risk results when the correlation between asset returns is +1. For any value of correlation less than +1, portfolio variance is reduced. Note that for a correlation of zero, the entire third term in the portfolio variance equation is zero. For negative values of correlation ρ_{12}, the third term becomes negative and further reduces portfolio variance and standard deviation.

We will illustrate this property with an example.

EXAMPLE: Portfolio risk as correlation varies

Consider two risky assets that have returns variances of 0.0625 and 0.0324, respectively. The assets' standard deviations of returns are then 25% and 18%, respectively. Calculate the variances and standard deviations of portfolio returns for an equal-weighted portfolio of the two assets when their correlation of returns is 1, 0.5, 0, and –0.5.

The calculations are as follows:

$$\text{variance}_{\text{portfolio}} = w_1^2\sigma_1^2 + w_2^2\sigma_2^2 + 2w_1w_2\rho_1\sigma_1\sigma_2$$

$$\sigma_{\text{portfolio}} = \sqrt{\text{variance}_{\text{portfolio}}}$$

$$\sigma_{\text{portfolio}} = \sqrt{w_1^2\sigma_1^2 + w_2^2\sigma_2^2 + 2w_1w_2\rho_{12}\sigma_1\sigma_2}$$

ρ = correlation = +1:

σ = portfolio standard deviation = 0.5(25%) + 0.5(18%) = **21.5%**

σ^2 = portfolio variance = 0.215^2 = 0.046225

ρ = correlation = 0.5:

$\sigma^2 = (0.5^2)0.0625 + (0.5^2)0.0324 + 2(0.5)(0.5)(\mathbf{0.5})(0.25)(0.18) =$ 0.034975

σ = **18.70%**

ρ = correlation = 0:

$\sigma^2 = (0.5^2)0.0625 + (0.5^2)0.0324 = 0.023725$

σ = **15.40%**

ρ = correlation = –0.5:

$\sigma^2 = (0.5^2)0.0625 + (0.5^2)0.0324 + 2(0.5)(0.5)(\mathbf{-0.5})(0.25)(0.18) =$ 0.012475

σ = **11.17%**

Note that portfolio risk falls as the correlation between the assets' returns decreases. This is an important result of the analysis of portfolio risk: The lower the correlation of asset returns, the greater the risk reduction (diversification) benefit of combining assets in a portfolio. If asset returns were perfectly negatively correlated, portfolio risk could be eliminated altogether for a specific set of asset weights.

We show these relations graphically in Figure 49.2 by plotting the portfolio risk and return for all portfolios of two risky assets, for assumed values of the assets' returns correlation.

Figure 49.2: Risk and Return for Different Values of ρ

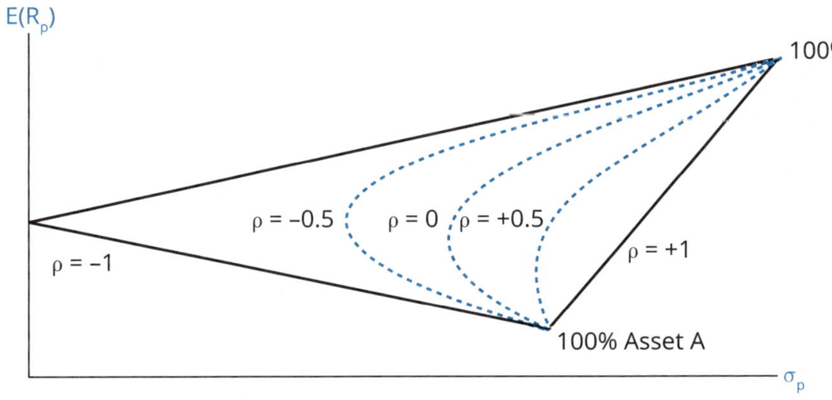

From these analyses, the risk-reduction benefits of investing in assets with low return correlations should be clear. The desire to reduce risk is what drives investors to invest in not just domestic stocks, but also bonds, foreign stocks, real estate, and other assets.

LOS 49.h: Describe and interpret the minimum-variance and efficient frontiers of risky assets and the global minimum-variance portfolio.

CFA® Program Curriculum, Volume 5, page 491

For each level of expected portfolio return, we can vary the portfolio weights on the individual assets to determine the portfolio that has the least risk. These portfolios that have the lowest standard deviation of all portfolios with a given expected return are known as **minimum-variance portfolios**. Together they make up the **minimum-variance frontier**.

Assuming that investors are risk averse, investors prefer the portfolio that has the greatest expected return when choosing among portfolios that have the same standard deviation of returns. Those portfolios that have the greatest expected return for each level of risk (standard deviation) make up the **efficient frontier**. The efficient frontier coincides with the top portion of the minimum-variance frontier. A risk-averse investor would only choose portfolios that are on the efficient frontier because all available portfolios that are not on the efficient frontier have lower expected returns than an efficient portfolio with the same risk. The portfolio on the efficient frontier that has the least risk is the **global minimum-variance portfolio**.

These concepts are illustrated in Figure 49.3.

Figure 49.3: Minimum-Variance and Efficient Frontiers

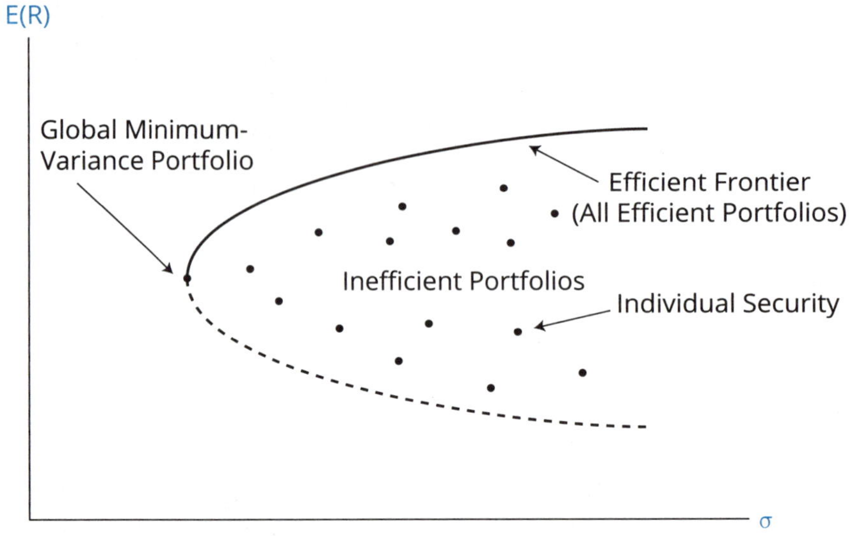

LOS 49.i: Explain the selection of an optimal portfolio, given an investor's utility (or risk aversion) and the capital allocation line.

CFA® Program Curriculum, Volume 5, page 473

An investor's **utility function** represents the investor's preferences in terms of risk and return (i.e., his degree of risk aversion). An **indifference curve** is a tool from economics that, in this application, plots combinations of risk (standard deviation) and expected return among which an investor is indifferent. In constructing indifference curves for portfolios based on only their expected return and standard deviation of returns, we are assuming that these are the only portfolio characteristics that investors care about. In Figure 49.4, we show three indifference curves for an investor. The investor's expected utility is the same for all points along a single indifference curve. Indifference curve I_1 represents the most preferred portfolios in Figure 49.4; our investor will prefer any portfolio along I_1 to any portfolio on either I_2 or I_3.

Figure 49.4: Risk-Averse Investor's Indifference Curves

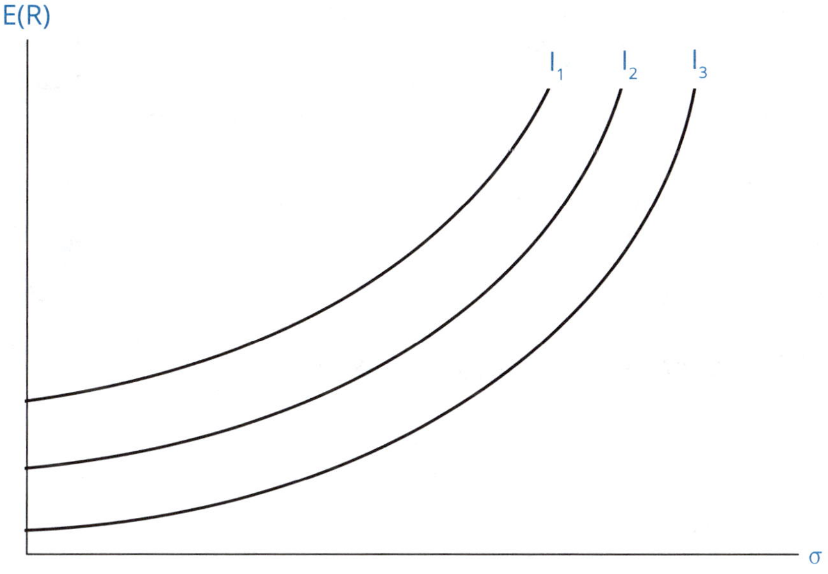

Indifference curves slope upward for risk-averse investors because they will only take on more risk (standard deviation of returns) if they are compensated with greater expected returns. An investor who is relatively more risk averse requires a relatively greater increase in expected return to compensate for a given increase in risk. In other words, a more risk-averse investor will have steeper indifference curves, reflecting a higher **risk aversion coefficient**.

In our previous illustration of efficient portfolios available in the market, we included only risky assets. Now we will introduce a risk-free asset into our universe of available assets, and we will consider the risk and return characteristics of a portfolio that combines a portfolio of risky assets and the risk-free asset. As we have seen, we can calculate the expected return and standard deviation of a portfolio with weight W_A allocated to risky Asset A and weight W_B allocated to risky Asset B using the following formulas:

$$E(R_{portfolio}) = W_A E(R_A) + W_B E(R_B)$$

$$\sigma_{portfolio} = \sqrt{W_A^2 \sigma_A^2 + W_B^2 \sigma_B^2 + 2 W_A W_B \rho_{AB} \sigma_A \sigma_B}$$

Allow Asset B to be the risk-free asset and Asset A to be the risky asset portfolio. Because a risk-free asset has zero standard deviation and zero correlation of returns with those of a risky portfolio, this results in the reduced equation:

$$\sigma_{portfolio} = \sqrt{W_A^2 \sigma_A^2} = W_A \sigma_A$$

The intuition of this result is quite simple: If we put X% of our portfolio into the risky asset portfolio, the resulting portfolio will have standard deviation of returns equal to X% of the standard deviation of the risky asset portfolio. The relationship between portfolio risk and return for various portfolio allocations is linear, as illustrated in Figure 49.5.

Combining a risky portfolio with a risk-free asset is the process that supports the **two-fund separation theorem**, which states that all investors' optimum portfolios will be made up of some combination of an optimal portfolio of risky assets and the risk-free asset. The line representing these possible combinations of risk-free assets and the optimal risky asset portfolio is referred to as the **capital allocation line**.

Point X on the capital allocation line in Figure 49.5 represents a portfolio that is 40% invested in the risky asset portfolio and 60% invested in the risk-free asset. Its expected return will be $0.40[E(R_{\text{risky asset portfolio}})] + 0.60(R_f)$, and its standard deviation will be $0.40(\sigma_{\text{risky asset portfolio}})$.

Figure 49.5: Capital Allocation Line and Risky Asset Weights

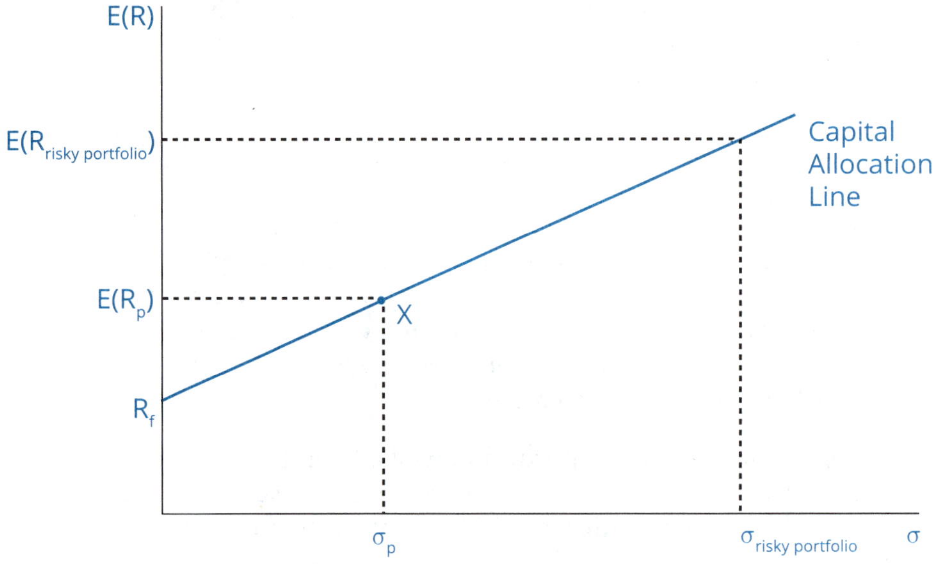

Now that we have constructed a set of the possible efficient portfolios (the capital allocation line), we can combine this with indifference curves representing an individual's preferences for risk and return to illustrate the logic of selecting an optimal portfolio (i.e., one that maximizes the investor's expected utility). In Figure 49.6, we can see that Investor A, with preferences represented by indifference curves I_1, I_2, and I_3, can reach the level of expected utility on I_2 by selecting portfolio X. This is the optimal portfolio for this investor, as any portfolio that lies on I_2 is preferred to all portfolios that lie on I_3 (and in fact to any portfolios that lie between I_2 and I_3). Portfolios on I_1 are preferred to those on I_2, but none of the portfolios that lie on I_1 are available in the market.

Figure 49.6: Risk-Averse Investor's Indifference Curves

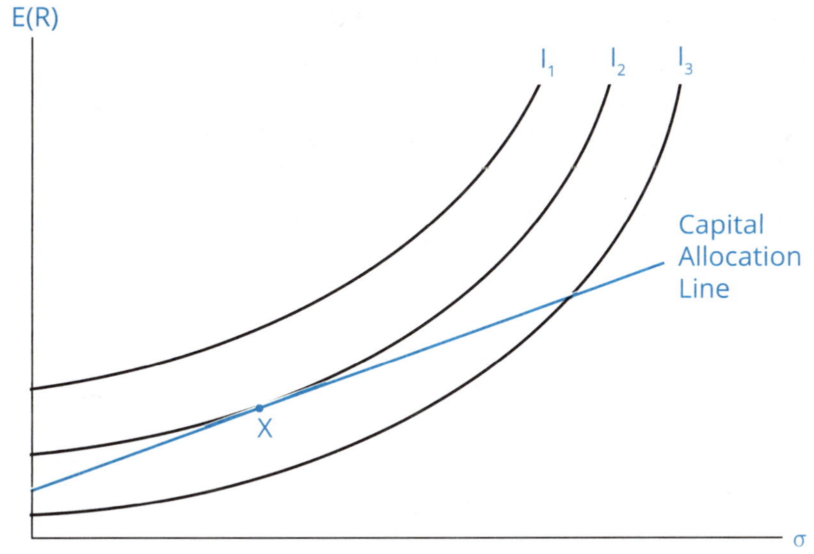

The final result of our analysis here is not surprising; investors who are less risk averse will select portfolios that are more risky. Recall that the less an investor's risk aversion, the flatter his indifference curves. As illustrated in Figure 49.7, the flatter indifference curve for Investor B (I_B) results in an optimal (tangency) portfolio that lies to the right of the one that results from a steeper indifference curve, such as that for Investor A (I_A). An investor who is less risk averse should optimally choose a portfolio with more invested in the risky asset portfolio and less invested in the risk-free asset.

Figure 49.7: Portfolio Choices Based on Investor's Indifference Curves

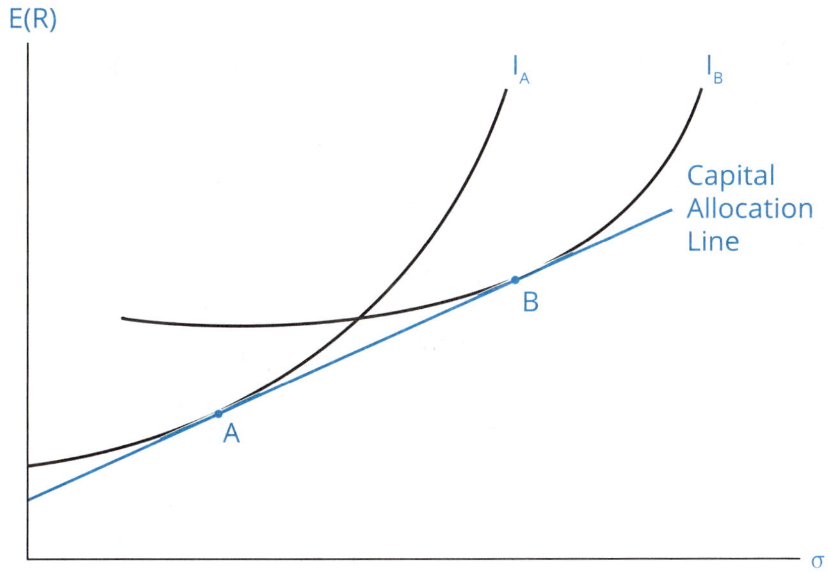

MODULE QUIZ 49.3

To best evaluate your performance, enter your quiz answers online.

Use the following data to answer Questions 1 and 2.

A portfolio was created by investing 25% of the funds in Asset A (standard deviation = 15%) and the balance of the funds in Asset B (standard deviation = 10%).

1. If the correlation coefficient is 0.75, what is the portfolio's standard deviation?
   A. 10.6%.
   B. 12.4%.
   C. 15.0%.
2. If the correlation coefficient is –0.75, what is the portfolio's standard deviation?
   A. 2.8%.
   B. 4.2%.
   C. 5.3%.
3. Which of the following statements about covariance and correlation is *least accurate*?
   A. A zero covariance implies there is no linear relationship between the returns on two assets.
   B. If two assets have perfect negative correlation, the variance of returns for a portfolio that consists of these two assets will equal zero.
   C. The covariance of a 2-stock portfolio is equal to the correlation coefficient times the standard deviation of one stock's returns times the standard deviation of the other stock's returns.
4. Which of the following available portfolios *most likely* falls below the efficient frontier?

	Portfolio	Expected return	Expected standard deviation
A.	A	7%	14%
B.	B	9%	26%
C.	C	12%	22%

5. The capital allocation line is a straight line from the risk-free asset through:
   A. the global maximum-return portfolio.
   B. the optimal risky portfolio.
   C. the global minimum-variance portfolio.

KEY CONCEPTS

LOS 49.a

Holding period return is used to measure an investment's return over a specific period. Arithmetic mean return is the simple average of a series of periodic returns. Geometric mean return is a compound annual rate.

Gross return is total return after deducting commissions on trades and other costs necessary to generate the returns, but before deducting fees for the management and administration of the investment account. Net return is the return after management and administration fees have been deducted.

Pretax nominal return is the numerical percentage return of an investment, without considering the effects of taxes and inflation. After-tax nominal return is the numerical return after the tax liability is deducted, without adjusting for inflation. Real return is the increase in an investor's purchasing power, roughly equal to nominal return minus inflation. Leveraged return is the gain or loss on an investment as a percentage of an investor's cash investment.

LOS 49.b

The money-weighted rate of return is the IRR calculated using periodic cash flows into and out of an account and is the discount rate that makes the PV of cash inflows equal to the PV of cash outflows.

The time-weighted rate of return measures compound growth. It is the rate at which $1 compounds over a specified performance horizon.

If funds are added to a portfolio just before a period of poor performance, the money-weighted return will be lower than the time-weighted return. If funds are added just prior to a period of high returns, the money-weighted return will be higher than the time-weighted return.

The time-weighted return is the preferred measure of a manager's ability to select investments. If the manager controls the money flows into and out of an account, the money-weighted return is the more appropriate performance measure.

LOS 49.c

As predicted by theory, asset classes with the greatest average returns have also had the highest risk.

Some of the major asset classes that investors consider when building a diversified portfolio include small-capitalization stocks, large-capitalization stocks, long-term corporate bonds, long-term Treasury bonds, and Treasury bills.

In addition to risk and return, when analyzing investments, investors also take into consideration an investment's liquidity, as well as non-normal characteristics such as skewness and kurtosis.

LOS 49.d

We can calculate the population variance, σ^2, when we know the return R_t for period t, the total number T of periods, and the mean μ of the population's distribution:

$$\text{population variance} = \sigma^2 = \frac{\sum_{t=1}^{T}(R_t - \mu)^2}{T}$$

In finance, we typically analyze only a sample of returns, so the sample variance applies instead:

$$\text{sample variance} = S^2 = \frac{\sum_{t=1}^{T}(R_t - \overline{R})^2}{T - 1}$$

Covariance measures the extent to which two variables move together over time. Positive covariance means the variables (e.g., rates of return on two stocks) tend to move together. Negative covariance means that the two variables tend to move in opposite directions. Covariance of zero means there is no linear relationship between the two variables.

Correlation is a standardized measure of co-movement that is bounded by –1 and +1:

$$\rho_{1,2} = \frac{Cov_{1,2}}{\sigma_1 \sigma_2}$$

LOS 49.e

A risk-averse investor is one that dislikes risk. Given two investments that have equal expected returns, a risk-averse investor will choose the one with less risk. However, a risk-averse investor will hold risky assets if he feels that the extra return he expects to earn is adequate compensation for the additional risk. Assets in the financial markets are priced according to the preferences of risk-averse investors.

A risk-seeking (risk-loving) investor actually prefers more risk to less and, given investments with equal expected returns, will choose the more risky investment.

A risk-neutral investor has no preference regarding risk and would be indifferent between two investments with the same expected return but different standard deviation of returns.

LOS 49.f

The standard deviation of returns for a portfolio of two risky assets is calculated as follows:

$$\sigma_{portfolio} = \sqrt{w_1^2\sigma_1^2 + w_2^2\sigma_2^2 + 2w_1w_2\rho_{1,2}\sigma_1\sigma_2}$$

LOS 49.g

The greatest portfolio risk will result when the asset returns are perfectly positively correlated. As the correlation decreases from +1 to –1, portfolio risk decreases. The lower the correlation of asset returns, the greater the risk reduction (diversification) benefit of combining assets in a portfolio.

LOS 49.h

For each level of expected portfolio return, the portfolio that has the least risk is known as a minimum-variance portfolio. Taken together, these portfolios form a line called the minimum-variance frontier.

On a risk versus return graph, the one risky portfolio that is farthest to the left (has the least risk) is known as the global minimum-variance portfolio.

Those portfolios that have the greatest expected return for each level of risk make up the efficient frontier. The efficient frontier coincides with the top portion of the minimum variance frontier. Risk-averse investors would only choose a portfolio that lies on the efficient frontier.

LOS 49.i

An indifference curve plots combinations of risk and expected return that an investor finds equally acceptable. Indifference curves generally slope upward because risk-averse investors will only take on more risk if they are compensated with greater expected returns. A more risk-averse investor will have steeper indifference curves.

Flatter indifference curves (less risk aversion) result in an optimal portfolio with higher risk and higher expected return. An investor who is less risk averse will optimally choose a portfolio with more invested in the risky asset portfolio and less invested in the risk-free asset.

ANSWER KEY FOR MODULE QUIZZES

Module Quiz 49.1, 49.2

1. **C** Using the cash flow functions on your financial calculator, enter $CF_0 = -40$; $CF_1 = -50 + 1 = -49$; $CF_2 = 60 \times 2 + 2 = 122$; CPT IRR = 23.82%. (Module 49.1, LOS 49.a)

2. **A** Small-cap stocks have had the highest annual return and standard deviation of return over time. Large-cap stocks and bonds have historically had lower risk and return than small-cap stocks. (Module 49.1, LOS 49.c)

3. **B** mean annual return = (5% – 3% – 4% + 2% + 6%) / 5 = 1.2%

   Squared deviations from the mean:

5% – 1.2% = 3.8%	$3.8^2 = 14.44$
–3% –1.2% = –4.2%	$-4.2^2 = 17.64$
–4% –1.2% = –5.2%	$-5.2^2 = 27.04$
2% –1.2% = 0.8%	$0.8^2 = 0.64$
6% –1.2% = 4.8%	$4.8^2 = 23.04$

   sum of squared deviations = 14.44 + 17.64 + 27.04 + 0.64 + 23.04 = 82.8

   sample variance = 82.8 / (5 – 1) = 20.7

   sample standard deviation = $20.7^{1/2} = 4.55\%$

   (Module 49.2, LOS 49.d)

4. **B** The covariance is defined as the co-movement of the returns of two assets or how well the returns of two risky assets move together. Range and standard deviation are measures of dispersion and measure risk, not how assets move together. (Module 49.2, LOS 49.d)

5. **B** A zero-variance portfolio can only be constructed if the correlation coefficient between assets is –1. Diversification benefits can be had when correlation is less than +1, and the lower the correlation, the greater the potential benefit. (Module 49.2, LOS 49.d)

6. **A** $\sqrt{A} = \sqrt{0.09} = 0.30$

   $\sqrt{B} = \sqrt{0.04} = 0.20$

   correlation = 0.006 / [(0.30)(0.20)] = 0.10

   (Module 49.2, LOS 49.d)

7. **B** Risk-averse investors are generally willing to invest in risky investments, if the return of the investment is sufficient to reward the investor for taking on this risk. Participants in securities markets are generally assumed to be risk-averse investors. (Module 49.2, LOS 49.e)

Module Quiz 49.3

1. **A** $\sqrt{(0.25)^2(0.15)^2 + (0.75)^2(0.10)^2 + 2(0.25)(0.75)(0.15)(0.10)(0.75)} =$
   $\sqrt{0.001406 + 0.005625 + 0.004219} = \sqrt{0.01125} = 0.106 = 10.6\%$
   (LOS 49.f)

2. **C** $\sqrt{(0.25)^2(0.15)^2 + (0.75)^2(0.10)^2 + 2(0.25)(0.75)(0.15)(0.10)(-0.75)} =$
   $\sqrt{0.001406 + 0.005625 - 0.004219} = \sqrt{0.002812} = 0.053 = 5.3\%$
   (LOS 49.f)

3. **B** If the correlation of returns between the two assets is –1, the set of possible portfolio risk/return combinations becomes two straight lines (see Figure 49.2). A portfolio of these two assets will have a positive returns variance unless the portfolio weights are those that minimize the portfolio variance. Covariance is equal to the correlation coefficient multiplied by the product of the standard deviations of the returns of the two stocks in a 2-stock portfolio. If covariance is zero, then correlation is also zero, which implies that there is no linear relationship between the two stocks' returns. (LOS 49.g)

4. **B** Portfolio B must be the portfolio that falls below the Markowitz efficient frontier because there is a portfolio (Portfolio C) that offers a higher return and lower risk. (LOS 49.h)

5. **B** An investor's optimal portfolio will lie somewhere on the capital allocation line, which begins at the risk-free asset and runs through the optimal risky portfolio. (LOS 49.i)

The following is a review of the Portfolio Management (1) principles designed to address the learning outcome statements set forth by CFA Institute. Cross-Reference to CFA Institute Assigned Reading #50.

READING 50

Portfolio Risk and Return: Part II

Study Session 17

EXAM FOCUS

The concepts developed here are very important to finance theory and are also used extensively in practice. You must know this material completely—not only the formulas and definitions, but the ideas that underlie their use. A model assumption that diversification is costless leads to the conclusion that only systematic risk (which cannot be reduced by further diversification) is priced in equilibrium, so that bearing nonsystematic risk does not increase expected returns.

MODULE 50.1: SYSTEMATIC RISK AND BETA

Video covering this content is available online.

LOS 50.a: Describe the implications of combining a risk-free asset with a portfolio of risky assets.

CFA® Program Curriculum, Volume 5, page 520

In the previous topic review, we covered the mathematics of calculating the risk and return of a portfolio with a percentage weight of W_A invested in a risky portfolio (P) and a weight of $W_B = 1 - W_A$ invested in a risk-free asset.

$$E(R_P) = W_A\,E(R_A) + W_B\,E(R_B)$$

$$\sigma_P = \sqrt{W_A^2\sigma_A^2 + W_B^2\sigma_B^2 + 2W_A W_B \rho_{AB}\sigma_A\sigma_B}$$

Because a risk-free asset has zero standard deviation and zero correlation of returns with a risky portfolio, allowing Asset B to be the risk-free asset and Asset A to be the risky asset portfolio results in the following reduced equation:

$$\sigma_P = \sqrt{W_A^2\sigma_A^2} = W_A\sigma_A$$

Our result is that the risk (standard deviation of returns) and expected return of portfolios with varying weights in the risk-free asset and a risky portfolio can be plotted as a line that begins at the risk-free rate of return and extends through the risky portfolio. This result is illustrated in Figure 50.1.

Figure 50.1: Combining a Risk-Free Asset With a Risky Asset

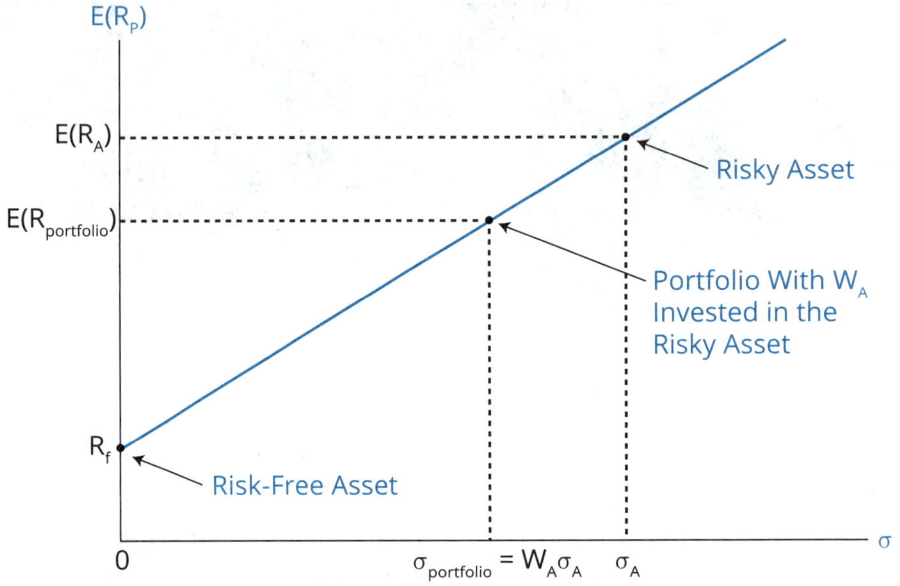

LOS 50.b: Explain the capital allocation line (CAL) and the capital market line (CML).

CFA® Program Curriculum, Volume 5, page 520

The line of possible portfolio risk and return combinations given the risk-free rate and the risk and return of a portfolio of risky assets is referred to as the **capital allocation line** (CAL). For an individual investor, the best CAL is the one that offers the most-preferred set of possible portfolios in terms of their risk and return. Figure 50.2 illustrates three possible investor CALs for three different risky portfolios A, B, and C. The optimal risky portfolio for this investor is Portfolio A because it results in the most preferred set of possible portfolios constructed by combining the risk-free asset with the risky portfolio. Of all the portfolios available to the investor, a combination of the risk-free asset with risky Portfolio A offers the investor the greatest expected utility.

Figure 50.2: Risky Portfolios and Their Associated Capital Allocation Lines

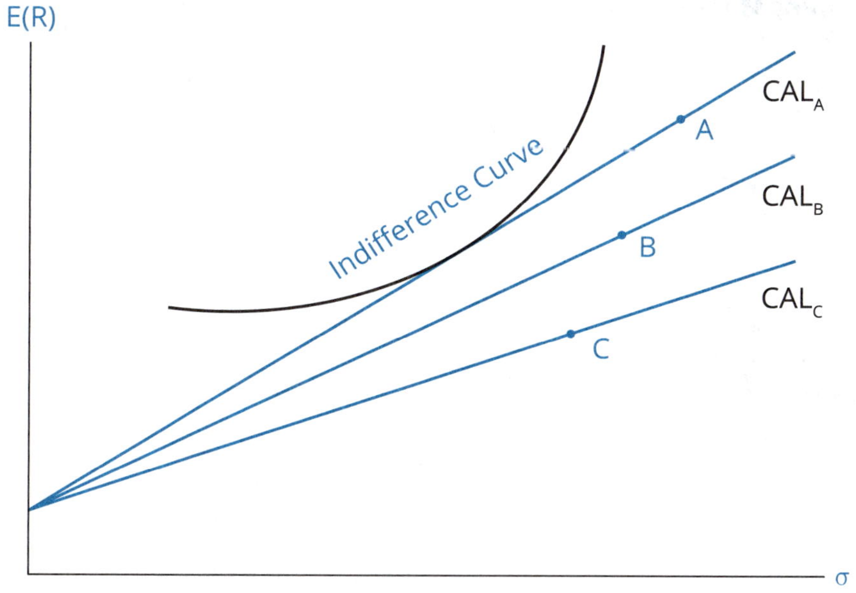

If each investor has different expectations about the expected returns of, standard deviations of, or correlations between risky asset returns, each investor will have a different optimal risky asset portfolio and a different CAL.

A simplifying assumption underlying modern portfolio theory (and the capital asset pricing model, which is introduced later in this topic review) is that investors have homogeneous expectations (i.e., they all have the same estimates of risk, return, and correlations with other risky assets for all risky assets). Under this assumption, all investors face the same efficient frontier of risky portfolios and will all have the same optimal risky portfolio and CAL.

Figure 50.3 illustrates the determination of the optimal risky portfolio and optimal CAL for all investors under the assumption of homogeneous expectations. Note that, under this assumption, the optimal CAL for any investor is the one that is just tangent to the efficient frontier. Depending on their preferences for risk and return (their indifference curves), investors may choose different portfolio weights for the risk-free asset and the risky (tangency) portfolio. Every investor, however, will use the same risky portfolio. When this is the case, that portfolio must be the **market portfolio** of all risky assets because all investors that hold any risky assets hold the same portfolio of risky assets.

Reading 50

Figure 50.3: Determining the Optimal Risky Portfolio and Optimal CAL Assuming Homogeneous Expectations

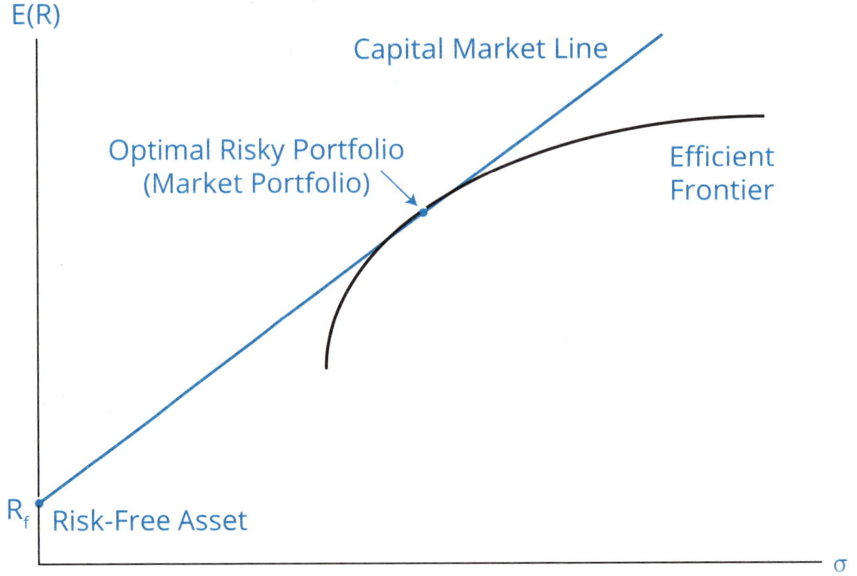

Under the assumption of homogeneous expectations, this optimal CAL for all investors is termed the **capital market line** (CML). Along this line, expected portfolio return, $E(R_P)$, is a linear function of portfolio risk, σ_P. The equation of this line is as follows:

$$E(R_P) = R_f + \left(\frac{E(R_M) - R_f}{\sigma_M}\right)\sigma_P$$

The *y*-intercept of this line is R_f and the slope (rise over run) of this line is as follows:

$$\left(\frac{E(R_M) - R_f}{\sigma_M}\right)$$

The intuition of this relation is straightforward. An investor who chooses to take on no risk ($\sigma_P = 0$) will earn the risk-free rate, R_f. The difference between the expected return on the market and the risk-free rate is termed the **market risk premium**. If we rewrite the CML equation as

$$E(R_P) = R_f + \left(E(R_M) - R_f\right)\left(\frac{\sigma_P}{\sigma_M}\right)$$

we can see that an investor can expect to get one unit of market risk premium in additional return (above the risk-free rate) for every unit of market risk, σ_M, that the investor is willing to accept.

If we assume that investors can both lend (invest in the risk-free asset) at the risk-free rate and borrow (as with a margin account) at the risk-free rate, they can select portfolios to the right of the market portfolio, as illustrated in Figure 50.4.

Figure 50.4: Borrowing and Lending Portfolios

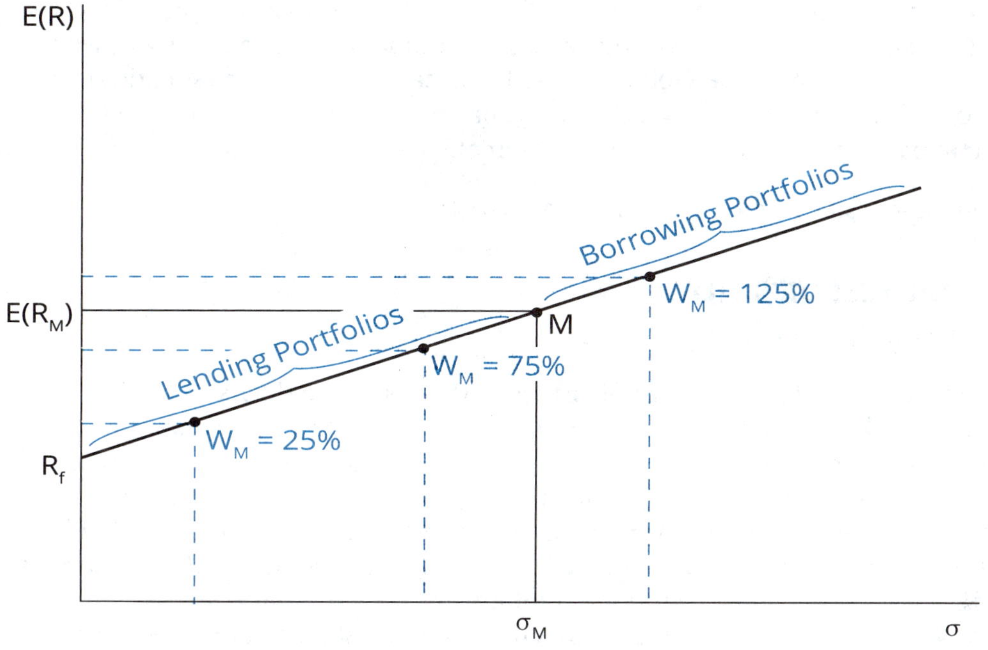

Investors who believe market prices are informationally efficient often follow a **passive investment strategy** (i.e., invest in an index of risky assets that serves as a proxy for the market portfolio and allocate a portion of their investable assets to a risk-free asset, such as short-term government securities). In practice, many investors and portfolio managers believe their estimates of security values are correct and market prices are incorrect. Such investors will not use the weights of the market portfolio but will invest more than the market weights in securities that they believe are undervalued and less than the market weights in securities which they believe are overvalued. This is referred to as **active portfolio management** to differentiate it from a passive investment strategy that utilizes a market index for the optimal risky asset portfolio.

LOS 50.c: Explain systematic and nonsystematic risk, including why an investor should not expect to receive additional return for bearing nonsystematic risk.

CFA® Program Curriculum, Volume 5, page 532

When an investor diversifies across assets that are not perfectly correlated, the portfolio's risk is less than the weighted average of the risks of the individual securities in the portfolio. The risk that is eliminated by diversification is called **unsystematic risk** (also called *unique, diversifiable,* or *firm-specific risk*). Because the market portfolio contains *all* risky assets, it must be a well-diversified portfolio. All the risk that can be diversified away has been. The risk that remains cannot be diversified away and is called the **systematic risk** (also called *nondiversifiable risk* or *market risk*).

The concept of systematic risk applies to individual securities as well as to portfolios. Some securities' returns are highly correlated with overall market returns. Examples of firms that are highly correlated with market returns are luxury goods manufacturers such as Ferrari automobiles and Harley Davidson motorcycles. These firms have high systematic risk (i.e., they are very responsive to market, or systematic, changes). Other firms, such as utility companies, respond very little to changes in the systematic risk factors. These firms have very little systematic risk. Hence, total risk (as measured by standard deviation) can be broken down into its component parts: unsystematic risk and systematic risk. Mathematically:

total risk = systematic risk + unsystematic risk

PROFESSOR'S NOTE

Know this concept!

Do you actually have to buy all the securities in the market to diversify away unsystematic risk? No. Academic studies have shown that as you increase the number of stocks in a portfolio, the portfolio's risk falls toward the level of market risk. One study showed that it only took about 12 to 18 stocks in a portfolio to achieve 90% of the maximum diversification possible. Another study indicated it took 30 securities. Whatever the number, it is significantly less than *all* the securities. Figure 50.5 provides a general representation of this concept. Note, in the figure, that once you get to 30 or so securities in a portfolio, the standard deviation remains constant. The remaining risk is systematic, or nondiversifiable, risk. We will develop this concept later when we discuss beta, a measure of systematic risk.

Figure 50.5: Risk vs. Number of Portfolio Assets

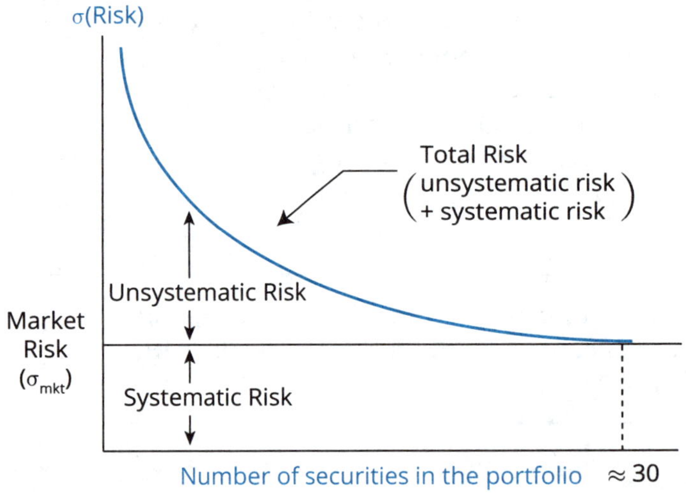

Systematic Risk Is Relevant in Portfolios

One important conclusion of capital market theory is that equilibrium security returns depend on a stock's or a portfolio's systematic risk, not its total risk as measured by standard deviation. One of the assumptions of the model is that diversification is free. The reasoning is that investors will not be compensated for bearing risk that can be eliminated at no cost. If you think about the costs of a no-load index fund compared to buying individual stocks, diversification is actually very low cost if not actually free.

The implications of this conclusion are very important to asset pricing (expected returns). The riskiest stock, with risk measured as standard deviation of returns, does not necessarily have the greatest expected return. Consider a biotech stock with one new drug product that is in clinical trials to determine its effectiveness. If it turns out that the drug is effective and safe, stock returns will be quite high. If, on the other hand, the subjects in the clinical trials are killed or otherwise harmed by the drug, the stock will fall to approximately zero and returns will be quite poor. This describes a stock with high standard deviation of returns (i.e., high total risk).

The high risk of our biotech stock, however, is primarily from firm-specific factors, so its unsystematic risk is high. Because market factors such as economic growth rates have little to do with the eventual outcome for this stock, systematic risk is a small proportion of the total risk of the stock. Capital market theory says that the equilibrium return on this stock may be less than that of a stock with much less firm-specific risk but more sensitivity to the factors that drive the return of the overall market. An established manufacturer of machine tools may not be a very risky investment in terms of total risk, but may have a greater sensitivity to market (systematic) risk factors (e.g., GDP growth rates) than our biotech stock. Given this scenario, the stock with more total risk (the biotech stock) has less systematic risk and will therefore have a lower equilibrium rate of return according to capital market theory.

Note that holding many biotech firms in a portfolio will diversify away the firm-specific risk. Some will have blockbuster products and some will fail, but you can imagine that when 50 or 100 such stocks are combined into a portfolio, the uncertainty about the portfolio return is much less than the uncertainty about the return of a single biotech firm stock.

To sum up, unsystematic risk is not compensated in equilibrium because it can be eliminated for free through diversification. Systematic risk is measured by the contribution of a security to the risk of a well-diversified portfolio, and the expected equilibrium return (required return) on an individual security will depend only on its systematic risk.

LOS 50.d: Explain return generating models (including the market model) and their uses.

CFA® Program Curriculum, Volume 5, page 534

Return generating models are used to estimate the expected returns on risky securities based on specific factors. For each security, we must estimate the sensitivity of its returns to each specific factor. Factors that explain security returns can be classified as macroeconomic, fundamental, and statistical factors. **Multifactor models** most commonly use macroeconomic factors such as GDP growth, inflation, or consumer confidence, along with fundamental factors such as earnings, earnings growth, firm size, and research expenditures. Statistical factors often have no basis in finance theory and are suspect in that they may represent only relations for a specific time period which have been identified by data mining (repeated tests on a single dataset).

The general form of a multifactor model with *k* factors is as follows:

$$E(R_i) - R_f = \beta_{i1} \times E(\text{Factor 1}) + \beta_{i2} \times E(\text{Factor 2}) + \ldots + \beta_{ik} \times E(\text{Factor k})$$

This model states that the expected excess return (above the risk-free rate) for Asset *i* is the sum of each **factor sensitivity** or **factor loading** (the βs) for Asset *i* multiplied by the expected value of that factor for the period. The first factor is often the expected excess return on the market, $E(R_m - R_f)$.

One multifactor model that is often used is that of Fama and French. They estimated the sensitivity of security returns to three factors: firm size, firm book value to market value ratio, and the return on the market portfolio minus the risk-free rate (excess return on the market portfolio). Carhart suggests a fourth factor that measures price momentum using prior period returns. Together, these four factors do a relatively good job of explaining returns differences for U.S. equity securities over the period for which the model has been estimated.

The simplest factor model is a single-factor model. A single-factor model with the return on the market, R_m, as its only risk factor can be written (in excess returns form) as:

$$E(R_i) - R_f = \beta_i \times [E(R_m) - R_f]$$

Here, the expected excess return (return above the risk-free rate) is the product of the factor weight or factor sensitivity, Beta i, and the risk factor, which in this model is the excess return on the market portfolio or market index, so that this is also sometimes called a **single-index model**.

A simplified form of a single-index model is the **market model**, which is used to estimate a security's (or portfolio's) beta and to estimate a security's abnormal return (return above its expected return) based on the actual market return.

The form of the market model is as follows:

$$R_i = \alpha_i + \beta_i R_m + e_i$$

where:
R_i = return on Asset *i*
R_m = market return
β_i = slope coefficient
α_i = intercept
e_i = abnormal return on Asset *i*

The intercept α_i and slope coefficient β_i are estimated from historical return data. We can require that α_i is the risk-free rate times $(1 - \beta_i)$ to be consistent with the general form of a single-index model in excess returns form.

The expected return on Asset *i* is $\alpha_i + \beta_i E(R_m)$. A deviation from the expected return in a given period is the abnormal return on Asset i, e_i, or $R_i - (\alpha_i + \beta_i R_m)$.

In the market model, the factor sensitivity or beta for Asset *i* is a measure of how sensitive the return on Asset *i* is to the return on the overall market portfolio (market index).

LOS 50.e: Calculate and interpret beta.

CFA® Program Curriculum, Volume 5, page 541

The sensitivity of an asset's return to the return on the market index in the context of the market model is referred to as its **beta**. Beta is a standardized measure of the covariance of the asset's return with the market return. Beta can be calculated as follows:

$$\beta_i = \frac{\text{covariance of Asset } i\text{'s return with the market return}}{\text{variance of the market return}} = \frac{Cov_{im}}{\sigma_m^2}$$

We can use the definition of the correlation between the returns on Asset *i* with the returns on the market index:

$$\rho_{im} = \frac{Cov_{im}}{\sigma_i \sigma_m}$$

to get $Cov_{im} = \rho_{im}\sigma_i\sigma_m$

Substituting for Cov_{im} in the equation for B_i, we can also calculate beta as:

$$\beta_i = \frac{\rho_{im}\sigma_i\sigma_m}{\sigma_m^2} = \rho_{im}\left(\frac{\sigma_i}{\sigma_m}\right)$$

EXAMPLE: Calculating an asset's beta

The standard deviation of the return on the market index is estimated as 20%.

1. If Asset A's standard deviation is 30% and its correlation of returns with the market index is 0.8, what is Asset A's beta?

   Using the formula $\beta_i = \rho_{im}\left(\frac{\sigma_i}{\sigma_m}\right)$, we have: $\beta_i = 0.80\left(\frac{0.30}{0.20}\right) = 1.2$.

2. If the covariance of Asset A's returns with the returns on the market index is 0.048, what is the beta of Asset A?

   Using the formula $\beta_i = \frac{Cov_{im}}{\sigma_m^2}$, we have $\beta_i = \frac{0.048}{0.2^2} = 1.2$.

PROFESSOR'S NOTE

Candidates should be prepared to calculate beta in either of the two ways in the example.

In practice, we estimate asset betas by regressing returns on the asset on those of the market index. While regression is a Level II concept, for our purposes, you can think of it as a mathematical estimation procedure that fits a line to a data plot. In Figure 50.5, we represent the excess returns on Asset *i* as the dependent variable and the excess returns on the market index as the independent variable. The *least squares regression line* is the line that minimizes the sum of the squared distances of the points plotted from the line (this is what is meant by the line of *best fit*). The slope of this line is our estimate of beta. In Figure 50.6, the line is steeper than 45 degrees, the slope is greater than one, and the asset's estimated beta is greater than one. Our interpretation is that the returns on Asset *i* are more variable in response to systematic risk factors than is the overall market, which has a beta of one.

Figure 50.6: Regression of Asset Excess Returns Against Market Asset Returns

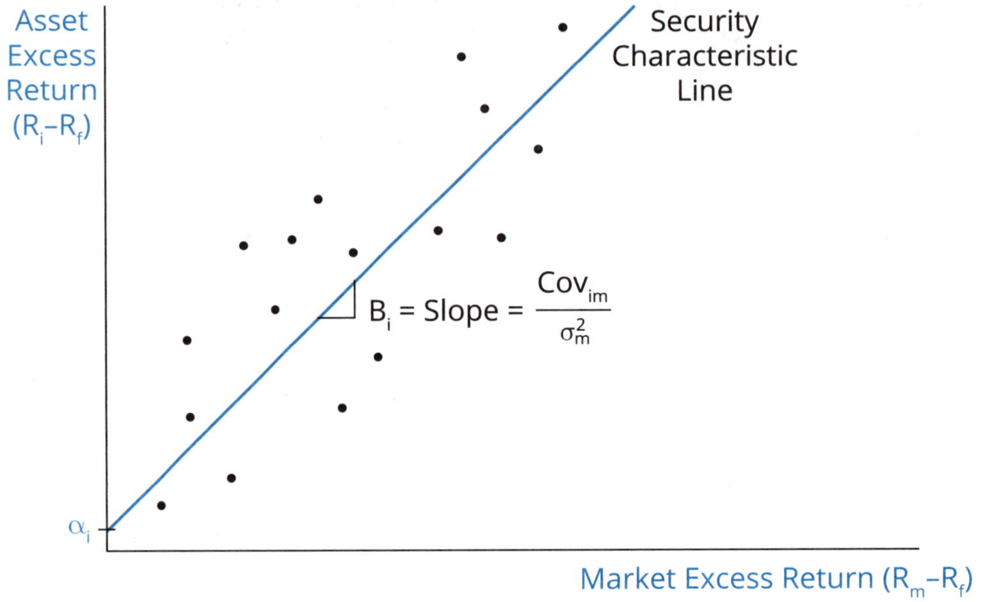

This regression line is referred to as the asset's **security characteristic line**. Mathematically, the slope of the security characteristic line is $\frac{Cov_{im}}{\sigma_m^2}$, which is the same formula we used earlier to calculate beta.

MODULE QUIZ 50.1

To best evaluate your performance, enter your quiz answers online.

1. An investor put 60% of his portfolio into a risky asset offering a 10% return with a standard deviation of returns of 8% and put the balance of his portfolio in a risk-free asset offering 5%. What is the expected return and standard deviation of his portfolio?

	Expected return	Standard deviation
A.	6.0%	6.8%
B.	8.0%	4.8%
C.	10.0%	6.6%

2. What is the risk measure associated with the capital market line (CML)?
   A. Beta risk.
   B. Unsystematic risk.
   C. Total risk.

3. A portfolio to the right of the market portfolio on the CML is:
   A. a lending portfolio.
   B. a borrowing portfolio.
   C. an inefficient portfolio.

4. As the number of stocks in a portfolio increases, the portfolio's systematic risk:
   A. can increase or decrease.
   B. decreases at a decreasing rate.
   C. decreases at an increasing rate.
5. Total risk equals:
   A. unique plus diversifiable risk.
   B. market plus nondiversifiable risk.
   C. systematic plus unsystematic risk.
6. A return generating model is *least likely* to be based on a security's exposure to:
   A. statistical factors.
   B. macroeconomic factors.
   C. fundamental factors.
7. The covariance of the market's returns with a stock's returns is 0.005 and the standard deviation of the market's returns is 0.05. What is the stock's beta?
   A. 1.0.
   B. 1.5.
   C. 2.0.

MODULE 50.2: THE CAPM AND THE SML

Video covering this content is available online.

LOS 50.f: Explain the capital asset pricing model (CAPM), including its assumptions, and the security market line (SML).

LOS 50.g: Calculate and interpret the expected return of an asset using the CAPM.

CFA® Program Curriculum, Volume 5, page 541

Given that the only relevant (priced) risk for an individual Asset *i* is measured by the covariance between the asset's returns and the returns on the market, $Cov_{i,mkt}$, we can plot the relationship between risk and return for individual assets using $Cov_{i,mkt}$ as our measure of systematic risk. The resulting line, plotted in Figure 50.7, is one version of what is referred to as the **security market line (SML).**

Figure 50.7: Security Market Line

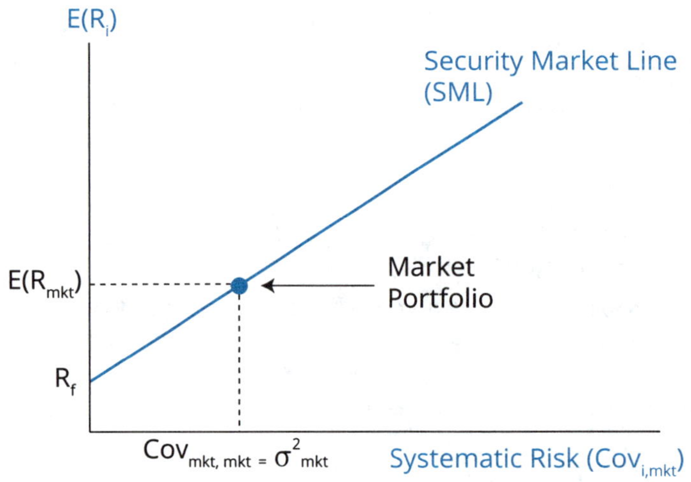

The equation of the SML is:

$$E(R_i) = R_f + \frac{E(R_{mkt}) - R_f}{\sigma^2_{mkt}}(Cov_{i,mkt})$$

which can be rearranged and stated as:

$$E(R_i) = R_f + \frac{Cov_{i,mkt}}{\sigma^2_{mkt}}[E(R_{mkt}) - R_f]$$

The line described by this last equation is presented in Figure 50.8, where we let the standardized covariance term, $\frac{Cov_{i,mkt}}{\sigma^2_{mkt}}$, be defined as beta, β_i.

This is the most common means of describing the SML, and this relation between beta (systematic risk) and expected return is known as the **capital asset pricing model** (CAPM).

Figure 50.8: The Capital Asset Pricing Model

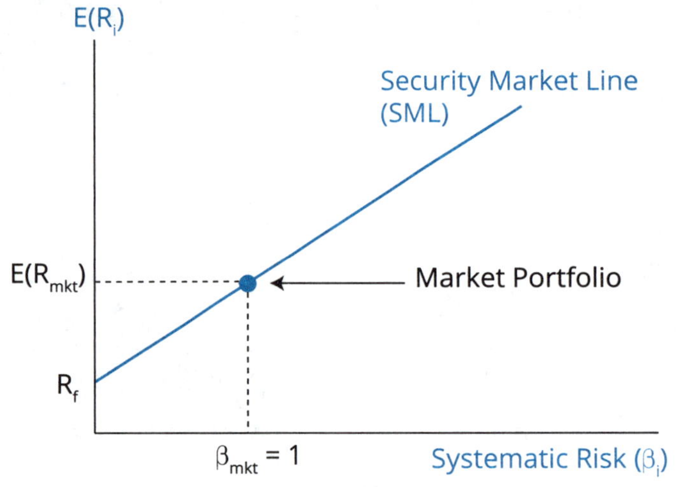

So, we can define beta, $\beta = \frac{Cov_{i,mkt}}{\sigma^2_{mkt}}$, as a standardized measure of systematic risk.

Beta measures the relation between a security's excess returns and the excess returns to the market portfolio.

Formally, the CAPM is stated as:

$$E(R_i) = R_f + \beta_i[E(R_{mkt}) - R_f]$$

The CAPM holds that, in equilibrium, the expected return on risky asset $E(R_i)$ is the risk-free rate (R_f) plus a beta-adjusted market risk premium, $\beta_i[E(R_{mkt}) - R_f]$. Beta measures systematic (market or covariance) risk.

EXAMPLE: Capital asset pricing model

The expected return on the market is 8%, the risk-free rate is 2%, and the beta for Stock A is 1.2. Compute the rate of return that would be expected (required) on this stock.

Answer:

$E(R_A) = 2\% + 1.2(8\% - 2\%) = 9.2\%$

Note: $\beta_A > 1$, so $E(R_A) > E(R_{mkt})$

The **assumptions of the CAPM** are:

- *Risk aversion*. To accept a greater degree of risk, investors require a higher expected return.
- *Utility maximizing investors*. Investors choose the portfolio, based on their individual preferences, with the risk and return combination that maximizes their (expected) utility.
- *Frictionless markets*. There are no taxes, transaction costs, or other impediments to trading.
- *One-period horizon*. All investors have the same one-period time horizon.
- *Homogeneous expectations*. All investors have the same expectations for assets' expected returns, standard deviation of returns, and returns correlations between assets.
- *Divisible assets*. All investments are infinitely divisible.
- *Competitive markets*. Investors take the market price as given and no investor can influence prices with their trades.

Comparing the CML and the SML

It is important to recognize that the CML and SML are very different. Recall the equation of the CML:

$$E(R_P) = R_f + \sigma_P\left\{\frac{[E(R_M) - R_f]}{\sigma_M}\right\}$$

Reading 50

The CML uses total risk = σ_p on the x-axis. Hence, only efficient portfolios will plot on the CML. On the other hand, the SML uses beta (systematic risk) on the x-axis. So in a CAPM world, *all properly priced securities and portfolios of securities will plot on the SML*, as shown in Figure 50.9.

Figure 50.9: Comparing the CML and the SML

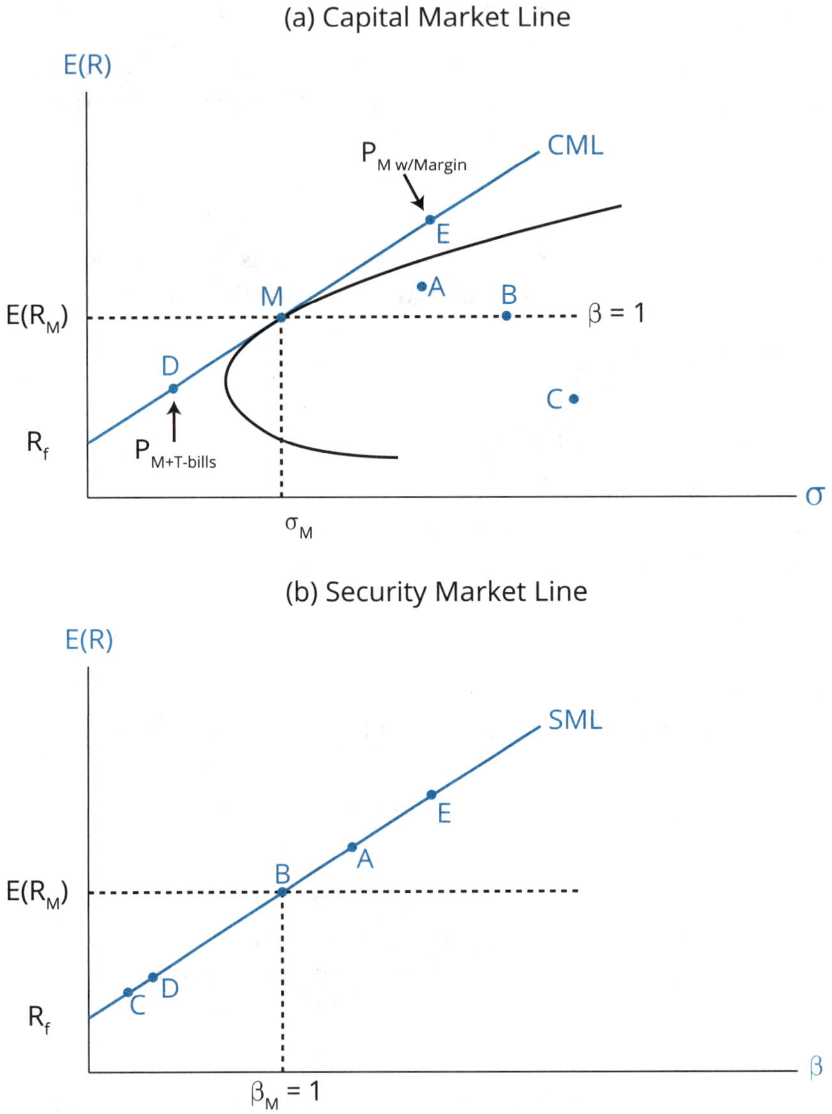

Portfolios that are not well diversified (efficient) plot inside the efficient frontier and are represented by risk-return combinations such as points A, B, and C in panel (a) of Figure 50.9. Individual securities are one example of such inefficient portfolios. According to the CAPM, the expected returns on all portfolios, well diversified or not, are determined by their systematic risk. Thus, according to the CAPM, Point A represents a high-beta stock or portfolio, Point B a stock or portfolio with a beta of one, and Point C a low-beta stock or portfolio. We know this because the expected return at Point B is equal to the expected return on the market, and the expected returns at Point A and C are greater and less than the expected return on the market (tangency) portfolio, respectively.

Note that a low-beta stock, such as represented by Point C, is not necessarily low-risk when total risk is considered. While its contribution to the risk of a well-diversified portfolio may be low, its risk when held by itself can be considered quite high. A firm whose only activity is developing a new, but as yet unproven, drug may be quite speculative with highly uncertain returns. It may also have quite low systematic risk if the uncertainty about its future returns depends primarily on firm-specific factors.

All stocks and portfolios that plot along the line labeled $\beta = 1$ in Figure 50.9 have the same expected return as the market portfolio and, thus, according to the CAPM, have the same systematic risk as the market portfolio (i.e., they all have betas of one).

All points on the CML (except the tangency point) represent the risk-return characteristics of portfolios formed by either combining the market portfolio with the risk-free asset or borrowing at the risk-free rate in order to invest more than 100% of the portfolio's net value in the risky market portfolio (investing on margin). Point D in Figure 50.9 represents a portfolio that combines the market portfolio with the risk-free asset, while points above the point of tangency, such as Point E, represent portfolios created by borrowing at the risk-free rate to invest in the market portfolio. Portfolios that do not lie on the CML are not efficient and therefore have risk that will not be rewarded with higher expected returns in equilibrium.

According to the CAPM, all securities and portfolios, diversified or not, will plot on the SML in equilibrium. In fact, all stocks and portfolios along the line labeled $\beta = 1$ in Figure 50.9, including the market portfolio, will plot at the same point on the SML. They will plot at the point on the SML with beta equal to one and expected return equal to the expected return on the market, regardless of their total risk.

Reading 50

LOS 50.h: Describe and demonstrate applications of the CAPM and the SML.

CFA® Program Curriculum, Volume 5, page 546

We have used beta to estimate a security's expected return based on our estimate of the risk-free rate and the expected return on the market. In equilibrium, a security's expected return and its required return (by investors) are equal. Therefore, we can use the CAPM to estimate a security's required return.

Because the SML shows the equilibrium (required) return for any security or portfolio based on its beta (systematic risk), analysts often compare their forecast of a security's return to its required return based on its beta risk. The following example illustrates this technique.

EXAMPLE: Identifying mispriced securities

The following figure contains information based on analyst's forecasts for three stocks. Assume a risk-free rate of 7% and a market return of 15%. Compute the expected and required return on each stock, determine whether each stock is undervalued, overvalued, or properly valued, and outline an appropriate trading strategy.

Forecast Data

Stock	Price Today	E(Price) in 1 Year	E(Dividend) in 1 Year	Beta
A	$25	$27	$1.00	1.0
B	40	45	2.00	0.8
C	15	17	0.50	1.2

Answer:

Expected and required returns computations are shown in the following figure.

Forecasts vs. Required Returns

Stock	Forecast Return	Required Return
A	($27 – $25 + $1) / $25 = 12.0%	0.07 + (1.0)(0.15 – 0.07) = 15.0%
B	($45 – $40 + $2) / $40 = 17.5%	0.07 + (0.8)(0.15 – 0.07) = 13.4%
C	($17 – $15 + $0.5) / $15 = 16.6%	0.07 + (1.2)(0.15 – 0.07) = 16.6%

- Stock A is *overvalued*. It is expected to earn 12%, but based on its systematic risk, it should earn 15%. It plots *below* the SML.
- Stock B is *undervalued*. It is expected to earn 17.5%, but based on its systematic risk, it should earn 13.4%. It plots *above* the SML.
- Stock C is *properly valued*. It is expected to earn 16.6%, and based on its systematic risk, it should earn 16.6%. It plots *on* the SML.

The appropriate trading strategy is:

- Short sell Stock A.
- Buy Stock B.
- Buy, sell, or ignore Stock C.

We can do this same analysis graphically. The expected return/beta combinations of all three stocks are graphed in the following figure relative to the SML.

Identifying Mispriced Securities

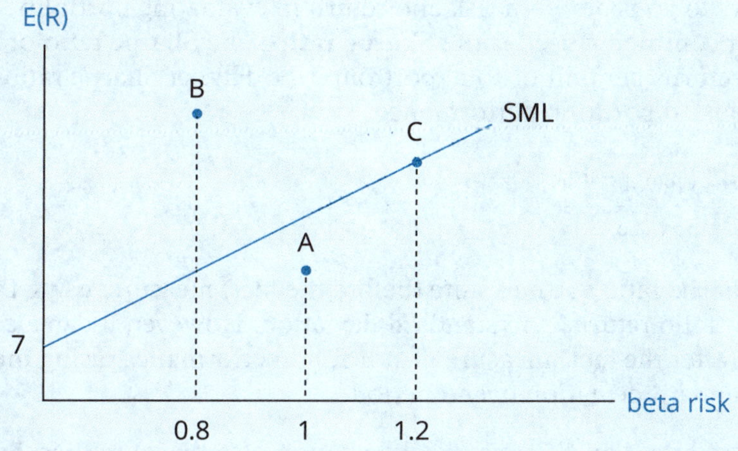

PROFESSOR'S NOTE

If the estimated return plots "over" the SML, the security is "under" valued. If the estimated return plots "under" the SML, the security is "over" valued.

Remember, all stocks should plot on the SML; any stock not plotting on the SML is mispriced. Notice that Stock A falls below the SML, Stock B lies above the SML, and Stock C is on the SML. If you plot a stock's expected return and it falls below the SML, the stock is overpriced. That is, the stock's expected return is too low given its systematic risk. If a stock plots above the SML, it is underpriced and is offering an expected return greater than required for its systematic risk. If it plots on the SML, the stock is properly priced.

Because the equation of the SML is the capital asset pricing model, you can determine if a stock is over- or underpriced graphically or mathematically. Your answers will always be the same.

LOS 50.i: Calculate and interpret the Sharpe ratio, Treynor ratio, M^2, and Jensen's alpha.

CFA® Program Curriculum, Volume 5, page 551

Performance evaluation of an active manager's portfolio choices refers to the analysis of the risk and return of the portfolio. **Attribution analysis**, an analysis of the sources of returns differences between active portfolio returns and those of a passive benchmark portfolio, is part of performance evaluation. Success in active portfolio management cannot be determined simply by comparing portfolio returns to benchmark portfolio returns; the risk taken to achieve returns must also be considered. A portfolio with greater risk than the benchmark portfolio (especially beta risk) is expected to produce higher returns over time than the benchmark portfolio.

When evaluating the performance of a portfolio with risk that differs from that of a benchmark portfolio, we need to adjust the active portfolio return's risk. Of the alternative ways to consider both risk and return in evaluating portfolio performance, the most commonly used is the **Sharpe ratio**. The Sharpe ratio of a portfolio is its excess returns per unit of total portfolio risk. Higher Sharpe ratios indicate better risk-adjusted portfolio performance.

$$\text{Sharpe ratio} = \frac{E[R_{\text{portfolio}}] - R_f}{\sigma_{\text{portfolio}}}$$

We have shown the Sharpe ratio as an ex ante (before the fact) measure, using the expected values of portfolio returns and standard deviation. However, it can also be used as an ex post (after the fact) measure of portfolio performance, using mean returns and sample standard deviation over a period.

The Sharpe ratio is based on total risk (standard deviation of returns), rather than systematic risk (beta). For this reason, the Sharpe ratio can be used to evaluate the performance of concentrated portfolios (those affected by unsystematic risk) as well as well-diversified portfolios (those with only systematic, or beta, risk). Note that the value of the Sharpe ratio is only useful for comparison with the Sharpe ratio of another portfolio.

In Figure 50.10, we illustrate that the Sharpe ratio of a portfolio is the slope of the CAL for that portfolio and can be compared to the slope of the CML, which is the Sharpe ratio for portfolios that lie on the CML.

Figure 50.10: Sharpe Ratios as Slopes

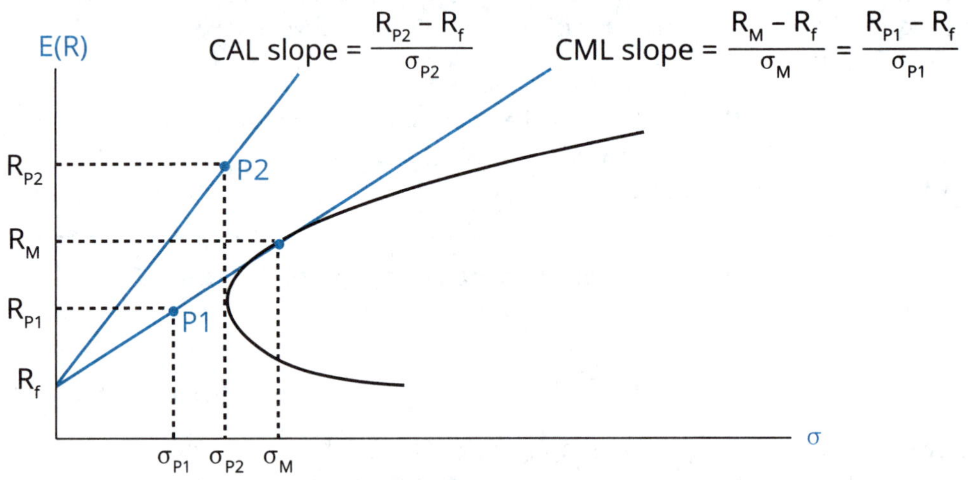

The **M-squared** (M^2) measure produces the same portfolio rankings as the Sharpe ratio but is stated in percentage terms. It is calculated as $\left(R_P - R_f\right)\frac{\sigma_M}{\sigma_P} - \left(R_M - R_f\right)$.

The first term is the excess return on a Portfolio P*, constructed by taking a leveraged position in Portfolio P so that P* has the same total risk, σ_M, as the market portfolio. As shown in Figure 50.11, the excess return on such a leveraged portfolio differs from the return on the market portfolio by the vertical distance M^2.

Figure 50.11: M-Squared for a Portfolio

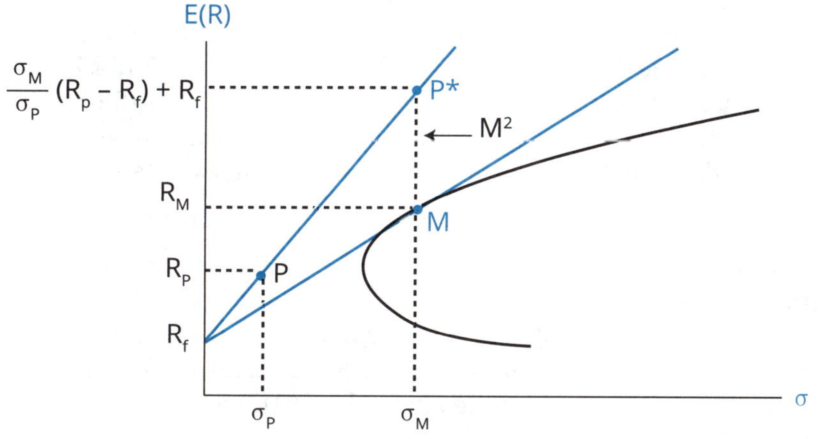

The difference between the Sharpe ratio and M^2 measure is that the Sharpe is a slope measure and M^2 is measured in percentage terms. M^2 is considered a measure of **risk-adjusted performance** (RAP). The intuition is that M^2 is the additional return that could have been earned by leveraging the active portfolio (borrowing at Rf) so that its risk is equal to that of the market portfolio.

Two measures of portfolio performance based on systematic (beta) risk rather than total risk are the **Treynor measure** and **Jensen's alpha**. They are analogous to the Sharpe ratio and M^2 in that the Treynor measure is a measure of slope and Jensen's alpha is a measure of percentage returns in excess of those from a portfolio that has the same risk (beta) but lies on the SML.

The Treynor measure is calculated as $\frac{R_P - R_f}{\beta_P}$, interpreted as excess returns per unit of systematic risk, and represented by the slope of a line as illustrated in Figure 50.12. Jensen's alpha for Portfolio P is calculated as

$$\alpha_P = R_p - [R_f + \beta_P(R_M - R_f)]$$

and is the percentage portfolio return above that of a portfolio (or security) with the same beta as the portfolio that lies on the SML, as illustrated in Figure 50.12.

Figure 50.12: Treynor Measure and Jensen's Alpha

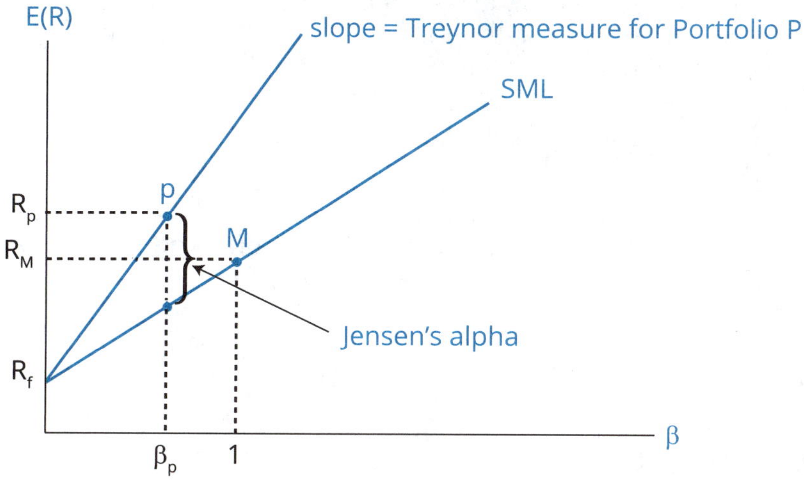

Whether risk adjustment should be based on standard deviation of returns or portfolio beta depends on whether a manager's portfolio bears unsystematic risk. If a single manager is used, then the total risk (including any nonsystematic risk) is the relevant measure and risk adjustment using total risk, as with the Sharpe and M^2 measures, is appropriate. If a fund uses multiple managers so that the overall fund portfolio is well diversified (has no unsystematic risk), then performance measures based on systematic (beta) risk, such as the Treynor measure and Jensen's alpha, are appropriate.

These measures of risk-adjusted returns are often used to compare the performance of actively managed funds to passively managed funds. Note in Figure 50.10 and Figure 50.11 that portfolios that lie above the CML have Sharpe ratios greater than those of any portfolios along the CML and have positive M^2 measures. Similarly, in Figure 50.12, we can see that portfolios that lie above the SML have Treynor measures greater than those of any security or portfolio that lies along the SML and also have positive values for Jensen's alpha.

One final note of caution is that estimating the values needed to apply these theoretical models and performance measures is often difficult and is done with error. The expected return on the market, and thus the market risk premium, may not be equal to its average historical value. Estimating security and portfolio betas is done with error as well.

MODULE QUIZ 50.2

To best evaluate your performance, enter your quiz answers online.

1. Which of the following statements about the SML and the CML is *least accurate*?
   A. Securities that plot above the SML are undervalued.
   B. Investors expect to be compensated for systematic risk.
   C. Securities that plot on the SML have no value to investors.
2. According to the CAPM, what is the expected rate of return for a stock with a beta of 1.2, when the risk-free rate is 6% and the market rate of return is 12%?
   A. 7.2%.
   B. 12.0%.
   C. 13.2%.
3. According to the CAPM, what is the required rate of return for a stock with a beta of 0.7, when the risk-free rate is 7% and the expected market rate of return is 14%?
   A. 11.9%.
   B. 14.0%.
   C. 16.8%.
4. The risk-free rate is 6%, and the expected market return is 15%. A stock with a beta of 1.2 is selling for $25 and will pay a $1 dividend at the end of the year. If the stock is priced at $30 at year-end, it is:
   A. overpriced, so short it.
   B. underpriced, so buy it.
   C. underpriced, so short it.

5. A stock with a beta of 0.7 currently priced at $50 is expected to increase in price to $55 by year-end and pay a $1 dividend. The expected market return is 15%, and the risk-free rate is 8%. The stock is:
   A. overpriced, so do not buy it.
   B. underpriced, so buy it.
   C. properly priced, so buy it.
6. Which of these return metrics is defined as excess return per unit of systematic risk?
   A. Sharpe ratio.
   B. Jensen's alpha.
   C. Treynor measure.

KEY CONCEPTS

LOS 50.a

The availability of a risk-free asset allows investors to build portfolios with superior risk-return properties. By combining a risk-free asset with a portfolio of risky assets, the overall risk and return can be adjusted to appeal to investors with various degrees of risk aversion.

LOS 50.b

On a graph of return versus risk, the various combinations of a risky asset and the risk-free asset form the capital allocation line (CAL). In the specific case where the risky asset is the market portfolio, the combinations of the risky asset and the risk-free asset form the capital market line (CML).

LOS 50.c

Systematic (market) risk is due to factors, such as GDP growth and interest rate changes, that affect the values of all risky securities. Systematic risk cannot be reduced by diversification. Unsystematic (firm-specific) risk can be reduced by portfolio diversification.

Because one of the assumptions underlying the CAPM is that portfolio diversification to eliminate unsystematic risk is costless, investors cannot increase expected equilibrium portfolio returns by taking on unsystematic risk.

LOS 50.d

A return generating model is an equation that estimates the expected return of an investment, based on a security's exposure to one or more macroeconomic, fundamental, or statistical factors.

The simplest return generating model is the market model, which assumes the return on an asset is related to the return on the market portfolio in the following manner:

$$R_i = \alpha_i + \beta_i R_m + e_i$$

LOS 50.e

Beta can be calculated using the following equation:

$$\beta_i = \frac{[\text{Cov}(R_i, R_m)]}{\sigma_m^2} = \rho_{im}\left(\frac{\sigma_i}{\sigma_m}\right)$$

where $[\text{Cov}(R_i, R_m)]$ and $\rho_{i,m}$ are the covariance and correlation between the asset and the market, and σ_i and σ_m are the standard deviations of asset returns and market returns.

The theoretical average beta of stocks in the market is 1. A beta of zero indicates that a security's return is uncorrelated with the returns of the market.

LOS 50.f

The capital asset pricing model (CAPM) requires several assumptions:

- Investors are risk averse, utility maximizing, and rational.
- Markets are free of frictions like costs and taxes.
- All investors plan using the same time period.
- All investors have the same expectations of security returns.
- Investments are infinitely divisible.
- Prices are unaffected by an investor's trades.

The security market line (SML) is a graphical representation of the CAPM that plots expected return versus beta for any security.

LOS 50.g

The CAPM relates expected return to the market factor (beta) using the following formula:

$$E(R_i) - R_f = \beta_i[E(R_m) - R_f]$$

LOS 50.h

The CAPM and the SML indicate what a security's equilibrium required rate of return should be based on the security's exposure to market risk. An analyst can compare his expected rate of return on a security to the required rate of return indicated by the SML to determine whether the security is overvalued, undervalued, or properly valued.

LOS 50.i

The Sharpe ratio measures excess return per unit of total risk and is useful for comparing portfolios on a risk-adjusted basis. The M-squared measure provides the same portfolio rankings as the Sharpe ratio but is stated in percentage terms:

$$\text{Sharpe ratio} = \left(\frac{R_P - R_f}{\sigma_P}\right)$$

$$\text{M-squared} = (R_P - R_f)\frac{\sigma_M}{\sigma_P} - (R_M - R_f)$$

The Treynor measure measures a portfolio's excess return per unit of systematic risk. Jensen's alpha is the difference between a portfolio's return and the return of a portfolio on the SML that has the same beta:

$$\text{Treynor measure} = \frac{R_P - R_f}{\beta_P}$$

$$\text{Jensen's alpha} = \alpha_P = R_P - [R_f + \beta_P(R_M - R_f)]$$

ANSWER KEY FOR MODULE QUIZZES

Module Quiz 50.1

1. **B** Expected return: (0.60 × 0.10) + (0.40 × 0.05) = 0.08, or 8.0%

   Standard deviation: 0.60 × 0.08 = 0.048, or 4.8%

   (LOS 50.a)

2. **C** The capital market line (CML) plots return against *total risk*, which is measured by standard deviation of returns. (LOS 50.b)

3. **B** A portfolio to the right of a portfolio on the CML has more risk than the market portfolio. Investors seeking to take on more risk will *borrow* at the risk-free rate to purchase more of the market portfolio. (LOS 50.b)

4. **A** When you increase the number of stocks in a portfolio, *unsystematic risk* will decrease at a decreasing rate. However, the portfolio's *systematic risk* can be increased by adding higher-beta stocks or decreased by adding lower-beta stocks. (LOS 50.c)

5. **C** Total risk equals systematic plus unsystematic risk. Unique risk is diversifiable and is unsystematic. Market (systematic) risk is nondiversifiable risk. (LOS 50.c)

6. **A** Macroeconomic, fundamental, and statistical factor exposures can be included in a return generating model to estimate the expected return of an investment. However, statistical factors may not have any theoretical basis, so analysts prefer macroeconomic and fundamental factor models. (LOS 50.d)

7. **C** beta = covariance / market variance

   market variance = 0.05^2 = 0.0025

   beta = 0.005 / 0.0025 = 2.0

   (LOS 50.e)

Module Quiz 50.2

1. **C** Securities that plot on the SML are expected to earn their equilibrium rate of return and, therefore, do have value to an investor and may have diversification benefits as well. The other statements are true. (LOS 50.f)

2. **C** 6 + 1.2(12 – 6) = 13.2% (LOS 50.g)

3. **A** 7 + 0.7(14 – 7) = 11.9% (LOS 50.g)

4. **B** required rate = 6 + 1.2(15 – 6) = 16.8%

   return on stock = (30 – 25 + 1) / 25 = 24%

   Based on risk, the stock plots above the SML and is underpriced, so buy it. (LOS 50.h)

5. **A** required rate = 8 + 0.7(15 – 8) = 12.9%

   return on stock = (55 – 50 + 1) / 50 = 12%

   The stock falls below the SML, so it is *overpriced*. (LOS 50.h)

6. **C** The Treynor measure is excess return (return in excess of the risk-free rate) per unit of systematic risk (beta). The Sharpe ratio is excess return per unit of total risk (portfolio standard deviation). Jensen's alpha is the difference between a portfolio's actual rate of return and the equilibrium rate of return for a portfolio with the same level of beta (systematic) risk. (LOS 50.i)

The following is a review of the Portfolio Management (2) principles designed to address the learning outcome statements set forth by CFA Institute. Cross-Reference to CFA Institute Assigned Reading #51.

READING 51

Basics of Portfolio Planning and Construction

Study Session 18

EXAM FOCUS

There is nothing difficult here, but the material is important because it is the foundation for the portfolio construction material at Level II and especially Level III. You should be ready to explain why investment policy statements are created and what their major components are. You should be familiar with the objectives (risk and return) and the constraints: liquidity, legal, time horizon, tax treatment, and unique circumstances. Know the difference between ability and willingness to take risk, the factors that define an asset class, and how asset allocation is used in constructing portfolios.

MODULE 51.1: PORTFOLIO PLANNING AND CONSTRUCTION

Video covering this content is available online.

LOS 51.a: Describe the reasons for a written investment policy statement (IPS).

CFA® Program Curriculum, Volume 6, page 6

An investment manager is very unlikely to produce a good result for a client without understanding that client's needs, circumstances, and constraints.

A written **investment policy statement** will typically begin with the investor's goals in terms of risk and return. These should be determined jointly, as the goals of high returns and low risk (while quite popular) are likely to be mutually exclusive in practice. Investor expectations in terms of returns must be compatible with investor's tolerance for risk (uncertainty about portfolio performance).

LOS 51.b: Describe the major components of an IPS.

CFA® Program Curriculum, Volume 6, page 6

The major components of an IPS typically address the following:

- *Description of Client* circumstances, situation, and investment objectives.
- *Statement of the Purpose* of the IPS.
- *Statement of Duties and Responsibilities* of investment manager, custodian of assets, and the client.
- *Procedures* to update IPS and to respond to various possible situations.
- *Investment Objectives* derived from communications with the client.
- *Investment Constraints* that must be considered in the plan.
- *Investment Guidelines* such as how the policy will be executed, asset types permitted, and leverage to be used.
- *Evaluation of Performance*, the benchmark portfolio for evaluating investment performance, and other information on evaluation of investment results.
- *Appendices* containing information on strategic (baseline) asset allocation and permitted deviations from policy portfolio allocations, as well as how and when the portfolio allocations should be rebalanced.

In any case, the IPS will, at a minimum, contain a clear statement of client circumstances and constraints, an investment strategy based on these, and some benchmark against which to evaluate the account performance.

LOS 51.c: Describe risk and return objectives and how they may be developed for a client.

CFA® Program Curriculum, Volume 6, page 8

The **risk objectives** in an IPS may take several forms. An **absolute risk objective** might be to "have no decrease in portfolio value during any 12-month period" or to "not decrease in value by more than 2% at any point over any 12-month period." Low absolute percentage risk objectives such as these may result in portfolios made up of securities that offer guaranteed returns (e.g., U.S. Treasury bills).

Absolute risk objectives can also be stated in terms of the probability of specific portfolio results, either percentage losses or dollar losses, rather than strict limits on portfolio results. Examples are as follows:

- "No greater than a 5% probability of returns below –5% in any 12-month period."
- "No greater than a 4% probability of a loss of more than $20,000 over any 12-month period."

An absolute return objective may be stated in nominal terms, such as "an overall return of at least 6% per annum," or in real returns, such as "a return of 3% more than the annual inflation rate each year."

Relative risk objectives relate to a specific benchmark and can also be strict, such as, "Returns will not be less than 12-month euro LIBOR over any 12-month period," or stated in terms of probability, such as, "No greater than a 5% probability of returns more than 4% below the return on the MSCI World Index over any 12-month period."

Return objectives can be relative to a benchmark portfolio return, such as, "Exceed the return on the S&P 500 Index by 2% per annum." For a bank, the return objective may be relative to the bank's cost of funds (deposit rate). While it is possible for an institution to use returns on peer portfolios, such as an endowment with a stated objective to be in the top quartile of endowment fund returns, peer performance benchmarks suffer from not being *investable* portfolios. There is no way to match this investment return by portfolio construction before the fact.

In any event, the account manager must make sure that the stated risk and return objectives are compatible, given the reality of expected investment results and uncertainty over time.

LOS 51.d: Explain the difference between the willingness and the ability (capacity) to take risk in analyzing an investor's financial risk tolerance.

CFA® Program Curriculum, Volume 6, page 8

An investor's **ability to bear risk** depends on financial circumstances. Longer investment horizons (20 years rather than 2 years), greater assets versus liabilities (more wealth), more insurance against unexpected occurrences, and a secure job all suggest a greater ability to bear investment risk in terms of uncertainty about periodic investment performance.

An investor's **willingness to bear risk** is based primarily on the investor's attitudes and beliefs about investments (various asset types). The assessment of an investor's attitude about risk is quite subjective and is sometimes done with a short questionnaire that attempts to categorize the investor's risk aversion or risk tolerance.

When the adviser's assessments of an investor's ability and willingness to take investment risk are compatible, there is no real problem selecting an appropriate level of investment risk. If the investor's willingness to take on investment risk is high but the investor's ability to take on risk is low, the low ability to take on investment risk will prevail in the adviser's assessment.

In situations where ability is high but willingness is low, the adviser may attempt to educate the investor about investment risk and correct any misconceptions that may be contributing to the investor's low stated willingness to take on investment risk. However, the adviser's job is not to change the investor's personality characteristics that contribute to a low willingness to take on investment risk. The approach will most likely be to conform to the lower of the investor's ability or willingness to bear risk, as constructing a portfolio with a level of risk that the client is clearly uncomfortable with will not likely lead to a good outcome in the investor's view.

LOS 51.e: Describe the investment constraints of liquidity, time horizon, tax concerns, legal and regulatory factors, and unique circumstances and their implications for the choice of portfolio assets.

CFA® Program Curriculum, Volume 6, page 15

PROFESSOR'S NOTE

When I was studying for the CFA exams over 20 years ago, we memorized R-R-T-T-L-L-U as a checklist for addressing the important points of portfolio construction, and it still works today. Then, as now, the important points to cover in an IPS were Risk, Return, Time horizon, Tax situation, Liquidity, Legal restrictions, and the Unique constraints of a specific investor.

Investment constraints include the investor's liquidity needs, time horizon, tax considerations, legal and regulatory constraints, and unique needs and preferences.

Liquidity: Liquidity refers to the ability to turn investment assets into spendable cash in a short period of time without having to make significant price concessions to do so. Investor needs for money to pay tuition, to pay for a parent's assisted living expenses, or to fund other possible spending needs may all require that some liquid assets be held. As we noted in an earlier topic review discussing property and casualty insurance companies, claims arrive unpredictably to some extent and therefore their portfolios must hold a significant proportion of liquid (or maturing) securities in order to be prepared to honor these claims. Illiquid investments in hedge funds and private equity funds, which typically are not traded and have restrictions on redemptions, are not suitable for an investor who may unexpectedly need access to the funds.

Time horizon: In general, the longer an investor's time horizon, the more risk and less liquidity the investor can accept in the portfolio. While the expected returns on a broad equities portfolio may not be too risky for an investor with a 20-year investment horizon, they likely are too risky for an investor who must fund a large purchase at the end of this year. For such an investor, government securities or a bank certificate of deposit may be the most appropriate investments because of their low risk and high liquidity at the time when the funds will be needed.

Tax situation: Besides an individual's overall tax rate, the tax treatment of various types of investment accounts is also a consideration in portfolio construction. For a fully taxable account, investors subject to higher tax rates may prefer tax-free bonds (U.S.) to taxable bonds or prefer equities that are expected to produce capital gains, which are often taxed at a lower rate than other types of income. A focus on expected after-tax returns over time in relation to risk should correctly account for differences in tax treatments as well as investors' overall tax rates.

Some types of investment accounts, such as retirement accounts, may be tax exempt or tax deferred. Investors with such accounts may choose to put securities that generate fully taxed income, such as corporate bond interest, in accounts that are tax deferred, while seeking long-term capital gains, tax-exempt interest income, and dividend income (in jurisdictions where dividends receive preferential tax treatment) in their personal accounts, which have no tax deferral benefit.

Legal and regulatory: In addition to financial market regulations that apply to all investors, more specific legal and regulatory constraints may apply to particular investors. Trust, corporate, and qualified investment accounts may all be restricted by law from investing in particular types of securities and assets. There may also be restrictions on percentage allocations to specific types of investments in such accounts. Corporate officers and directors face legal restrictions on trading in the securities of their firms that the account manager should be aware of.

Unique circumstances: Each investor, whether individual or institutional, may have specific preferences or restrictions on which securities and assets may be purchased for the account. Some of these may be nonfinancial considerations, which are commonly categorized as **responsible investing**. Ethical preferences, such as prohibiting investment in securities issued by tobacco or firearms producers, are not uncommon. Restrictions on investments in companies or countries where human rights abuses are suspected or documented would also fall into this category. Religious preferences may preclude investment in securities that make explicit interest payments.

Unique investor preferences may also be based on diversification needs when the investor's income depends heavily on the prospects for one company or industry. An investor who has founded or runs a company may not want any investment in securities issued by a competitor to that company.

LOS 51.f: Explain the specification of asset classes in relation to asset allocation.

CFA® Program Curriculum, Volume 6, page 23

After having determined the investor objectives and constraints through the exercise of creating an IPS, a **strategic asset allocation** is developed which specifies the percentage allocations to the included asset classes. In choosing which asset classes to consider when developing the strategic asset allocation for the account, the correlations of returns *within* an asset class should be relatively high, indicating that the assets within the class are similar in their investment performance. On the other hand, it is low correlations of returns *between* asset classes that leads to risk reduction through portfolio diversification.

Historically, only the broad categories of equities, bonds, cash, and real estate were considered. More recently, a group of several investable asset classes, referred to collectively as alternative investments, has gained more prominence. Alternative investment asset classes include hedge funds of various types, private equity funds, managed or passively constructed commodity funds, artwork, and intellectual property rights.

We can further divide equities by whether the issuing companies are domestic or foreign, large or small, or whether they are traded in emerging or developed markets. An example of specifying asset classes is world equities. A U.S. investor may want to divide world equities into different regions.

With bonds, we can divide the overall universe of bonds into asset classes based on maturities or on criteria such as whether they are foreign or domestic, government or corporate, or investment grade or speculative (high yield). Overall, the asset classes considered should approximate the universe of permissible investments specified in the IPS.

Once the universe of asset classes has been specified, the investment manager will collect data on the returns, standard deviation of returns, and correlations of returns with those of other asset classes for each asset class.

Figure 51.1 illustrates the strategic asset allocation for a pension fund.

Figure 51.1: Strategic Asset Allocation

The Vermont Pension Investment Committee manages more than $4 billion in retirement assets for various teachers and state and municipal employees in that state. VPIC's investment policy specifies the following strategic asset allocation:

Asset Class	Target
Growth assets	
Passive global equities	24%
Active global equities	5%
Large cap U.S. equities	4%
Small-/mid-cap U.S. equities	3%
Non–U.S. developed market equities	5%
International small-cap equities	2%
Private equity	10%
Core plus fixed income	6%
Emerging market debt	4%
Private debt	5%
Non-core real estate	3%
Total growth assets	**71%**
Downturn hedging assets	
Core fixed income	14%
Short-term quality credit	5%
Total downturn hedging	**19%**
Inflation hedging assets	
Core real estate	5%
U.S. TIPS	3%
Infrastructure/farmland	2%
Total inflation hedging	**10%**

Source: State of Vermont, Office of the State Treasurer. Target allocation as of March 25, 2019. www.vermonttreasurer.gov/content/pension.

LOS 51.g: Describe the principles of portfolio construction and the role of asset allocation in relation to the IPS.

CFA® Program Curriculum, Volume 6, page 23

Once the portfolio manager has identified the investable asset classes for the portfolio and the risk, return, and correlation characteristics of each asset class, an *efficient frontier*, analogous to one constructed from individual securities, can be constructed using a computer program. By combining the return and risk objectives from the IPS with the actual risk and return properties of the many portfolios along the efficient frontier, the manager can identify that portfolio which best meets the risk and return requirements of the investor. The asset allocation for the efficient portfolio selected is then the strategic asset allocation for the portfolio.

So far, we have not concerned ourselves with deviations from strategic asset allocations or with selection of individual securities within individual asset classes. These activities are referred to as active (versus passive) portfolio management strategies. A manager who varies from strategic asset allocation weights in order to take advantage of perceived short-term opportunities is adding **tactical asset allocation** to the portfolio strategy. **Security selection** refers to deviations from index weights on individual securities within an asset class. For example, a portfolio manager might overweight energy stocks and underweight financial stocks, relative to the index weights for U.S. large-cap equities as an asset class. For some asset classes, such as hedge funds, individual real estate properties, and artwork, investable indexes are not available. For these asset classes, selection of individual assets is required by the nature of the asset class.

While each of these active strategies may produce higher returns, they each also increase the risk of the portfolio compared to a passive portfolio of asset class indexes. A practice known as **risk budgeting** sets an overall risk limit for the portfolio and budgets (allocates) a portion of the permitted risk to the systematic risk of the strategic asset allocation, the risk from tactical asset allocation, and the risk from security selection.

Active portfolio management has two specific issues to consider.

1. An investor may have multiple managers actively managing to the same benchmark for the same asset class (or may have significant benchmark overlap). In this case, one manager may overweight an index stock while another may underweight the same stock. Taken together, there is no net active management risk, although each manager has reported active management risk. Overall, the risk budget is underutilized as there is less net active management than gross active management.
2. When all managers are actively managing portfolios relative to an index, trading may be excessive overall. This extra trading could have negative tax consequences, specifically potentially higher capital gains taxes, compared to an overall efficient tax strategy.

One way to address these issues is to use a **core-satellite approach**. The core-satellite approach invests the majority, or core, portion of the portfolio in passively managed indexes and invests a smaller, or satellite, portion in active strategies. This approach reduces the likelihood of excessive trading and offsetting active positions.

Clearly, the success of security selection will depend on the manager's skill and the opportunities (mispricings or inefficiencies) within a particular asset class. Similarly, the success of tactical asset allocation will depend both on the existence of short-term opportunities in specific asset classes and on the manager's ability to identify them.

LOS 51.h: Describe how environmental, social, and governance (ESG) considerations may be integrated into portfolio planning and construction.

CFA® Program Curriculum, Volume 6, page 37

In our Corporate Issuers review of "Introduction to Corporate Governance and Other ESG Considerations," we described several approaches to ESG investing. Briefly, these approaches include:

- **Negative screening**, excluding specific companies or industries based on ESG factors.
- **Positive screening**, investing in companies that have positive ESG practices.
- **Thematic investing**, selecting sectors or companies to promote specific ESG-related goals.
- **Impact investing**, selecting investments both to provide a return and to promote positive ESG practices.
- **Engagement/active ownership**, using share ownership as a platform to promote improved ESG practices at a company.
- **ESG integration**, considering ESG factors throughout the asset allocation and security selection process.

Here, we look at some issues these approaches raise for portfolio management.

If a portfolio's investment universe is constrained by negative screening, measuring its performance against a broad market index is unlikely to be appropriate. Indexes excluding companies or industries that investors with ESG concerns commonly avoid are available.

While many investors use positive screening, thematic, or impact investing approaches, choices of which specific companies to invest in and which ESG factors to focus on differ among investors. Thus, portfolios and performance benchmarks must be customized under these approaches, and they may require investment managers who specialize in these styles of investing.

For investment managers with clients who wish to engage in active ownership, it is important to clarify whether the clients intend to vote their shares themselves or direct the managers to vote the shares according to specified ESG factors.

Regardless of the approach chosen, investors should be aware that imposing constraints based on ESG factors will likely affect portfolio performance. How these constraints will affect portfolio performance in practice is uncertain. Both limiting the universe of investment choices and incurring the costs involved in considering

ESG factors may decrease returns. On the other hand, investing in companies with good corporate governance practices and avoiding those that face ESG-related risks may increase portfolio returns.

MODULE QUIZ 51.1

To best evaluate your performance, enter your quiz answers online.

1. The investment policy statement is *most accurately* considered:
   A. the starting point of the portfolio management process.
   B. the key intermediate step in the portfolio management process.
   C. the end product of the portfolio management process.
2. The component of an investment policy statement that defines the investment objectives is *most likely* to include information about:
   A. the investor's risk tolerance.
   B. unique needs and preferences of the investor.
   C. permitted asset types and use of leverage in the investment account.
3. When an investment advisor is developing return and risk objectives for a client:
   A. return objectives should be absolute and risk objectives should be relative.
   B. risk objectives should be absolute and return objectives should be relative.
   C. both return and risk objectives may be stated in absolute or relative terms.
4. A client exhibits an above-average willingness to take risk but a below-average ability to take risk. When assigning an overall risk tolerance, the investment adviser is *most likely* to assess the client's overall risk tolerance as:
   A. above average.
   B. average.
   C. below average.
5. Which of the following is *least likely* an example of a portfolio constraint?
   A. Higher tax rate on dividend income than on capital gains.
   B. Significant spending requirements in the near future.
   C. Minimum total return requirement of 8%.
6. For asset allocation purposes, asset classes should be specified such that correlations of returns are relatively:
   A. low within each asset class and low among asset classes.
   B. high within each asset class and low among asset classes.
   C. low within each asset class and high among asset classes.
7. In determining the appropriate asset allocation for a client's investment account, the manager should:
   A. consider only the investor's risk tolerance.
   B. incorporate forecasts of future economic conditions.
   C. consider the investor's risk tolerance and future needs, but not forecasts of market conditions.

KEY CONCEPTS

LOS 51.a

A written investment policy statement, the first step in the portfolio management process, is a plan for achieving investment success. An IPS forces investment discipline and ensures that goals are realistic by requiring investors to articulate their circumstances, objectives, and constraints.

LOS 51.b

Many IPS include the following sections:

- Introduction—Describes the client.
- Statement of Purpose—The intentions of the IPS.
- Statement of Duties and Responsibilities—Of the client, the asset custodian, and the investment managers.
- Procedures—Related to keeping the IPS updated and responding to unforeseen events.
- Investment Objectives—The client's investment needs, specified in terms of required return and risk tolerance.
- Investment Constraints—Factors that may hinder the ability to meet investment objectives; typically categorized as time horizon, taxes, liquidity, legal and regulatory, and unique needs.
- Investment Guidelines—For example, whether leverage, derivatives, or specific kinds of assets are allowed.
- Evaluation and Review—Related to feedback on investment results.
- Appendices—May specify the portfolio's strategic asset allocation (policy portfolio) or the portfolio's rebalancing policy.

LOS 51.c

Risk objectives are specifications for portfolio risk that are developed to embody a client's risk tolerance. Risk objectives can be either absolute (e.g., no losses greater than 10% in any year) or relative (e.g., annual return will be within 2% of FTSE return).

Return objectives are typically based on an investor's desire to meet a future financial goal, such as a particular level of income in retirement. Return objectives can be absolute (e.g., 9% annual return) or relative (e.g., outperform the S&P 500 by 2% per year).

The achievability of an investor's return expectations may be hindered by the investor's risk objectives.

LOS 51.d

Willingness to take financial risk is related to an investor's psychological factors, such as personality type and level of financial knowledge.

Ability or capacity to take risk depends on financial factors, such as wealth relative to liabilities, income stability, and time horizon.

A client's overall risk tolerance depends on both his ability to take risk and his willingness to take risk. A willingness greater than ability, or vice versa, is typically resolved by choosing the more conservative of the two and counseling the client.

LOS 51.e

Investment constraints include:

- Liquidity—The need to draw cash from the portfolio for anticipated or unexpected future spending needs. High liquidity needs often translate to a high portfolio allocation to bonds or cash.
- Time horizon—Often the period over which assets are accumulated and before withdrawals begin. Risky or illiquid investments may be inappropriate for an investor with a short time horizon.
- Tax considerations—Concerns the tax treatments of the investor's various accounts, the relative tax treatment of capital gains and income, and the investor's marginal tax bracket.
- Legal and regulatory—Constraints such as government restrictions on portfolio contents or laws against insider trading.
- Unique circumstances—Restrictions due to investor preferences (religious, ethical, etc.) or other factors not already considered.

LOS 51.f

An asset class is a group of securities with similar risk and performance characteristics. Examples of major asset classes include equity, fixed income, cash, and real estate. Portfolio managers also use more narrowly defined asset classes, such as large-cap U.S. equities or speculative international bonds, and alternative asset classes, such as commodities or investments in hedge funds.

LOS 51.g

Strategic asset allocation is a set of percentage allocations to various asset classes that is designed to meet the investor's objectives. The strategic asset allocation is developed by combining the objectives and constraints in the IPS with the performance expectations of the various asset classes. The strategic asset allocation provides the basic structure of a portfolio.

Tactical asset allocation refers to an allocation that deviates from the baseline (strategic) allocation in order to profit from a forecast of shorter-term opportunities in specific asset classes.

LOS 51.h

Imposing portfolio constraints based on ESG factors may affect performance. Limiting the universe of investment choices may decrease returns, but good corporate governance and low ESG-related risks may increase returns.

If a portfolio's investment universe is constrained by negative screening, its performance should be measured against a benchmark that excludes companies with negative ESG factors.

Positive screening, best-in-class, or thematic investing approaches typically require portfolio construction to be customized for the investor's choices of which ESG factors to focus on.

For active ownership, it is important to clarify whether investors intend to vote their shares themselves or direct managers to vote the shares according to specified ESG factors.

ANSWER KEY FOR MODULE QUIZZES

Module Quiz 51.1

1. **A** An investment policy statement is considered to be the starting point of the portfolio management process. The IPS is a plan for achieving investment success. (LOS 51.a)

2. **A** Investment objectives are defined based on both the investor's return requirements and risk tolerance. Investment constraints include the investor's time horizon, liquidity needs, tax considerations, legal and regulatory requirements, and unique needs and preferences. Policies regarding permitted asset types and the amount of leverage to use are best characterized as investment guidelines. (LOS 51.b)

3. **C** Both risk and return objectives can be defined either in absolute terms or relative to some benchmark. (LOS 51.c)

4. **C** When assigning an overall risk tolerance, the prudent approach is to use the lower of ability to take risk and willingness to take risk. (LOS 51.d)

5. **C** Return objectives are part of a policy statement's objectives, not constraints. (LOS 51.e)

6. **B** Asset classes should be defined such that correlations of returns within the asset class are relatively high (because assets within a class should perform alike over time), while correlations of returns among asset classes are relatively low (to benefit from diversification). (LOS 51.f)

7. **B** An adviser's forecasts of the expected returns and expected volatilities (risk) of different asset classes are an important part of determining an appropriate asset allocation. (LOS 51.g)

The following is a review of the Portfolio Management (2) principles designed to address the learning outcome statements set forth by CFA Institute. Cross-Reference to CFA Institute Assigned Reading #52.

READING 52

The Behavioral Biases of Individuals

Study Session 18

EXAM FOCUS

Behavioral finance investigates ways in which human behavior differs from the rationality assumed by traditional economic models. Some believe these irrational behaviors or biases lead to predictable deviations of financial markets from the implications of financial models of security price behavior. Here, candidates must learn some of the terminology of behavioral finance and examples that support a belief in irrational investor behavior. Additionally, we cover how investor biases and irrationality may explain certain anomalous results of tests of market efficiency.

MODULE 52.1: COGNITIVE ERRORS VS. EMOTIONAL BIASES

Video covering this content is available online.

Traditional finance assumes that individuals act as perfectly rational economic beings who objectively consider all relevant information to make rational decisions, and that this process results in efficient markets. Research results have called these assumptions into question. Kahneman and Tversky pioneered this work in the early 1970s, initially setting logic tests where individuals' intuitive answers were predictably flawed. This supported the idea that human decision-making has systematic biases that lead to irrational decisions.

This work was extended by Kahneman, Tversky, and others, who have suggested that a better understanding of these biases by clients (and by the professionals who work with those clients) should produce securities prices and returns over time that better match the informationally efficient markets of traditional finance theory.

LOS 52.a: Compare and contrast cognitive errors and emotional biases.

CFA® Program Curriculum, Volume 6, page 50

Individuals, when facing complex decision-making, often lack the time or ability to derive the optimal course of action prescribed by traditional finance. Cognitive limitations and emotional responses introduce bias into the decision-making process, leading to decisions that are biased (not perfectly rational). Behavioral finance asserts that certain biases, which are not simply random errors, are widespread and therefore predictable.

Cognitive errors are due primarily to faulty reasoning or irrationality. They can arise from not understanding statistical analysis, information processing errors, illogical reasoning, or memory errors. Such errors can possibly be reduced by increased awareness, better training, or more information.

Emotional biases are not related to conscious thought. Rather, they stem from feelings, impulses, or intuition. As such, they are difficult to overcome and may have to be accommodated.

Despite the distinction in grouping biases as either cognitive or emotional, a bias may have elements of both cognition and emotion. When trying to overcome or mitigate biases that are both emotional and cognitive, success is more likely by focusing on the cognitive issues.

LOS 52.b: Discuss commonly recognized behavioral biases and their implications for financial decision making.

CFA® Program Curriculum, Volume 6, page 50

Cognitive errors can be divided into *belief perseverance* biases that reflect an irrational reluctance to change prior conclusions and decisions, and *processing errors* where the information analysis is flawed.

Cognitive Errors: Belief Perseverance

Psychologists use the term **cognitive dissonance** to refer to a situation where an individual holds conflicting beliefs or receives information that causes a current belief to be questioned. Cognitive dissonance causes stress that individuals seek to reduce. They may do so by letting go of prior beliefs in favor of the conflicting belief. On the other hand, they might discount the conflicting information or viewpoints by questioning their truth, source, applicability, or significance. To the extent that it is easier to do the latter than the former, bias in favor of currently held beliefs is the result.

1. **Conservatism bias** occurs when market participants rationally form an initial view but then fail to change that view as new information becomes available. That is, they overweight their prior probabilities and do not adjust them appropriately as new information becomes available. Individuals displaying this bias tend to maintain prior forecasts and securities allocations, ignoring or failing to recognize the significance of new information. Individuals may react slowly to new data or ignore information that is complex to process.

EXAMPLE: Conservatism bias

John Molinari allocates assets based on his observation that over the last 80 years, recessions occurred in 20% of those years. When a coworker informs Molinari that the country's central bank has announced a policy change to a tightening of monetary conditions, Molinari does not adjust his recommended asset allocations. Does this reflect conservatism bias?

Answer:

Molinari should consider that the conditional probability of a recession, given that the central bank is tightening, may differ from the unconditional probability of a recession that he previously estimated. He is showing conservatism bias by not considering the impact of this new information.

Conservatism bias may result in market participants holding investments too long because they are unwilling or slow to update a view or forecast. They may be avoiding the mental effort or stress of updating prior beliefs by not considering the implications of new information.

2. **Confirmation bias** occurs when market participants focus on or seek information that supports prior beliefs, while avoiding or diminishing the importance of conflicting information or viewpoints. They may distort new information in a way that remains consistent with their prior beliefs.

   For example, after buying a car from a given manufacturer, the buyer would exhibit confirmation bias by reading articles about how great cars from that manufacturer are but avoiding news about problems with that particular brand. Because the buyer already purchased the car, information suggesting that it was a bad decision is unwelcome.

   Consequences and implications of confirmation bias may include market participants who:

   - Consider positive information but ignore negative information.
   - Set up a decision process or data screen incorrectly to support a preferred belief.
   - Become overconfident about the correctness of a presently held belief.

   Market participants can reduce confirmation bias by seeking out contrary views and information—for example, by reading analyses and viewpoints that disagree with a presently held belief, rather than only reading those that reinforce the belief.

3. **Representativeness bias** occurs when certain characteristics are used to put an investment in a category and the individual concludes that it will have the characteristics of investments in that category. Individuals systematically make the error of believing that two things that are similar in some respects are more similar in other respects than they actually are.

   Two forms of representativeness bias are base-rate neglect and sample-size neglect.

   Base-rate neglect refers to analyzing an individual member of a population without adequately considering the probability of a characteristic in that population (the base rate). Consider this example of base-rate neglect: a group was asked to identify the most likely occupation of a man who was

Reading 52

characterized as somewhat shy as a salesperson or a librarian. Most participants chose librarian, thinking that most librarians would tend to be more shy on average than salespeople, who tend to be outgoing. Their mistake was in not considering that there are relatively few male librarians and a great number of male salespeople. Even though a greater percentage of librarians may be characterized as somewhat shy, the absolute number of salespeople who could be characterized as somewhat shy is significantly greater.

Sample-size neglect refers to making a classification based on a small and potentially unrealistic data sample. The error is believing the population reflects the characteristics of the small sample.

For example, a fund manager may show strong performance over a three-year time horizon. This may lead investors to assume this is evidence of superior skill. However, examination of longer sample periods shows a lack of persistence; there will be some three-year "winners" even when annual returns results are actually random. The evidence of the lack of persistence of managers' relative performance over time does not support investors' conclusion that this manager will continue to outperform.

EXAMPLE: Representativeness bias

XYZ company has long been recognized as a growth stock, delivering superior earnings growth and stock price appreciation. While earnings have continued to grow, last year's revenue has not, and neither has the stock price. Under the following two conditions, would an analyst be more likely to buy or sell the stock?

1. The analyst suffers from base-rate and sample-size neglect.
2. The analyst treats the growth classification as representative.

Answer:

If the analyst exhibits sample-size neglect and base-rate neglect biases, the analyst will ignore XYZ's long record as a growth stock, focus on the short-term disappointing results, and may recommend selling the stock without considering the long-term possibility it will revert to growth behavior.

However, if the analyst over-relies on the initial growth classification, the analyst may assume that the stock will return to growth and recommend buying it, without properly considering the reasons for its recent results or their longer-term implications.

Representativeness bias may lead market participants to attach too much importance to a few characteristics based on a small sample size or make decisions based on simple rules and classifications rather than conducting a more-thorough and complex analysis.

4. **Illusion of control bias** exists when market participants believe they can control or affect outcomes when they cannot. It is often associated with emotional biases: *illusion of knowledge* (belief you know things you do not know), *self-attribution* (belief you personally caused something to happen), and *overconfidence* (an unwarranted belief that your beliefs will prove to be correct).

An example of control bias can be seen in humans' attempts to control the weather using ritual ceremonies. This allowed them to believe they had some control of the environment, when in fact it is highly unlikely that a ceremony can influence the weather.

Illusion of control may cause market participants to overweight securities for which they believe they have control over outcomes, such as a company they work for or are otherwise associated with. This can result in their portfolios being inadequately diversified.

5. **Hindsight bias** is a selective memory of past events, actions, or what was knowable in the past, resulting in an individual's tendency to see things as more predictable than they really are. People tend to remember their correct predictions and forget their incorrect ones. They also overestimate what could have been known. This behavior results from individuals being able to observe outcomes that did occur but not the outcomes that did not materialize. Hindsight bias is sometimes referred to as the *I-knew-it-all-along phenomenon*.

   Hindsight bias is caused by three types of errors:

   1. Individuals distort their earlier predictions when looking back. This is the tendency to believe that we knew the outcome of an uncertain event all along.
   2. Individuals tend to view events that have occurred as inevitable.
   3. Individuals assume they could have foreseen the outcomes of uncertain events.

   Hindsight bias can lead to overconfidence in ability to predict outcomes. It may also cause investors to cast aside valid analysis techniques that did not turn out to be correct in favor of poor techniques that turned out well by chance.

Cognitive Errors: Information-Processing Biases

These are related more to the processing of information and less to the decision-making process.

Anchoring and adjustment bias refers to basing expectations on a prior number and overweighting its importance, making adjustments in relation to that number as new information arrives. Examples would be estimating the value of a security relative to its current value or making estimates of earnings per share relative to a previously reported value or relative to a prior estimate. Anchoring leads to underestimating the implications of new information. New data should be considered objectively without regard to any initial anchor point.

Mental accounting bias refers to viewing money in different accounts or from different sources differently when making investment decisions. This conflicts with the idea that security decisions should be made in the context of the investor's overall portfolio of assets based on their financial goals and risk tolerance.

An example of mental accounting is an investor who receives an unexpected bonus at work and chooses to invest it in a very risky biotechnology stock, reasoning that the bonus is "found money" that can acceptably be risked on speculation. In fact, while such a stock may have a place in the investor's portfolio, decisions about whether and how much of it to include should be based on a total portfolio approach.

Another example may be an investor who receives an inheritance from a parent and segregates those funds into low-risk bonds out of a desire to "not lose any of the money the parent worked so hard to save." This behavior also conflicts with the principle that investments should be considered in the context of the entire portfolio.

The result of such mental accounting may be that an investor's overall portfolio is not optimal given the investor's circumstances, investment goals, and risk tolerance. It can cause an investor to hold positions that offset each other, rather than considering investments in the context of their correlation of returns. One common form of mental accounting bias is a tendency to view income differently from capital appreciation. This may cause an investor to hold a mix of income-producing and non-income-producing securities that does not match the investor's circumstances.

A study by Camerer et al. (1997)[1] investigated behavior of New York taxi drivers. The study suggests that each new day was a separate account in the minds of the taxi drivers. It appears that New York taxi drivers have a reference rate for daily income and perceive a loss if they fail to meet it (which we may also view as an example of anchoring). On rainy days, demand for taxis is high, while on sunny days, the demand is low. Logically, you would expect taxi drivers to work more hours on rainy days to maximize their incomes. In reality, the opposite was true. Taxi drivers worked longer hours on sunny days as they strove to hit their target income. On rainy days, once the target was achieved, the taxi drivers stopped working.

Framing bias occurs when decisions are affected by the way in which the question or data is "framed." In other words, the way a question is phrased can influence the answer given. Tversky and Kahneman (1980)[2] illustrate framing bias with the following example.

EXAMPLE: Framing bias (framing as a gain)

The United States is preparing for the outbreak of an unusual disease, which is expected to kill 600 people. Two alternative programs have been proposed. If Program A is adopted, 200 people will be saved. If Program B is adopted, there is a one-third probability that 600 people will be saved and a two-thirds probability that no one will be saved. Which program will people choose?

Answer:

Program A is typically selected. Although the expected value of both Program A and Program B is 200 lives saved, the majority choice is risk averse. The prospect of saving 200 lives with certainty is more attractive than the risky option with the same expected value.

1. Colin Camerer, Linda Babcock, George Loewenstein, and Richard Thaler, "Labor Supply of New York City Cab Drivers: One Day at a Time," *Quarterly Journal of Economics* 112 (1997): 407–442.
2. Amos Tversky and Daniel Kahneman, "The Framing of Decisions and the Rationality of Choice," Stanford University Department of Psychology, Defense Technical Information Center – Technical Report (1980).

EXAMPLE: Framing bias (framing as a loss)

A different group of individuals is given the same issue, but the two programs are framed differently. If Program A is adopted, 400 people will die. If Program B is adopted, there is a one-third probability that nobody will die and a two-thirds probability that 600 will die. Which program will people choose?

Answer:

In this situation, Program B is typically selected. The majority choice is now risk-taking, with the certain death of 400 people being less acceptable than a two-thirds chance that 600 people will die.

In these examples, the two programs presented (A and B) are identical for both groups, but the framing of the information results in different choices. For the first group, the information was presented in the context of a gain, while for the second group, it was in the context of a loss. Loss aversion—the idea that we fear losses more than we value gains—is then demonstrated by the choices made.

An example of framing bias in an investment context is overestimating the significance of short-term price volatility (risk) without weighing it against long-term considerations. This may result in overly conservative portfolios.

Investment managers must take care to avoid framing bias when creating questions to assess an investor's risk tolerance. Failing to properly assess risk tolerance may identify investors as more or less risk averse than they actually are, resulting in portfolios that are inconsistent with the investors' needs.

Availability bias refers to putting undue emphasis on information that is readily available, easy to recall, or based narrowly on personal experience or knowledge. Availability bias occurs when individuals judge the probability of an event occurring by the ease with which examples and instances come to mind. By the very nature of memory, more-recent events are typically easier to recall than events further in the past, which leads to the bias of attaching too much significance to events that have occurred recently and too little to events that occurred further in the past. People also tend to assume that if something is easily remembered, it must occur with a higher probability.

EXAMPLE: Availability bias

Imagine a word is picked at random from a dictionary. Is it more likely that the word has the letter *r* as the first letter in the word or the third letter?

Answer:

When faced with this problem, most individuals state that it is more likely the letter *r* will be the first letter. In fact, in the English language, there are approximately three times more words with *r* as the third letter than the first. Individuals find it easier to recall words that begin with *r* than words with *r* as the third letter, which distorts their estimation of probabilities.

Availability bias may lead market participants to choose a manager or investment based on advertising or recalling they have heard the name. They may limit their universe of potential investments to familiar firms, resulting in inappropriate asset allocations and lack of diversification. They may also overreact to recent market conditions while ignoring data on historical market performance, or they may place too much emphasis on events that receive a large amount of media attention.

MODULE 52.2: EMOTIONAL BIASES

Video covering this content is available online.

PROFESSOR'S NOTE

Some of the terms we are about to discuss have already come up in the discussion of cognitive biases. In general, if an investor's view is based on unconscious emotion that the holder is unwilling or unable to change, we should regard it as an emotional bias. If a bias can be overcome with a relatively simple change in thought process or information, we should regard it as a cognitive bias.

While there is no formally accepted definition, these six biases generally arise from emotion and feelings rather than through conscious thought:

1. **Loss-aversion bias** arises from feeling more pain from a loss than pleasure from an equal gain. Kahneman and Tversky (1979)[3] investigated differences between how people feel when they gain and when they lose and how that affects behavior when faced with risk. They found that individuals' willingness to take a gamble (risk) was very different when facing a loss or a gain.

   Consider the following two scenarios:

   Scenario 1: An individual is given $10. The individual is then given the following options:

   – Take an additional $5 with certainty.

   – Flip a coin and win an additional $10 if it lands heads up or nothing if it lands tails up.

   Both options represent a gain relative to the original $10, and the expected value of the gain is $5 for either option. Option 1 creates a guaranteed outcome of $15. Option 2 introduces uncertainty, with equal probabilities of an outcome of $10 or $20. Most individuals chose the riskless Option 1 over the riskier Option 2.

   Scenario 2: An individual is given $20. The individual is then given the following options:

   – Take a $5 loss with certainty.

   – Flip a coin and lose nothing if it lands heads up, but lose $10 if it lands tails up.

   Both options represent a potential loss relative to the original $20, and the expected loss is $5 for either option. Most individuals chose risky Option 2 over the riskless certain loss of Option 1.

---

3. Daniel Kahneman and Amos Tversky, "Prospect Theory: An Analysis of Decision Under Risk," *Econometrica* 47, no. 2 (1979): 263–91.

In both scenarios, the expected value of the individual's wealth is $15. The options given to the individuals are also identical, with Option 1 resulting in a guaranteed outcome of $15 and Option 2 providing equal probabilities of either $10 or $20. Yet, when faced with gains, people preferred certainty, and when faced with losses, they preferred risk.

The conclusion is that individuals display asymmetrical responses to gains and losses. Kahneman and Tversky suggested that people look at decisions relative to a reference rate. Anything below the reference rate is seen as a loss, and anything above the reference rate is seen as a gain. The reference rate in scenario 1 was the $10 initially given to the individual, and in scenario 2, it was $20. The conflicting responses to the scenarios are explained by attitudes toward gains and losses. Crucially, people fear losses far more than they value gains. Thus, in scenario 2, they were willing to take the risk in the hope of avoiding a loss.

PROFESSOR'S NOTE

Be sure to understand the difference between risk aversion and loss aversion. A risk-averse investor is simply an investor who, given two investments with the same expected returns, would select the investment with the lowest risk. A loss-averse investor is one who feels greater pain (decreases in utility) from losses than satisfaction (increase in utility) from gains. As a result, the individual is more likely to take a risk in the hope of avoiding losses than in the hope of achieving gains.

Consequences of loss-aversion bias may include trading too much by selling for small gains, which increases transaction costs and decreases returns, or incurring too much risk by continuing to hold assets that have deteriorated in quality and lost value. If an initial decline in value occurs, loss-averse investors may take excessive risk in the hope of recovering (investment managers may be particularly susceptible to this behavior). A loss-averse investor might view a position inappropriately as a gain or a loss based on the framing of the reference point.

2. **Overconfidence bias** occurs when market participants overestimate their own intuitive ability or reasoning. It can show up as *illusion of knowledge* when they think they do a better job of predicting than they actually do. Combined with *self-attribution bias*, individuals may give themselves personal credit when things go right (*self-enhancing*) but blame others or circumstances when things go wrong (*self-protecting*). *Prediction overconfidence* leads individuals to underestimate uncertainty and the standard deviation of their predictions, while *certainty overconfidence* occurs when they overstate the probability they will be right.

   While overconfidence is both cognitive and emotional, it is more emotional in nature because it is difficult for most individuals to correct and is rooted in the desire to feel good. Overconfidence bias may cause market participants to underestimate risk, overestimate return, and fail to diversify sufficiently.

3. **Self-control bias** occurs when individuals lack self-discipline and favor short-term satisfaction over long-term goals. Often, individuals are not prepared to make short-term sacrifices to meet their long-term goals. They may favor small payoffs now at the expense of larger payoffs in the future, which is known as *hyperbolic discounting*.

   Self-control bias may result in insufficient savings to fund retirement needs, which in turn may cause an investor to take excessive risk to try to compensate for insufficient savings accumulation. It may also result in overemphasis on income-producing assets to meet short-term needs.

Self-control bias might be mitigated by establishing an appropriate investment plan (asset allocation) and a budget to achieve sufficient savings. Both should be reviewed on a regular basis.

4. **Status quo bias** occurs when comfort with an existing situation causes an individual to be resistant to change. If investment choices include the option to maintain existing investments or allocations, or if a choice will happen unless the participant opts out, status quo choices become more likely.

   Companies have found that automatically enrolling workers in retirement savings schemes, with the option to opt out, increases participation compared with making it necessary for employees to opt in. Thaler and Sunstein (2008)[4] argue for framing choices in this way to achieve better participation rates in retirement plans, as well as other choices, such as whether to register as an organ donor.

   Consequences of status quo bias may include holding portfolios with inappropriate risk and not considering other, better investment alternatives.

5. **Endowment bias** occurs when an asset is felt to be special and more valuable simply because it is already owned. For example, a spouse may hold on to securities the deceased spouse purchased, for reasons like sentiment that are unrelated to the current merits of the securities. Endowment bias is common with inherited assets and might be detected or mitigated by asking a question such as "Would you make this same investment with new money today?"

   In studies, individuals have been asked to state their minimum sales price for an asset they own (say $25) and the maximum price they would pay now to buy the same asset (say $23). The price at which they would be willing to sell tended to be higher than the price they would pay. This has been explained as an endowment effect. Once they own an asset, they act as if it is worth more than they would pay.

   Market participants who exhibit endowment bias may be failing to sell assets that are no longer appropriate for their investment needs, or they hold assets with which they are familiar because they provide some intangible sense of comfort.

6. **Regret-aversion bias** occurs when market participants do nothing out of excessive fear that actions could be wrong. They attach undue weight to errors of commission (doing something that turns out wrong) and not enough weight to errors of omission (not doing something that would have turned out right). Their sense of regret and pain is stronger for acts of commission. This is quite similar to status quo bias.

   Herding behavior is a form of regret aversion where participants go with the consensus or popular opinion. Essentially, participants tell themselves they are not to blame if others are wrong too.

   Consequences of regret-aversion bias may include excess conservatism in the portfolio because it is easy to see that riskier assets do at times underperform. Therefore, an investor might not buy riskier assets so as not to experience regret when they decline.

---

4. Richard H. Thaler and Cass R. Sunstein, *Nudge: Improving Decisions About Health, Wealth, and Happiness* (New York: Penguin Group, 2008).

LOS 52.c: Describe how behavioral biases of investors can lead to market characteristics that may not be explained by traditional finance.

CFA® Program Curriculum, Volume 6, page 72

In our Equity Investments topic review of market efficiency, we developed the ideas of anomalies (results that do not fit the prevailing model of securities risks and returns) and market inefficiencies (anomalies that present opportunities to earn positive risk-adjusted returns). Many market anomalies have been explained by small sample size, time period bias, or inadequacies in the specification of prevailing models of returns. In the same way, some anomalies once considered evidence of market inefficiency have been explained by the possible misspecification of risk, leading to inaccurate risk adjustment of returns.

Bubbles and subsequent crashes have been with us as long as trading markets have existed. Some have offered explanations for these extremes of valuation based on rational behavior. Investors who leave markets that they determine are exhibiting characteristics of a bubble may miss out on high returns over extended periods. On the other hand, investors who stay invested based on a belief that they will be able to get out at or near the market top often find that that is not realistic. Either type of mistake, leaving the market too early or staying fully invested too long, can be quite damaging to a fund manager's career. Exploiting the fact that a market is "in a bubble" for an arbitrage profit may not be possible due to the restrictions on and risk of short selling in a rapidly rising market.

While behavioral finance does not provide an overall explanation for bubbles and their aftermath, some have claimed that cognitive and emotional biases exhibited during such periods may have some causal effects. These claims include the following:

- *Overconfidence* may lead to overtrading, underestimation of risk, and lack of diversification.
- Persistently good results combined with *self-attribution* bias can fuel overconfidence, as can *hindsight* bias (as investors give themselves credit for choosing profitable stocks in a bull market).
- *Confirmation bias* may lead investors to ignore or misinterpret new information suggesting that valuations will not continue to rise, or to misinterpret initial decreases in asset values as simply another buying opportunity.
- *Anchoring* may cause investors to believe recent highs are rational prices even after prices begin their eventual decline.
- Fear of *regret* may keep even very skeptical investors in the market.

One anomaly that has been persistent over time is the value/growth anomaly. Value stocks (low market-book, low P/E, high dividend yield stocks) have outperformed growth stocks (high P/E, low dividend yield stocks) over long periods. Fama and French (1992) found that adding risk factors for firm size and book-to-market ratio to a model of stock returns eliminated the evidence of value stock outperformance. These results suggest that the extra returns to value stocks were compensation for additional risks captured by firm size and book-to-market ratios.

Reading 52

Others have suggested behavioral factors as the cause of the seeming outperformance of value stocks. The **halo effect** is a version of representativeness in which a company's good characteristics, such as fast growth and a rising stock price, are extended into a conclusion that it is a good stock to own, leading to overvaluation of growth stocks.

The fact that investors tend to invest heavily in firms in their domestic country in a global portfolio, or more heavily in firms operating in their region of a country, is considered anomalous in that rationality suggests greater diversification. Such **home bias**, it is claimed, may result from a belief that they have better access to information or simply an emotional desire to invest in companies "closer to home." Similarly, investors may underestimate the risk or overestimate the future returns of firms whose products they use or firms for which they are exposed to a great amount of positive marketing messages.

MODULE QUIZ 52.1, 52.2

To best evaluate your performance, enter your quiz answers online.

1. Which of the following would *most likely* be classified as an emotional bias?
   A. The investor has difficulty interpreting complex new information.
   B. The investor only partially adjusts forecasts when he receives new information.
   C. The investor has a tendency to value the same assets higher if he owns them than if he does not own them.
2. Which of the following would *most likely* indicate that an investor is subject to an emotional bias?
   A. Regularly basing decisions on only a subset of available information.
   B. Reacting spontaneously to a negative earnings announcement by quickly selling a stock.
   C. Remaining invested in a profitable technology stock even though new information indicates its P/E ratio is too high.
3. A cognitive error is *most likely* indicated by which of the following?
   A. A client is the chief executive officer of a public company that she founded and insists she will not diversify her holding of the company stock.
   B. The spouse of a now-deceased company founder becomes upset when it is recommended the portfolio holdings in that company need to be diversified.
   C. A client who initially resists recommendations to diversify the portfolio later thanks the manager for explaining the benefits of diversification.

4. Abby Lane has investments scattered across many different accounts, from bank savings to before- and after-tax retirement accounts to taxable nonretirement accounts. She has multiple investing goals ranging from important short-term goals to longer-term "wish list" goals. She looks at her financial assets and views each holding as designed to meet specific goals. Lane has been very successful in her investment decisions for several decades and believes she can continue to achieve reasonable results. Lane *most likely* exhibits:
   A. framing bias.
   B. mental accounting.
   C. overconfidence bias.

5. Twenty years ago, Jane Ivy set up her initial asset allocation in her defined contribution plan by placing an equal amount in each asset class and never changed it. Over time, she increased her contribution by 1% per year until she reached the maximum amount allowed by law. Due to her steadfastness and good fortune, coupled with matching funds from her employer, she now finds herself in her early 40s with a million-dollar retirement account. Which of the following biases does Ivy *most likely* exhibit?
   A. Representativeness.
   B. Status quo bias.
   C. Availability bias.

6. The halo effect suggests that investors tend to overvalue stocks:
   A. from their own country or region.
   B. with which the investors are most familiar.
   C. that have experienced rapid growth and price appreciation.

KEY CONCEPTS

LOS 52.a

Cognitive errors result from the inability to analyze information or from basing decisions on partial information. Individuals try to process information and make rational decisions, but they may lack the capacity or sufficient information to do so. Cognitive errors can be divided into belief perseverance errors and processing errors.

Emotional biases are caused by the way individuals frame information and decisions, rather than the process used to analyze and interpret information. Emotional bias is more of a spontaneous reaction.

LOS 52.b

Cognitive Errors: Belief Perseverance

- Conservatism bias.
- Confirmation bias.
- Representativeness bias.
- Control bias.
- Hindsight bias.

Cognitive Errors: Information Processing

- Anchoring and adjustment.
- Mental accounting bias.
- Framing bias.
- Availability bias.

Emotional Biases

- Loss-aversion bias.
- Overconfidence bias.
- Self-control bias.
- Status quo bias.
- Endowment bias.
- Regret-aversion bias.

LOS 52.c

Many reported anomalies have been explained by inadequate specification of security risk, but some have attempted to explain the existence of persistent anomalies as the results of cognitive errors and emotional biases.

Behavioral finance has not explained bubbles and crashes, but some cognitive errors and emotional biases may be exhibited during bubbles and crashes.

ANSWER KEY FOR MODULE QUIZZES

Module Quiz 52.1, 52.2

1. **C** This describes the *endowment bias*, where individuals place a higher value on assets they own than if they did not own those same assets. The other two answer choices describe cognitive errors that are due to the inability to analyze all the information. (Modules 52.1, 52.2, LOS 52.a, 52.b)

2. **B** Emotional biases tend to elicit more of a spontaneous reaction than cognitive errors. Making a decision based only on partial information is indicative of a cognitive error. Ignoring a high P/E ratio could be indicative of the conservatism bias, which is reacting slowly to new information or avoiding analyzing new information. It could also indicate confirmation bias, where the investor focuses on positive information and ignores negative information. Both conservatism and confirmation biases are cognitive errors. (Modules 52.1, 52.2, LOS 52.a, 52.b)

3. **C** Individuals making cognitive errors are more likely to respond rationally when new information is provided. The client initially resists a rational recommendation but then reverses their thoughts when given more information.

   There are rational reasons a CEO may want to hold a large block of her company's stock. Those include legal restrictions on sale or a desire to take concentrated risk in a situation where she has a lot of control. A rational decision is not an error. Alternatively, the "insists" could indicate an emotional bias. Neither interpretation suggests a cognitive error.

   The spouse who becomes upset at a rational recommendation to diversify is likely showing an emotional bias. (Module 52.1, LOS 52.a)

4. **B** Viewing each asset in light of meeting a specific goal is mental accounting. There was no indication of framing (the way data is provided overly affects the decision process). An investor with decades-long success who expects to produce reasonable results is acting rationally and is not necessarily overconfident. (Module 52.2, LOS 52.b)

5. **B** Ivy is exhibiting *status quo bias*, where investors leave their asset allocation alone and don't change it according to changing market conditions or changes in their own circumstances. Her actions do not suggest representativeness (placing something in a category and assuming it will have the characteristics associated with that category) or availability (putting undue emphasis on information readily available or easily recalled). (Module 52.2, LOS 52.b)

6. **C** The halo effect suggests investors will view a stock that has experienced rapid growth and price appreciation as a good stock to own, which may result in these stocks being overvalued. Home bias is the tendency for investors to favor stocks from their own country or region because they are more familiar with those stocks. (Module 52.2, LOS 52.c)

The following is a review of the Portfolio Management (2) principles designed to address the learning outcome statements set forth by CFA Institute. Cross-Reference to CFA Institute Assigned Reading #53.

READING 53

Introduction to Risk Management

Study Session 18

EXAM FOCUS

Here we present a framework for risk management that is broad enough to be applied to corporations in general, financial firms, and individuals, as well as to the management of securities portfolios in any context. The main idea is that organizations should estimate the various risks they face and then reduce some risks and accept or increase other risks. The result should be a bundle of risks that simultaneously matches the risk tolerance of the organization and provides the greatest benefits in terms of reaching the organization's goals. Note that risk is not minimized though this process. The concept of risk budgeting, the categorization of types of risks, and the various methods of risk mitigation all offer testable material.

MODULE 53.1: INTRODUCTION TO RISK MANAGEMENT

Video covering this content is available online.

LOS 53.a: Define risk management.

CFA® Program Curriculum, Volume 6, page 85

The **risk management** process seeks to 1) identify the risk tolerance of the organization, 2) identify and measure the risks that the organization faces, and 3) modify and monitor these risks.

The process does not seek to minimize or eliminate all of these risks. The organization may increase its exposure to risks it decides to take because it is better able to manage and respond to them. The organization may decrease its exposure to risks that it is less well able to manage and respond to by making organizational changes, purchasing insurance, or entering into hedging transactions. Through these choices the firm aligns the risks it takes with its risk tolerances for these various types of risk.

Risk (uncertainty) is not something to be avoided by an organization or in an investment portfolio. Returns above the risk-free rate are earned by taking on risk. While returns for any period are not under the control of managers, the specific risks and overall level of risk the organization takes are under their control. We can think of risk management as determining organizational risks, determining the optimal bundle of risks for the organization, and implementing risk mitigation strategies to achieve that bundle of risks.

We describe the principles of risk management here in a framework that can be applied broadly, not only to firms or organizations in general, but also to the management of investment portfolios and financial firms, and even to individuals deciding how much risk and which specific risks they will take. Individuals follow a similar approach, selecting a bundle of risks that is optimal for maximizing their expected utility (rather than returns or profit).

LOS 53.b: Describe features of a risk management framework.

CFA® Program Curriculum, Volume 6, page 87

An overall **risk management framework** encompasses several activities, including:

- Establishing processes and policies for risk governance.
- Determining the organization's risk tolerance.
- Identifying and measuring existing risks.
- Managing and mitigating risks to achieve the optimal bundle of risks.
- Monitoring risk exposures over time.
- Communicating across the organization.
- Performing strategic risk analysis.

This framework is general, but all of these elements should be addressed in any comprehensive risk management framework. Only by understanding the risks the organization faces, and having the processes and procedures in place to effectively manage and monitor these risks, can an organization align its risk exposures to the goals of the organization.

LOS 53.c: Define risk governance and describe elements of effective risk governance.

CFA® Program Curriculum, Volume 6, page 87

Risk governance refers to senior management's determination of the risk tolerance of the organization, the elements of its optimal risk exposure strategy, and the framework for oversight of the risk management function. Risk governance seeks to manage risk in a way that supports the overall goals of the organization so it can achieve the best business outcome consistent with the organization's overall risk tolerance. Risk governance provides organization-wide guidance on the risks that should be pursued in an efficient manner, risks that should be subject to limits, and risks that should be reduced or avoided.

A risk management committee can provide a way for various parts of the organization to bring up issues of risk measurement, integration of risks, and the best ways to mitigate undesirable risks.

LOS 53.d: Explain how risk tolerance affects risk management.

CFA® Program Curriculum, Volume 6, page 96

Determining an organization's **risk tolerance** involves setting the overall risk exposure the organization will take by identifying the risks the firm can effectively take and the risks that the organization should reduce or avoid. Some of the factors that determine an organization's risk tolerance are its expertise in its lines of business, its skill at responding to negative outside events, its regulatory environment, and its financial strength and ability to withstand losses.

When analyzing risk tolerance, management should examine risks that may exist within the organization as well as those that may arise from outside. The various risks the firm is exposed to must each be considered and weighted against the expected benefits of bearing those risks and how these fit the overall goals of the organization.

LOS 53.e: Describe risk budgeting and its role in risk governance.

CFA® Program Curriculum, Volume 6, page 98

Risk budgeting is the process of allocating firm resources to assets (or investments) by considering their various risk characteristics and how they combine to meet the organization's risk tolerance. The goal is to allocate the overall amount of acceptable risk to the mix of assets or investments that have the greatest expected returns over time.

The risk budget may be a single metric, such as portfolio beta, value at risk, portfolio duration, or returns variance. A risk budget may be constructed based on categories of investments, such as domestic equities, domestic debt securities, international equities, and international debt securities. Another way to allocate a risk budget is to identify specific risk factors that comprise the overall risk of the portfolio or organization. In this case, specific risk factors that affect asset classes to varying degrees, such as interest rate risk, equity market risk, and foreign exchange rate risk, are estimated and aggregated to determine whether they match the overall risk tolerance of the organization.

LOS 53.f: Identify financial and non-financial sources of risk and describe how they may interact.

CFA® Program Curriculum, Volume 6, page 101

Financial risks are those that arise from exposure to financial markets. Examples are:

- **Credit risk.** This is the uncertainty about whether the counterparty to a transaction will fulfill its contractual obligations.

- **Liquidity risk.** This is the risk of loss when selling an asset at a time when market conditions make the sales price less than the underlying fair value of the asset.
- **Market risk.** This is the uncertainty about market prices of assets (stocks, commodities, and currencies) and interest rates.

Non-financial risks arise from the operations of the organization and from sources external to the organization. Examples are:

- **Operational risk.** This is the risk that human error, faulty organizational processes, inadequate security, or business interruptions will result in losses. An example of an operational risk is **cyber risk**, which refers to disruptions of an organization's information technology.
- **Solvency risk.** This is the risk that the organization will be unable to continue to operate because it has run out of cash.
- **Regulatory risk.** This is the risk that the regulatory environment will change, imposing costs on the firm or restricting its activities.
- **Governmental or political risk** (including **tax risk**). This is the risk that political actions outside a specific regulatory framework, such as increases in tax rates, will impose significant costs on an organization.
- **Legal risk.** This is the uncertainty about the organization's exposure to future legal action.
- **Model risk.** This is the risk that asset valuations based on the organization's analytical models are incorrect.
- **Tail risk.** This is the risk that extreme events (those in the tails of the distribution of outcomes) are more likely than the organization's analysis indicates, especially from incorrectly concluding that the distribution of outcomes is normal.
- **Accounting risk.** This is the risk that the organization's accounting policies and estimates are judged to be incorrect.

For individuals, risks, such as risk of death (**mortality risk**) prior to providing for their families' future needs and the risk of living longer than anticipated (**longevity risk**) so that assets run out, are very important in financial planning. Mortality risk is most often addressed with life insurance, and longevity risk can be reduced by purchasing a lifetime annuity. Risk of health care expenses is addressed with health insurance. Although the risks for an individual are in some ways different from those of organizations, the overall approach is the same, choosing which risks to bear (self-insure), which risks to prevent or avoid, and which risks to take in order to maximize the expected outcome in terms of personal utility or satisfaction.

The various risks an organization faces are not independent; they interact in many ways. Consider a firm with market risk that it reduces with option contracts. If markets decline significantly, the firm is owed a payment from the firm on the other side of the option trade, so now there is significant counterparty or credit risk. There also may be legal risks if the counterparty seeks to avoid the payment through loopholes in the contract. Credit losses and legal losses may result in greater liquidity risk as positions must be sold. Additional losses from selling in a declining or less liquid market may increase solvency risk because of the negative impact on the firm's cash position.

Interactions among risks must be considered because such interactions are many and frequent. They can be especially important during periods of stress in financial markets, when risk management is most important to the health and possibly the survival of the organization.

LOS 53.g: Describe methods for measuring and modifying risk exposures and factors to consider in choosing among the methods.

CFA® Program Curriculum, Volume 6, page 110

Measures of risk for specific asset types include standard deviation, beta, and duration.

- **Standard deviation** is a measure of the volatility of asset prices and interest rates. Standard deviation may not be the appropriate measure of risk for non-normal probability distributions, especially those with negative skew or positive excess kurtosis (fat tails).
- **Beta** measures the market risk of equity securities and portfolios of equity securities. This measure considers the risk reduction benefits of diversification and is appropriate for securities held in a well-diversified portfolio, whereas standard deviation is a measure of risk on a stand-alone basis.
- **Duration** is a measure of the price sensitivity of debt securities to changes in interest rates.

PROFESSOR'S NOTE

We describe and calculate standard deviation in Quantitative Methods; duration in Fixed Income; and beta in the current topic area, Portfolio Management.

Derivatives risks (sometimes referred to as "the Greeks") include:

- **Delta.** This is the sensitivity of derivatives values to the price of the underlying asset.
- **Gamma.** This is the sensitivity of delta to changes in the price of the underlying asset.
- **Vega.** This is the sensitivity of derivatives values to the volatility of the price of the underlying asset.
- **Rho.** This is the sensitivity of derivatives values to changes in the risk-free rate.

Tail risk is the uncertainty about the probability of extreme (negative) outcomes. Commonly used measures of tail risk (sometimes referred to as **downside risk**) include Value at Risk and Conditional VaR.

Value at risk (VaR) is the minimum loss over a period that will occur with a specific probability. Consider a bank that has a one-month VaR of $1 million with a probability of 5%. That means that a one-month loss of at least $1 million is expected to occur 5% of the time. Note that this is not the maximum one-month loss the bank will experience; it is the minimum loss that will occur 5% of the time. VaR does not provide a maximum loss for a period. VaR has become accepted as a risk measure for banks and is used in establishing minimum capital requirements.

There are various methods of calculating VaR, and both the inputs and models used will affect the calculated value, perhaps significantly. As is always the case with estimates of risk, incorrect inputs or inappropriate distribution assumptions will lead to misleading results. Given these limitations, VaR should be used in conjunction with other risk measures.

Conditional VaR (CVaR) is the expected value of a loss, *given* that the loss exceeds a minimum amount. Relating this to the VaR measure presented previously, the CVaR would be the expected loss, given that the loss was at least \$1 million. It is calculated as the probability-weighted average loss for all losses expected to be at least \$1 million. CVaR is similar to the measure of loss given default that is used in estimating risk for debt securities.

Subjective and Market-Based Estimates of Risk

Two methods of risk assessment that are used to supplement measures such as VaR and CVaR are stress testing and scenario analysis. **Stress testing** examines the effects of a specific (usually extreme) change in a key variable such as an interest rate or exchange rate. **Scenario analysis** refers to a similar what-if analysis of expected loss but incorporates changes in multiple inputs. A given scenario might combine an interest rate change with a significant change in oil prices or exchange rates.

Quantifying the risk to an organization of very infrequent events is quite difficult. The risk of the bankruptcy of a firm that has never experienced significant financial distress is often a subjective estimate rather than a data-driven estimate. Estimates of risk can also be based on the market prices of insurance, derivatives, or other securities that can be used to hedge those risks. These hedging costs provide information on market participants' aggregate estimate of the expected loss of specific risks.

Operational risks are difficult to quantify for a single organization because they are very difficult to predict and may result in very large costs to the organization. One way to approach this problem is to examine a large sample of firms in order to determine an overall probability of significant losses due to operational risks and the average loss of firms that have experienced such losses.

Unexpected changes in tax laws or the regulatory environment can impose large costs on an organization. The political nature of such changes makes them quite difficult to predict. Subjective estimates, rather than data-driven quantitative estimates, are necessary. As is often the case, even a subjective, non-quantitative estimate of risk probabilities and magnitudes is better than not addressing the risk factor at all.

Modifying Risk Exposures

Risk management does not seek to eliminate all risks. The goal is to retain the optimal mix of risks for the organization. This may mean taking on more of some risks, decreasing others, and eliminating some altogether. Once the risk management team has estimated various risks, management may decide to prevent or avoid a risk, accept a risk, transfer a risk, or shift a risk.

One way to avoid a risk is to not engage in the activity with the uncertain outcome. If political risks in a country are to be avoided, simply not investing in securities of firms based in that country or not expanding a business enterprise to that country would avoid those risks. A decision to avoid certain risks typically would come from top management as a part of establishing the risk tolerance of the organization and would be instituted because the risks are judged to outweigh the potential benefits of specific activities.

Some risks can be prevented. The risk of a data breach can be prevented with a greater level of security for the data and stronger processes. In this case, the benefits of reducing or eliminating the risk are judged to be greater than the cost of doing so.

For risks that management has decided to bear, the organization will seek to bear them efficiently. **Diversification** may offer a way to more efficiently bear a specific risk.

PROFESSOR'S NOTE

We explain how diversification can reduce risk in our review of "Portfolio Risk and Return: Part I."

Sometimes the term **self-insurance** is used to describe a situation where an organization has decided to bear a risk. Note, however, that this simply means that it will bear any associated losses from this risk factor. It is possible that this represents inaction rather than the result of analysis and strategic decision-making. In some cases, the firm will establish a reserve account to cover losses as a way of mitigating the impact of losses on the organization.

For a risk an organization has decided not to bear, risk transfer or risk shifting can be employed. With a **risk transfer**, another party takes on the risk. Insurance is a type of risk transfer. The risk of fire destroying a warehouse complex is shifted to an insurance company by buying an insurance policy and paying the policy premiums. Insurance companies diversify across many risks so the premiums of some insured parties pay the losses of others. Ideally, the various risks the insurance company insures are not highly correlated, as that can reduce or eliminate any diversification benefits. An insurance company with highly correlated risks (or a single very large risk) may itself shift some of the resulting risk by buying reinsurance from another company.

With a **surety bond**, an insurance company has agreed to make a payment if a third party fails to perform under the terms of a contract or agreement with the organization. For example, a company may be exposed to losses if a key supplier does not deliver on time, slowing a project and resulting in penalty payments by the company. Insurers also issue **fidelity bonds**, which will pay for losses that result from employee theft or misconduct. Managements that purchase insurance, surety bonds, or fidelity bonds have determined that the benefits of risk reduction are greater than the cost of the insurance.

Risk shifting is a way to change the distribution of possible outcomes and is accomplished primarily with derivative contracts. For example, financial firms that do not want to bear currency risk on some foreign currency denominated debt securities can use forward currency contracts, futures contracts, or swaps to reduce or eliminate that risk. A firm with a large position in a specific stock can buy put options that provide a minimum sale price for the securities, altering the distribution of possible outcomes (in this case providing a floor value for the securities). On the other hand, a firm could sell call options on a specific stock, altering the distribution of possible outcomes by giving up some of the upside potential of the stock but decreasing its downside risk by the amount of the premiums received from the sale of the call options.

Choosing Among Risk Modification Methods

Organizations may use multiple methods of risk modification to reduce a single risk. The criterion is always a comparison of the costs and benefits of risk modification. Some risks may be mitigated by diversification, some shifted by insurance where it is available and economical, some shifted though the use of derivatives, and some simply borne or self-insured. The end result is a risk profile that matches the risk tolerance established for the organization and includes the risks that top management has determined match the goals of the organization in terms of cost versus potential returns.

MODULE QUIZ 53.1

To best evaluate your performance, enter your quiz answers online.

1. An investor has the *most* control over her portfolio's:
   A. risk.
   B. relative returns.
   C. risk-adjusted returns.
2. A risk management framework *least likely* includes:
   A. risk governance, risk mitigation, and strategic risk analysis.
   B. identifying and measuring risks, risk policies and processes, and risk governance.
   C. risk mitigation, tracking the organization's risk profile, and establishing position limits.
3. Risk governance should *most appropriately* be addressed within an organization at:
   A. the enterprise level.
   B. the business unit level.
   C. the individual employee level.
4. Effective risk management would *most likely* attempt to:
   A. maximize expected return for a given level of risk.
   B. minimize risk for a given level of expected return.
   C. reduce any significant risks the firm is exposed to.
5. Risk budgeting can *best* be described as:
   A. setting an annual limit on risk taken.
   B. selecting assets by their risk characteristics.
   C. establishing a maximum amount of risk to be taken.
6. Which of the following is *most appropriately* termed a financial risk?
   A. Credit risk.
   B. Solvency risk.
   C. Settlement risk.

7. Risk shifting is *most likely* achieved by:
    A. risk mitigation.
    B. using derivative securities.
    C. transferring risk to an insurance company.

KEY CONCEPTS

LOS 53.a

Risk management is the process of identifying and measuring the risks an organization (or portfolio manager or individual) faces, determining an acceptable level of overall risk (establishing risk tolerance), deciding which risks should be taken and which risks should be reduced or avoided, and putting the structure in place to maintain the bundle of risks that is expected to best achieve the goals of the organization.

LOS 53.b

An overall risk management framework should address the following activities:

- Identifying and measuring existing risks.
- Determining the organization's overall risk tolerance.
- Establishing the processes and policies for risk governance.
- Managing and mitigating risks to achieve the optimal bundle of risks.
- Monitoring risk exposures over time.
- Communicating across the organization.
- Performing strategic risk analysis.

LOS 53.c

Risk governance refers to senior management's determination of the risk tolerance of the organization, the elements of its optimal risk exposure strategy, and the framework for oversight of the risk management function.

LOS 53.d

The risk tolerance for an organization is the overall amount of risk it will take in pursuing its goals and is determined by top management.

LOS 53.e

Risk budgeting is the process of allocating the total risk the firm will take (risk tolerance) to assets or investments by considering the risk characteristics of each and how they can be combined to best meet the organization's goals. The budget can be a single risk measure or the sum of various risk factors.

LOS 53.f

Financial risks are those that arise from exposure to financial markets, including credit risk, liquidity risk, and market risk. Non-financial risks are the risks from the operation of the organization and from sources external to the organization. Individuals face mortality and longevity risk, in addition to financial risks.

Interactions among risks are frequent and can be especially significant during periods of stress in financial markets.

LOS 53.g

Risk of assets is measured by standard deviation, beta, or duration. Derivatives risk measures include delta, gamma, vega, and rho. Tail risk is measured with value at risk (VaR) or conditional VaR. Some risks must be measured subjectively.

An organization may decide to bear a risk (self-insurance), avoid or take steps to prevent a risk, efficiently manage a risk through diversification, transfer a risk with insurance or a surety bond, or shift a risk (change the distribution of uncertain outcomes) with derivatives.

Organizations may use multiple methods of risk modification after considering the costs and benefits of the various methods. The end result is a risk profile that matches the organization's risk tolerance and includes the risks that top management has determined match the organization's goals.

ANSWER KEY FOR MODULE QUIZZES

Module Quiz 53.1

1. **A** An investor can select securities to achieve a given level of portfolio risk. Returns cannot be controlled. (LOS 53.a)

2. **C** A risk management framework includes the procedures, analytical tools, and infrastructure to conduct the risk governance process. It includes all of the items listed with the exception of establishing position limits, which is an example of the operational implementation of a system of risk management. (LOS 53.b)

3. **A** Risk governance should be approached from an enterprise view, with senior management determining risk tolerance and a risk management strategy on an organization-wide level. (LOS 53.c)

4. **A** Risk management requires establishment of a risk tolerance (maximum acceptable level of risk) for the organization and will attempt to maximize expected returns for that level of risk. Some significant risks the firm is exposed to may be borne by the firm or even increased as a result of risk management. (LOS 53.d)

5. **B** Risk budgeting refers to selecting assets or securities by their risk characteristics up to the maximum allowable amount of risk. The maximum amount of risk to be taken is established through risk governance. (LOS 53.e)

6. **A** The main sources of financial risk are market risk, credit risk, and liquidity risk. Solvency risk and settlement risk are classified as non-financial risks. (LOS 53.f)

7. **B** Risk shifting changes the distribution of possible outcomes, typically through the use of derivative securities. Risk shifting is one technique for mitigating risk. Transferring risk to an insurance company is termed *risk transfer*. (LOS 53.g)

The following is a review of the Portfolio Management (2) principles designed to address the learning outcome statements set forth by CFA Institute. Cross-Reference to CFA Institute Assigned Reading #54.

READING 54

Technical Analysis

Study Session 18

EXAM FOCUS

This topic review introduces the "story" that underlies technical analysis, and you should understand how this differs from fundamental analysis. You should learn what the technical indicator names mean and how they are used, but don't worry about being able to calculate them. The LOS require you to be able to "explain" and "describe." You are responsible for knowing the assumptions and tools of technical analysis and understanding how technical analysts apply them in practice. You are not required to believe technical analysis can create positive risk-adjusted returns on average over time.

MODULE 54.1: TECHNICAL ANALYSIS

Video covering this content is available online.

LOS 54.a: Explain principles and assumptions of technical analysis.

CFA® Program Curriculum, Volume 6, page 332

Technical analysis is the study of collective market sentiment, as expressed in buying and selling of assets. It is based on the idea that prices are determined by the interaction of supply and demand. The market price equates supply and demand at any instant. Only participants who actually trade affect prices, and better-informed participants tend to trade in greater volume. Thus, price and volume reflect the collective behavior of buyers and sellers.

Technical analysis is based on three key principles:

1. *Market prices reflect all known information*, including economic factors, company fundamentals, and investor psychology.
2. *Market prices exhibit trends and countertrends* that tend to persist.
3. *Patterns and cycles repeat themselves in predictable ways.*

LOS 54.b: Describe potential links between technical analysis and behavioral finance.

CFA® Program Curriculum, Volume 6, page 332

A key assumption of technical analysis is that market prices reflect both rational and irrational investor behavior. This assumption implies that the *efficient markets hypothesis* does not hold.

Technical analysts believe investor behavior is reflected in trends and patterns that tend to repeat and can be identified and used for forecasting price movements. This behavior may reflect both rational and irrational decisions, as research in behavioral finance has indicated. Technical analysts believe investors respond in similar ways to similar situations over time, so that patterns in trading prices and volumes will repeat themselves. Further, they believe that recognizing these patterns will provide information about future price changes.

Price and volume data reflect all the reasons why investors buy and sell, whether or not their buying and selling is consistent with any measure of a security's intrinsic value. The data also reflect the **market microstructure**, which consists of specifications such as tick sizes and order types, that may influence how supply and demand manifest themselves in a market.

PROFESSOR'S NOTE

The efficient markets hypothesis is described in the Equity Investments topic area.

LOS 54.c: Compare principles of technical analysis and fundamental analysis.

CFA® Program Curriculum, Volume 6, page 332

Technical analysis can be contrasted with fundamental analysis, which attempts to determine the intrinsic value of an asset. While fundamental analysis of a firm uses the company's financial statements and other information to analyze its financial position and determine its value, technical analysis uses only the firm's share price and trading volume data to project a target price. Technical analysis is not concerned with identifying buyers' and sellers' reasons for trading, but only with the trades that have occurred.

An advantage of only using actual price and volume data is that they are observable. Much of the data used in fundamental analysis is subject to assumptions or restatements, and might not be available at all for assets such as currencies or commodities. (This does not, however, imply that technical analysis itself is objective; both kinds of analysis require subjective judgment.) Another advantage of technical analysis is that it can be applied to the prices of assets that do not produce future cash flows (dividends or interest), such as commodities. Technical analysis can also be useful when financial statement fraud occurs. Price and volume may reflect the true value of the company even before the fraud is widely known and before the financial statements are restated.

The usefulness of technical analysis is limited in markets where price and volume data might not truly reflect supply and demand. This may be the case in illiquid markets and in markets that are subject to outside manipulation (for example, currency market intervention by central banks). For stocks of bankrupt companies, short covering can create positive technical patterns even when it is known that the stock price will go to zero.

LOS 54.d: Describe and interpret different types of technical analysis charts.

CFA® Program Curriculum, Volume 6, page 339

Technical analysts primarily use charts of price and volume to analyze asset prices and overall market movement. Most of these charts have time on the horizontal axis. The time interval chosen (monthly, weekly, daily, or intraday periods) reflects the trading horizon of interest to the analyst. A technical analyst will typically start by observing longer-term trends on monthly and weekly charts, then look at recent activity on daily or intraday charts. If prices have changed exponentially (e.g., a stock index over several decades), an analyst may choose to draw charts on a logarithmic scale instead of the usual linear scale.

Line charts are the simplest technical analysis charts. They show closing prices for each period as a continuous line (see Figure 54.1).

Figure 54.1: Line Chart

Bar charts add the high and low prices for each trading period and often include the opening price as well. Each period is displayed as a vertical line, with the closing price indicated as a point or dash on the right side of the line. If the chart includes opening prices, these are shown on the left side of each vertical line.

Candlestick charts use the same data as bar charts but display a box bounded by the opening and closing prices. The box is clear if the closing price is higher than the opening price, or filled if the close is lower than the opening price. Candlestick charts can make patterns easier to recognize (see Figure 54.2).

Figure 54.2: Bar and Candlestick Charts

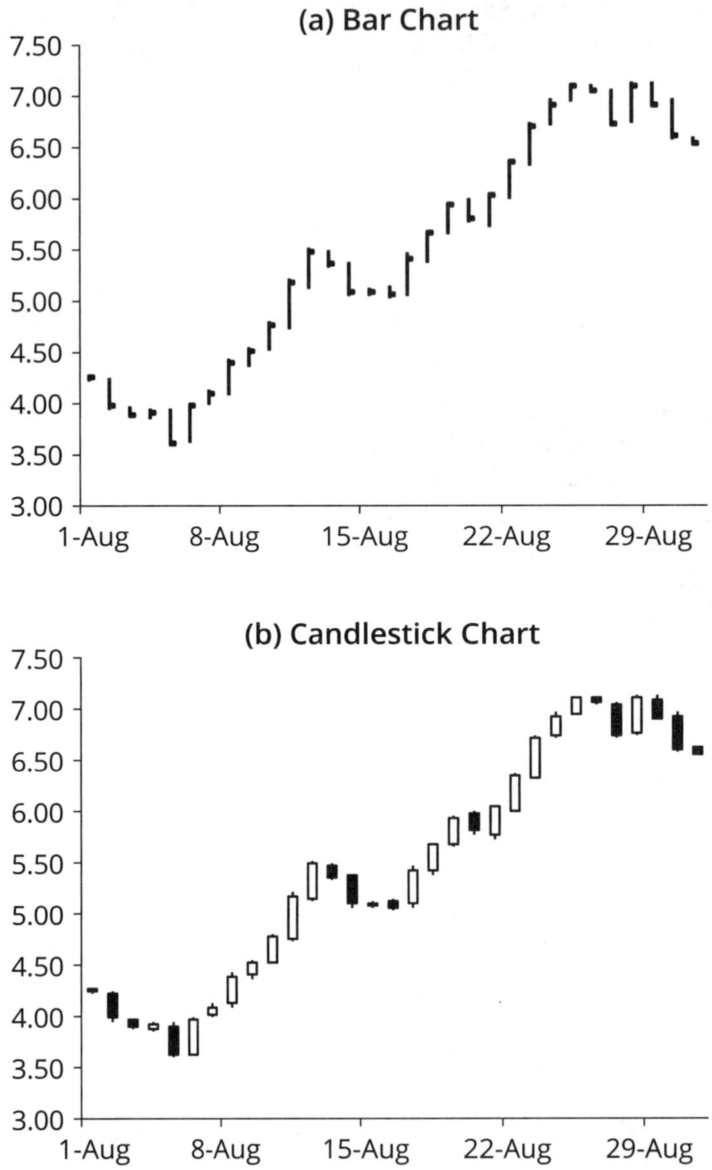

Technical analysts are concerned with volume as well as price. **Volume charts** are usually displayed below price charts with each period's volume shown as a vertical line (see Figure 54.3).

Figure 54.3: Volume Chart

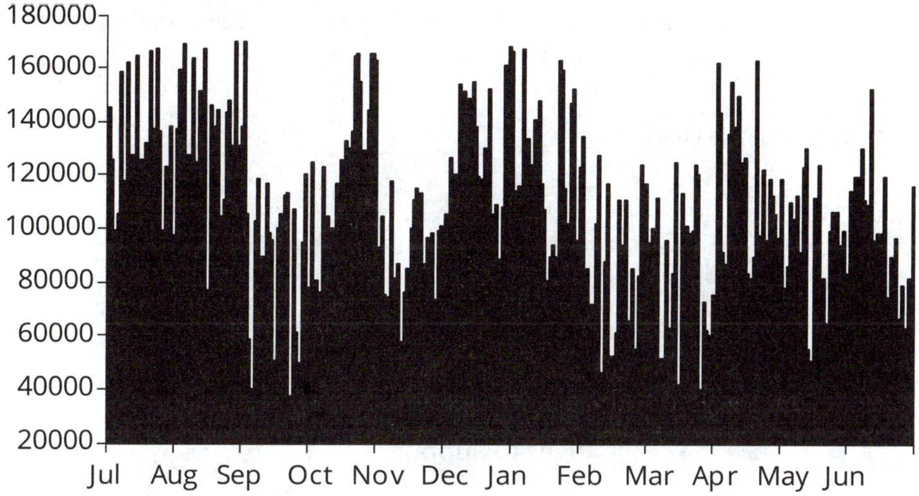

To perform **relative strength analysis**, an analyst calculates the ratios of an asset's closing prices to benchmark values, such as a stock index or comparable asset, and draws a line chart of the ratios. An increasing trend indicates that the asset is outperforming the benchmark (positive relative strength) and a decrease shows that the asset is underperforming the benchmark (negative relative strength).

LOS 54.e: Explain uses of trend, support, and resistance lines.

CFA® Program Curriculum, Volume 6, page 339

The most basic concept in technical analysis is the **trend** in prices. A market is said to be in an **uptrend** if prices are consistently reaching higher highs and retracing to higher lows. An uptrend means demand is increasing relative supply.

A market is in a **downtrend** if prices are consistently declining to lower lows and retracing to lower highs. A downtrend suggests supply (i.e., selling pressure) is increasing relative to demand. A period when neither an uptrend nor a downtrend is apparent is referred to as a period of **consolidation**.

Drawing a **trendline** on a chart can help to identify whether a trend is continuing or reversing. In an uptrend, a trendline connects the increasing lows in price. In a downtrend, the trendline connects the decreasing highs in price. When the price crosses the trendline by what the analyst considers a significant amount, a **breakout** from a downtrend or a **breakdown** from an uptrend is said to occur. Either a breakout or a breakdown may signal the end of the previous trend.

Breakouts and breakdowns are important because the trendline is thought to represent a level of support or resistance. At a **support level**, buying is expected to emerge that prevents further price decreases. At a **resistance level**, selling is expected to emerge that prevents further price increases. In addition to trendlines, support and resistance levels frequently appear at psychologically important prices such as round-number prices or historical highs and lows.

An important principle in technical analysis is the **change in polarity**. This refers to a belief that breached resistance levels become support levels and that breached support levels become resistance levels. In Figure 54.4, the area of 55 is viewed as a resistance level until the price breaks above that level, then 55 becomes a support level as prices decline from their new highs.

Figure 54.4: Change in Polarity

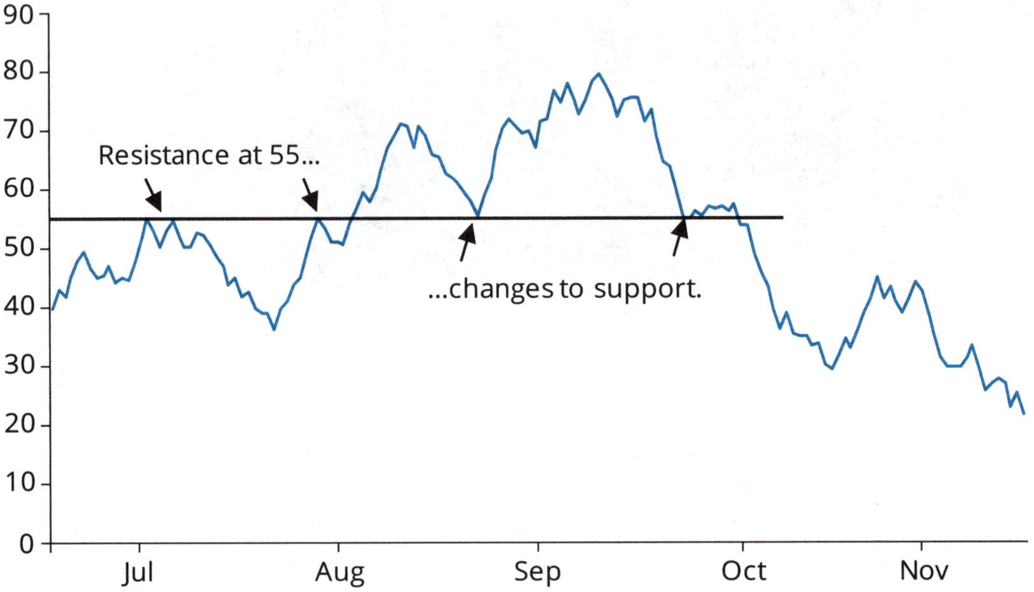

LOS 54.f: Explain common chart patterns.

CFA® Program Curriculum, Volume 6, page 339

Technical analysts look for recurring patterns in charts that suggest the future course of prices. Some patterns tend to appear at the end of trends, while other patterns indicate that a trend is likely to continue.

Reversal patterns occur when a trend approaches a range of prices but fails to continue beyond that range. A well-known example is the **head-and-shoulders pattern**, as shown in Figure 54.6. This pattern suggests the demand that has been driving the uptrend is fading, especially if each of the highs in the pattern occurs on declining volume.

Technical analysts commonly use the size of a head-and-shoulders pattern to project a price target for the ensuing downtrend. The size is the difference in price between the "head," the highest price reached, and the "neckline," the support level to which the price retraced after the left "shoulder" and the head have formed. If the price declines beyond the neckline after the right shoulder forms, the downtrend is projected to continue from that breakdown price by about the size of the head-and-shoulders pattern. In Figure 54.5, the top of the head is at 80 and the neckline is at 55, so the size of the pattern is 80 – 55 = 25. The price target for the ensuing downtrend is 55 – 25 = 30.

Figure 54.5: Reversal Patterns

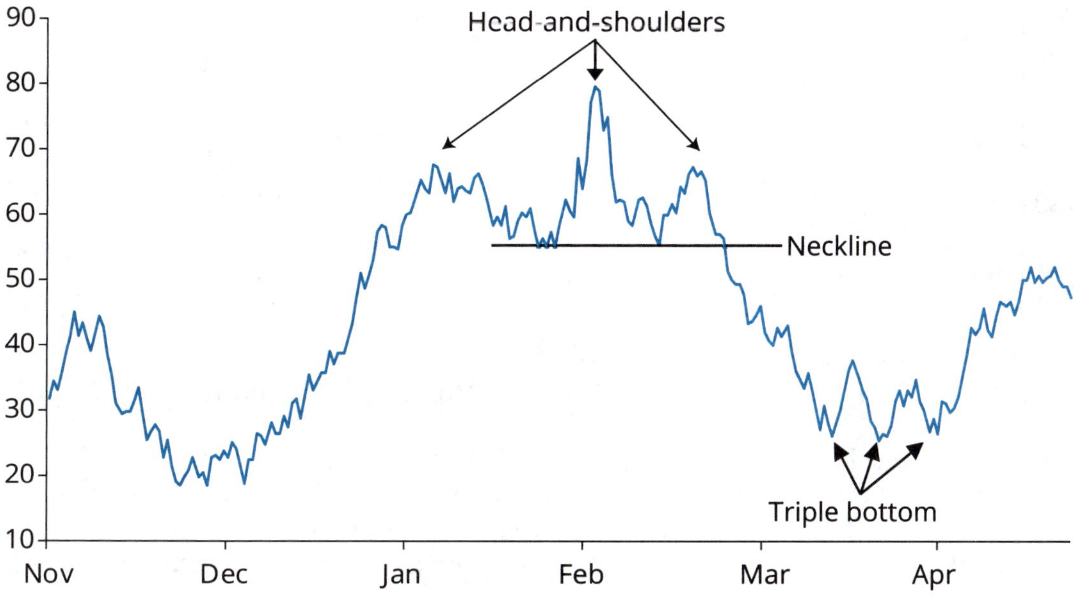

Double top and **triple top** patterns are similar to the head-and-shoulders pattern in that they indicate weakening in the buying pressure that has been driving an uptrend. In both cases, the price reaches a resistance level at which selling pressure appears repeatedly, preventing any further increase in the price. As with the head-and-shoulders, the size of a double or triple top pattern can be used to project a price target for the next downtrend.

Reversal patterns for downtrends are called **inverse head-and-shoulders**, **double bottom**, and **triple bottom** patterns and can be analyzed in the same way as the reversal patterns for uptrends.

Continuation patterns suggest a pause in a trend rather than a reversal. **Triangles** form when prices reach lower highs and higher lows over a period of time (see Figure 54.6). Trendlines on the highs and on the lows thus converge when they are projected forward. Triangles can be symmetrical (higher lows and lower highs), ascending (higher lows and a resistance level), or descending (lower highs and a support level).

Figure 54.6: Triangle Continuation Pattern

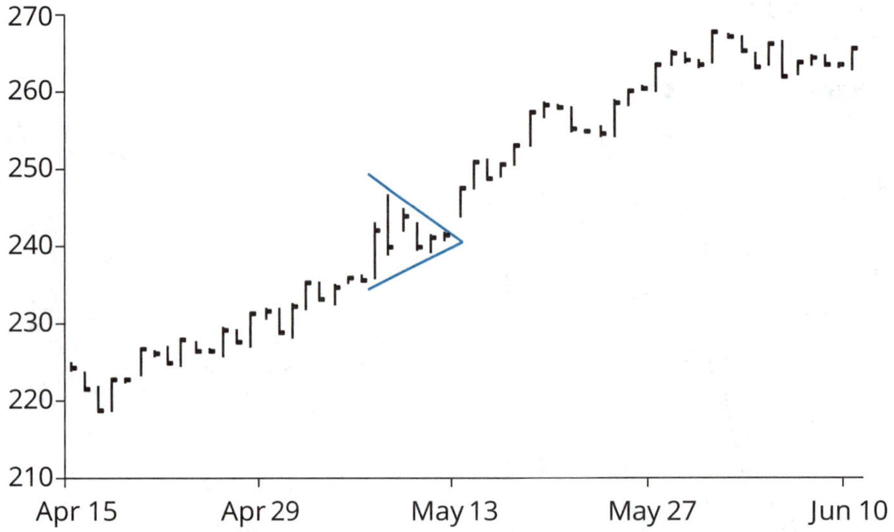

Triangles suggest buying and selling pressure have become roughly equal temporarily, but they do not imply a change in direction of the trend. The size of a triangle, or the difference between the two trendlines at the time when the pattern begins to form, can be used to set a price target, assuming the price breaks out of the triangle and the previous trend continues.

Rectangles form when trading temporarily forms a range between a support level and a resistance level. As with a triangle, a rectangle suggests the prevailing trend will resume and can be used to set a price target. **Flags** and **pennants** refer to rectangles and triangles that appear on short-term price charts.

LOS 54.g: Explain common technical indicators.

CFA® Program Curriculum, Volume 6, page 373

Price-Based Indicators

Moving average lines are frequently used to smooth the fluctuations in a price chart (or a chart of any time series). A moving average is simply the mean of the last n closing prices. The larger the chosen value of n, the smoother the moving average line. Analysts often use moving average periods that make intuitive sense, such as 20 days to represent the number of trading days in a month. In an uptrend, the price is higher than the moving average, and in a downtrend, the price is lower than the moving average. Moving average lines are often viewed as support or resistance levels.

Analysts use moving average lines to make changes in the trend easier to see. The longer the period used to calculate the moving average, the more short-term fluctuations are removed from the line. Overly long periods may, in fact, obscure changes in a price trend.

Moving averages for different periods can be used together, such as 20-day and 250-day averages. Points where the short-term average (more volatile) crosses the long-term average (smoother) can indicate changes in the price trend. When the short-term average crosses above long-term average (a "golden cross"), this is often viewed as an indicator of an emerging uptrend or a "buy" signal by technical analysts. The short-term average crossing below the long term average (a "dead cross") is often viewed as an indicator of an emerging downtrend or a "sell" signal.

Bollinger bands are constructed based on the standard deviation of closing prices over the last *n* periods. An analyst can draw high and low bands a chosen number of standard deviations (typically two) above and below the *n*-period moving average. The bands move away from one another when price volatility increases and move closer together when prices are less volatile (see Figure 54.7).

Figure 54.7: Moving Average and Bollinger Bands

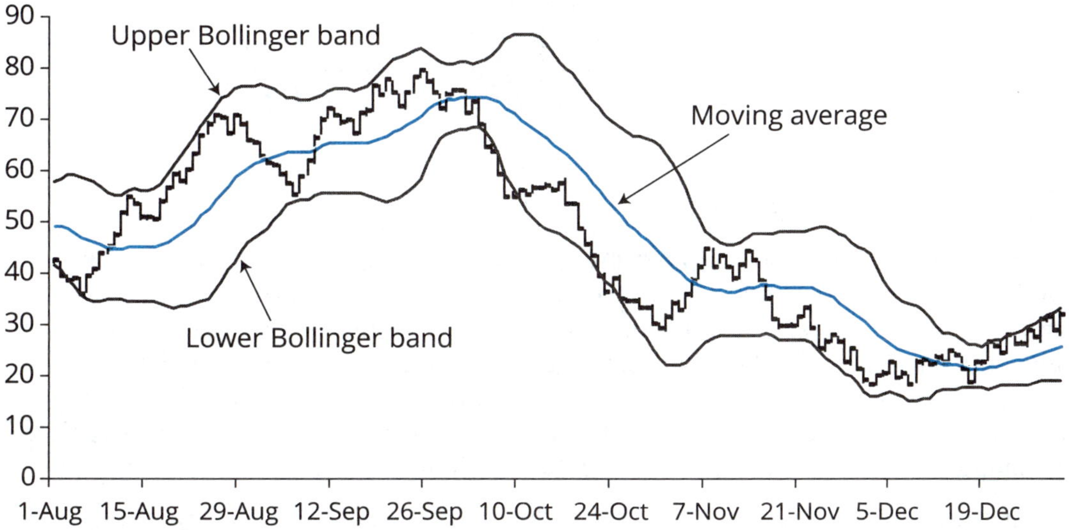

Bollinger bands can be used to identify prices that are "extreme" in terms of how many standard deviations they are above or below the moving average price. Prices at or above the upper Bollinger band may be viewed as indicating an **overbought** market, one that is "too high" and likely to decrease in the near term. Likewise, prices at or below the lower Bollinger band may be viewed as indicating an **oversold** market, one that is "too low" and likely to increase in the near term. A possible trading strategy using Bollinger bands is to buy when the price is at the lower band or sell when the price is at the upper band. This is an example of a **contrarian strategy**—one that buys when most traders are selling and sells when most traders are buying. Contrarians believe markets and individual assets become overbought or oversold because most investors tend to buy and sell at the wrong times, and thus it can be profitable to trade in the opposite direction.

The distance between the upper and lower Bollinger bands reflects changes in price volatility (standard deviation) over time. The **Bollinger band width indicator** is the difference between the upper and lower bands as a percentage of the moving average. Figure 54.8 illustrates the Bollinger band width indicator for the market shown in Figure 54.7. A period of low volatility, such as early October in Figure 54.8, is referred to as a **squeeze** and, according to technical analysts, will be followed by a period of increasing volatility.

Figure 54.8: Bollinger Band Width Indicator

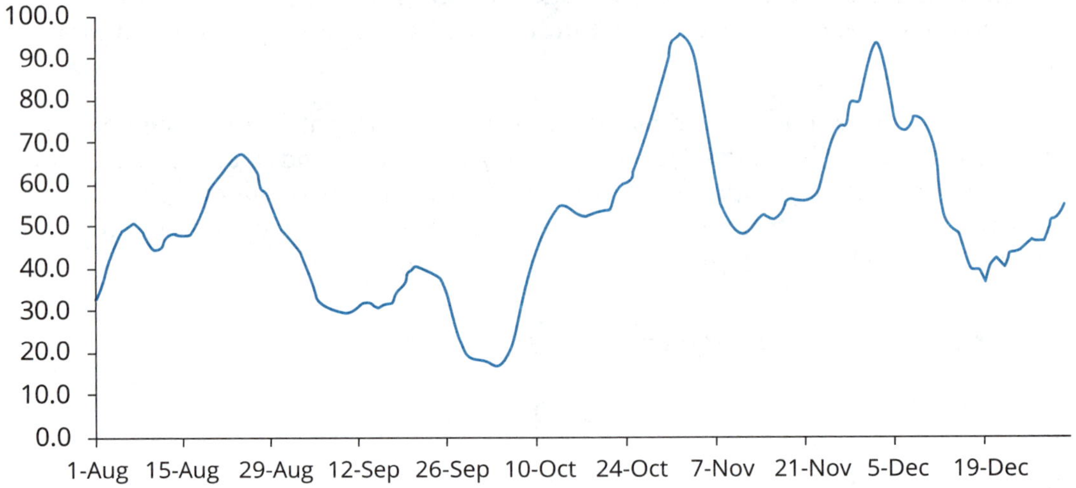

Momentum Oscillators

Momentum oscillators are another group of tools technical analysts use to identify overbought or oversold markets. These indicators are based on market prices but scaled so that they "oscillate" around a given value, such as zero, or between two values such as zero and 100. Extreme high values of an oscillator are viewed as indicating that a market is overbought, while extreme low values are viewed as indicating an oversold market. Technical analysts use charts of oscillators over time to highlight periods when they are near their high or low extremes.

Oscillator charts can also be used to identify **convergence** or **divergence** of the oscillator and market prices. Convergence occurs when the oscillator shows the same pattern as prices (e.g., both reaching higher highs), and divergence occurs when the oscillator shows a different pattern than prices (e.g., failing to reach a higher high when the price does). Convergence suggests the price trend is likely to continue, while divergence may indicate a potential change in the price trend.

Examples of oscillators include the rate of change (ROC) oscillator, Relative Strength Index (RSI), moving average convergence/divergence (MACD) lines, and the stochastic oscillator.

- **ROC oscillator.** An ROC is calculated as 100 times the difference between the latest closing price and the closing price *n* periods earlier. Thus, it oscillates around zero. One way technical analysts use the ROC is to buy when the oscillator changes from negative to positive during an uptrend in prices, and sell when the ROC changes from positive to negative during a downtrend. Some analysts prefer to use the ratio of the current price to the past price in place of the difference. Calculated this way, the ROC oscillates around 100.
- **RSI.** An RSI is based on the ratio of total price increases to total price decreases over a selected number of periods. This ratio is then scaled to oscillate between

0 and 100, with high values (typically those greater than 70) indicating an overbought market and low values (typically those less than 30) indicating an oversold market.

- **MACD.** MACD oscillators are drawn using exponentially smoothed moving averages, which place greater weight on more recent observations. The "MACD line" is the difference between two exponentially smoothed moving averages of the price, and the "signal line" is an exponentially smoothed moving average of the MACD line. The lines oscillate around zero but are not bounded. The MACD oscillator can be used to indicate overbought or oversold conditions or to identify convergence or divergence with the price trend. Points where the two lines cross can be used as trading signals, much like the use of two different moving averages discussed previously. The MACD line crossing above the smoother signal line is viewed as a buy signal and the MACD line crossing below the signal line is viewed as a sell signal.
- **Stochastic oscillator.** A stochastic oscillator is calculated from the latest closing price and highest and lowest prices reached in a recent period, such as 14 days. In a sustainable uptrend, prices tend to close nearer to the recent high, and in a sustainable downtrend, prices tend to close nearer to the recent low. Stochastic oscillators use two lines that are bounded by 0 and 100. The "%K" line is the difference between the latest price and the recent low as a percentage of the difference between the recent high and low. The "%D" line is a 3-period average of the %K line. Technical analysts typically use stochastic oscillators to identify overbought and oversold markets. Points where the %K line crosses the %D line can also be used as trading signals in the same way as the MACD lines.

PROFESSOR'S NOTE

Is this fun or what? Remember, no calculations are required. Just know the terms as best you can.

Non-Price-Based Indicators

While the technical indicators mentioned so far assume investor sentiment is reflected in price and volume data, technical analysts can also look at indicators of investor sentiment and capital flows to gain insight into potential emerging trends. **Sentiment indicators** can be used to discern the views of potential buyers and sellers. Market sentiment is said to be "bullish" when investors expect increasing prices and "bearish" when they expect decreasing prices.

Indicators can include opinion polls that try to measure investor sentiment directly, as well as several measures that are based on market data:

- **Put/call ratio.** Put options increase in value when the price of an underlying asset decreases, while call options increase in value if the price of the underlying asset increases. For financial assets that have actively traded options, the volume of put and call options reflects activity by investors with negative and positive outlooks, respectively, about the asset. The put/call ratio is put volume divided by call volume. Increases in the put/call ratio indicate a more negative outlook for the price of the asset. This ratio is generally viewed as a contrarian indicator. Extremely high ratios indicate strongly bearish investor sentiment and possibly an oversold market, while extremely low ratios indicate strongly bullish sentiment and perhaps an overbought market.

- **Volatility index (VIX)**. The Chicago Board Options Exchange calculates the VIX, which measures the volatility of options on the S&P 500 stock index. High levels of the VIX suggest investors fear declines in the stock market. Technical analysts most often interpret the VIX in a contrarian way, viewing a predominantly bearish investor outlook as a bullish sign.
- **Margin debt.** The amount of margin debt is a readily available indicator because brokers are required to report this data. Increases in total margin debt outstanding suggest aggressive buying by bullish margin investors. As margin investors reach their limits of margin credit, their ability to continue buying decreases, which can cause prices to begin declining. As prices decrease, investors may need to sell securities to meet margin calls, and these sales drive prices lower still. Increasing margin debt tends to coincide with increasing market prices and decreasing margin debt tends to coincide with decreasing prices.

LOS 54.h: Describe principles of intermarket analysis.

CFA® Program Curriculum, Volume 6, page 392

Intermarket analysis is an analysis of the interrelationships among the market values of major asset classes, such as stocks, bonds, commodities, and currencies. After identifying attractive asset classes, an analyst can apply relative strength analysis to identify which assets within these classes are outperforming others. This approach is also useful for comparing the relative performance of equity market sectors or industries, and of various international markets.

Relative strength charts are used to determine which assets, asset classes, or markets are outperforming others. Figure 54.9 shows a relative strength analysis of two hypothetical stocks, Made Up Data (MUD) and Random Time Series (RATS). Panels a and b are bar charts for each stock and panel c is the closing price of MUD as a ratio of the closing price of RATS. The relative strength chart indicates a clear breakout from a downtrend in early August. A technical analyst might have interpreted this as a signal to reduce the portfolio investment in RATS and increase the allocation to MUD.

Figure 54.9: Relative Strength Analysis

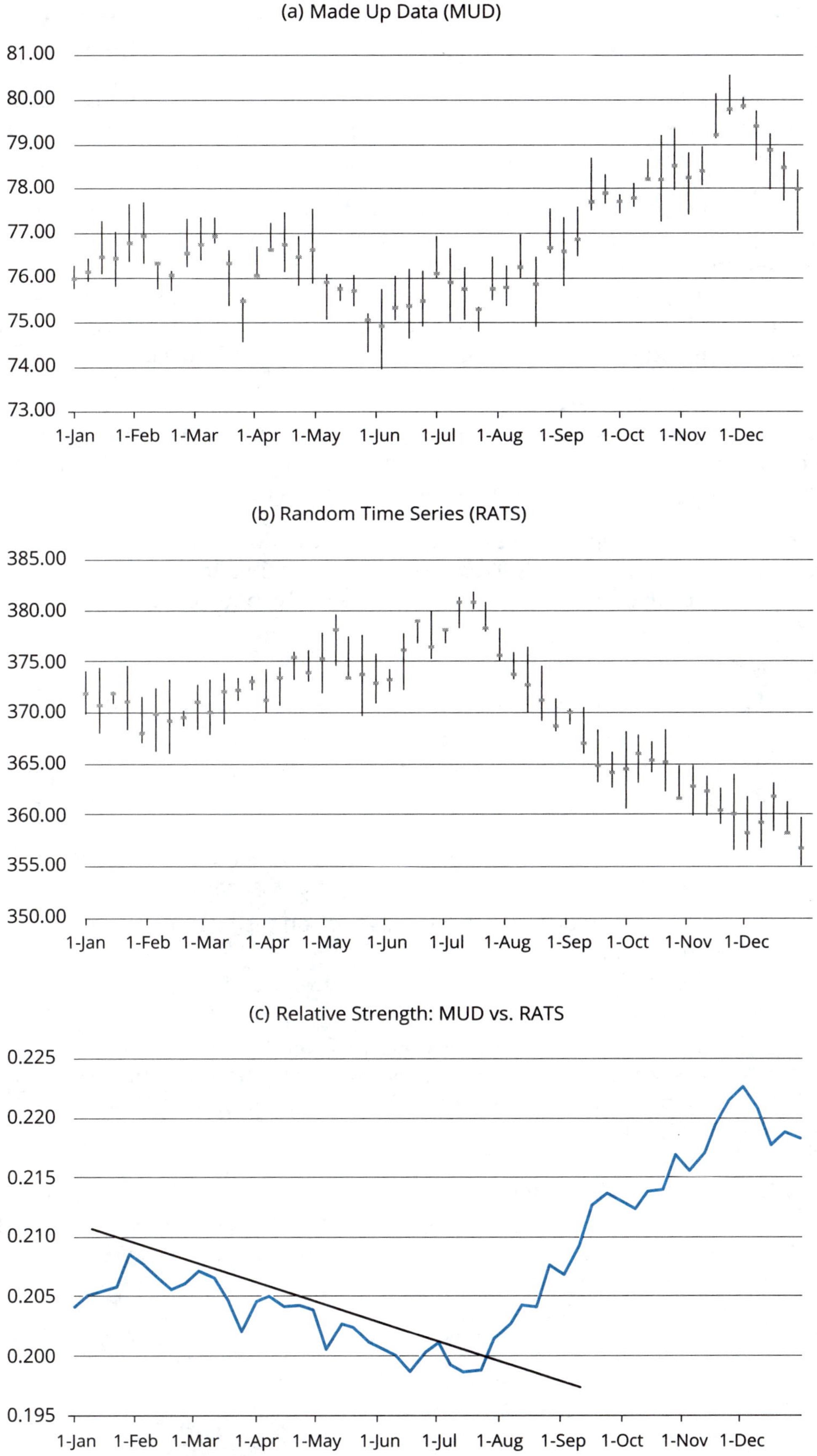

LOS 54.i: Explain technical analysis applications to portfolio management.

CFA® Program Curriculum, Volume 6, page 392

Recall that the execution step of a portfolio management process may involve top-down or bottom-up approaches to asset allocation and security selection. Technical analysis may be used to complement fundamental analysis using either approach.

A top-down approach begins by examining a country's or international region's economic growth, then analyzing how it is affecting the performance of market sectors, industry groups, and securities, and then using that analysis to identify attractive areas for investment. Intermarket analysis using relative strength charts can identify markets and sectors that have outperformed relative to others. Portfolio managers may use this analysis to make tactical asset allocation decisions.

Bottom-up analysis uses the opposite approach, taking economic and industry performance as given. Instead, this approach begins by identifying an investment universe or opportunity set, then narrowing it using criteria chosen by the analyst. These criteria may include technical analysis indicators or chart patterns.

At times, a bottom-up approach can complement a top-down approach. For example, if several stocks in an industry exhibit technical patterns indicating selling pressure, it may be that this industry as a whole is likely to underperform.

MODULE QUIZ 54.1

To best evaluate your performance, enter your quiz answers online.

1. An assumption of technical analysis is that market prices:
   A. exhibit identifiable trends and patterns that persist and repeat.
   B. are the only information necessary to analyze a freely trading market.
   C. reflect supply and demand conditions because actual transactions reflect rational decisions by buyers and sellers.
2. Which type of price chart requires data on the opening price?
   A. Bar chart.
   B. Line chart.
   C. Candlestick chart.
3. A stock has been in a downtrend for several days. When its price decreases to near \$30, many investors enter orders to buy the stock and the price increases to \$31. This is *most likely* an example of:
   A. a support level.
   B. a resistance level.
   C. a change in polarity.
4. An analyst who uses the standard deviation of recent prices to identify overbought or oversold conditions is *most likely* to employ:
   A. Bollinger bands.
   B. a Relative Strength Index (RSI).
   C. a rate of change (ROC) oscillator.

5. If a stock's relative strength chart shows an uptrend, the stock is:
   A. increasing in price.
   B. outperforming a benchmark.
   C. increasing on high volume or decreasing on low volume.

6. A technical analyst begins her evaluation of the U.S. equity market by using a computer algorithm to identify which stocks in the S&P 500 Index have shown uptrends on increasing volume over the last month. This analyst is *most accurately* said to be using:
   A. a top-down approach.
   B. a center-out approach.
   C. a bottom-up approach.

KEY CONCEPTS

LOS 54.a

Technical analysis is based on three key principles:

1. Market prices reflect all known information.
2. Prices exhibit trends that persist.
3. Investor behavior repeats itself, producing patterns and cycles that recur.

LOS 54.b

Technical analysts believe investor behavior is reflected in trends and patterns that repeat and can be used for forecasting. This behavior may reflect both rational and irrational motivations, as the theory of behavioral finance suggests.

LOS 54.c

Technical analysis can be contrasted with fundamental analysis, which attempts to determine the intrinsic value of an asset. While fundamental analysis uses a company's financial statements and other information to analyze its financial position and determine its value, technical analysis uses only the firm's share price and trading volume data to project a target price.

LOS 54.d

Technical analysts use charts to identify trends and patterns in prices over time. A line chart is a continuous line that connects closing prices for each period. Bar charts and candlestick charts show the open, high, low, and close for each period. Volume charts often accompany price charts.

LOS 54.e

In an uptrend, prices are reaching higher highs and higher lows. An uptrend line is drawn below the prices on a chart by connecting the increasing lows with a straight line. In a downtrend, prices are reaching lower lows and lower highs. A downtrend line is drawn above the prices on a chart by connecting the decreasing highs with a straight line.

Support and resistance are price levels or ranges at which buying or selling pressure is expected to limit price movement. Commonly identified support and resistance levels include trendlines and previous high and low prices. The change in polarity principle is the idea that breached resistance levels become support levels and breached support levels become resistance levels.

LOS 54.f

Technical analysts look for recurring patterns in price charts. Head-and-shoulders patterns, double tops, and triple tops are thought to be reversal patterns at the ends of uptrends. Inverse head-and-shoulders patterns, double bottoms, and triple bottoms are thought to be reversal patterns at the ends of downtrends. Triangles, rectangles, flags, and pennants are thought to be continuation patterns, which indicate that the trend in which they appear is likely to go further in the same direction.

LOS 54.g

Price-based indicators include moving averages, Bollinger bands, and momentum oscillators such as the Relative Strength Index (RSI), moving average convergence/divergence (MACD) lines, rate of change (ROC) oscillators, and stochastic oscillators. These indicators are commonly used to identify changes in price trends, as well as "overbought" markets that are likely to decrease in the near term and "oversold" markets that are likely to increase in the near term. Sentiment indicators include opinion polls, the put/call ratio, the volatility index, and margin debt.

LOS 54.h

Intermarket analysis refers to analysis of the relationships among the price behavior of major asset classes, such as stocks, bonds, commodities, and currencies. It uses relative strength charts to identify assets, asset classes, or markets that have outperformed others.

LOS 54.i

Technical analysis may be used in either a top-down or bottom-up approach to asset class allocation and security selection. In a top-down approach, intermarket analysis can be used to identify markets and sectors that have outperformed others. In a bottom-up approach, criteria for narrowing down an investment opportunity set may include technical indicators and chart patterns.

ANSWER KEY FOR MODULE QUIZZES

Module Quiz 54.1

1. **A** Technical analysis assumes persistent trends and repeating patterns in market prices can be used to forecast price behavior. Technical analysts believe prices reflect supply and demand, but that buying and selling can be motivated by both rational and irrational causes. Volume, along with price, is important information to a technical analyst. (LOS 54.a)

2. **C** Constructing a candlestick chart requires opening, high, low, and closing prices for each trading period. A line chart requires only the closing prices. A bar chart can be constructed using high, low, and closing prices. (LOS 54.c)

3. **A** The downtrend reached a support level where buying demand sustained the price. A resistance level is a price at which selling pressure emerges that stops an uptrend. The change in polarity principle holds that breached support levels become resistance and breached resistance levels become support. With no information given on the stock's history, we cannot determine whether $30 had once been a resistance level. (LOS 54.e)

4. **A** Bollinger bands are based on the standard deviation of prices over some number of the most recent periods. An RSI is based on the sums of positive and negative price changes during a period. An ROC oscillator is based on the difference between the most recent closing price and the closing price a given number of periods earlier. (LOS 54.g)

5. **B** If a relative strength chart shows an uptrend, the stock is outperforming the benchmark stock or index against which it is being measured. This does not imply that the stock is increasing in price; if the stock price is decreasing, but the benchmark is decreasing by a larger percentage, the relative strength chart will still trend upward. Volume is not an input into a relative strength ratio. (LOS 54.h)

6. **C** Using selected criteria to narrow an investment universe reflects a bottom-up approach. (LOS 54.i)

The following is a review of the Portfolio Management (2) principles designed to address the learning outcome statements set forth by CFA Institute. Cross-Reference to CFA Institute Assigned Reading #55.

READING 55

Fintech in Investment Management

Study Session 18

EXAM FOCUS

Fintech (financial technology) is increasing in its importance to the financial services industry. As terms like *Big Data*, *blockchain*, and *algorithmic trading* come into common use, CFA exam candidates are expected to be familiar with them and how they relate to investment management. That being said, we do not believe the exam writers expect finance professionals to become data scientists. The Learning Outcome Statements for this topic only ask candidates to describe these fintech concepts. Focus on their applications, such as cryptocurrencies and robo-advisors, the advantages of their use in finance, and the challenges their adoption may present.

MODULE 55.1: FINTECH IN INVESTMENT MANAGEMENT

Video covering this content is available online.

LOS 55.a: Describe "fintech."

CFA® Program Curriculum, Volume 6, page 225

The term **fintech** refers to developments in technology that can be applied to the financial services industry. Companies that are in the business of developing technologies for the finance industry are often referred to as fintech companies.

Some of the primary areas where fintech is developing include:

- Increasing functionality to handle large sets of data that may come from many sources and exist in a variety of forms.
- Tools and techniques such as artificial intelligence for analyzing very large datasets.

- Automation of financial functions such as executing trades and providing investment advice.
- Emerging technologies for financial recordkeeping that may reduce the need for intermediaries.

LOS 55.b: Describe Big Data, artificial intelligence, and machine learning.

CFA® Program Curriculum, Volume 6, page 227

Big Data is a widely used expression that refers to all the potentially useful information that is generated in the economy. This includes not only data from traditional sources, such as financial markets, company financial reports, and government economic statistics, but also **alternative data** from non-traditional sources. Some of these non-traditional sources are:

- Individuals who generate usable data such as social media posts, online reviews, email, and website visits.
- Businesses that generate potentially useful information such as bank records and retail scanner data. These kinds of data are referred to as **corporate exhaust**.
- Sensors, such as radio frequency identification chips, are embedded in numerous devices such as smart phones and smart buildings. The broad network of such devices is referred to as the **Internet of Things**.

Characteristics of Big Data include its volume, velocity, and variety.

The volume of data continues to grow by orders of magnitude. The units in which data can be measured have increased from megabytes and gigabytes to terabytes (1,000 gigabytes) and even petabytes (1,000 terabytes).

Velocity refers to how quickly data are communicated. Real-time data such as stock market price feeds are said to have low **latency**. Data that are only communicated periodically or with a lag are said to have high latency.

The variety of data refers to the varying degrees of structure in which data may exist. These range from structured forms such as spreadsheets and databases, to semistructured forms such as photos and web page code, to unstructured forms such as video.

The field of **data science** concerns how we extract information from Big Data. Data science describes methods for processing and visualizing data. Processing methods include:

- *Capture*—collecting data and transforming it into usable forms.
- *Curation*—assuring data quality by adjusting for bad or missing data.
- *Storage*—archiving and accessing data.
- *Search*—examining stored data to find needed information.
- *Transfer*—moving data from their source or a storage medium to where they are needed.

Visualization techniques include the familiar charts and graphs that display structured data. To visualize less-structured data requires other methods. Some examples of these are word clouds that illustrate the frequency that words appear in a sample of text, or mind maps that display logical relations among concepts.

Taking advantage of Big Data presents a number of challenges. Analysts must ensure that the data they use are of high quality, accounting for the possibilities of outliers, bad or missing data, or sampling biases. The volume of data collected must be sufficient and appropriate for its intended use.

The need to process and organize data before using it can be especially problematic with qualitative and unstructured data. This is a process to which **artificial intelligence**, or computer systems that can be programmed to simulate human cognition, may be applied usefully. **Neural networks** are an example of artificial intelligence in that they are programmed to process information in a way similar to the human brain.

An important development in the field of artificial intelligence is **machine learning**. In machine learning, a computer algorithm is given inputs of source data, with no assumptions about their probability distributions, and may be given outputs of target data. The algorithm is designed to learn, without human assistance, how to model the output data based on the input data or to learn how to detect and recognize patterns in the input data.

Machine learning typically requires vast amounts of data. A typical process begins with a *training* dataset in which the algorithm looks for relationships. A *validation* dataset is then used to refine these relationship models, which can then be applied to a *test* dataset to analyze their predictive ability.

In **supervised learning**, the input and output data are labelled, the machine learns to model the outputs from the inputs, and then the machine is given new data on which to use the model. In **unsupervised learning**, the input data are not labelled and the machine learns to describe the structure of the data. **Deep learning** is a technique that uses layers of neural networks to identify patterns, beginning with simple patterns and advancing to more complex ones. Deep learning may employ supervised or unsupervised learning. Some of the applications of deep learning include image and speech recognition.

Machine learning can produce models that overfit or underfit the data. **Overfitting** occurs when the machine learns the input and output data too exactly, treats noise as true parameters, and identifies spurious patterns and relationships. In effect, the machine creates a model that is too complex. **Underfitting** occurs when the machine fails to identify actual patterns and relationships, treating true parameters as noise. This means the model is not complex enough to describe the data. A further challenge with machine learning is that its results can be a "black box," producing outcomes based on relationships that are not readily explainable.

LOS 55.c: Describe fintech applications to investment management.

CFA® Program Curriculum, Volume 6, page 233

Applications of fintech that are relevant to investment management include text analytics, natural language processing, risk analysis, algorithmic trading, and robo-advisory services.

Text analytics refers to the analysis of unstructured data in text or voice forms. An example of text analytics is analyzing the frequency of words and phrases. In the finance industry, text analytics have the potential to partially automate specific tasks such as evaluating company regulatory filings.

Natural language processing refers to the use of computers and artificial intelligence to interpret human language. Speech recognition and language translation are among the uses of natural language processing. Possible applications in finance could be to check for regulatory compliance in an examination of employee communications, or to evaluate large volumes of research reports to detect more subtle changes in sentiment than can be discerned from analysts' recommendations alone.

As we saw in our topic review of "Risk Management: An Introduction," risk governance requires an understanding of a firm's exposure to a wide variety of risks. Financial regulators require firms to perform risk assessments and stress testing. The simulations, scenario analysis, and other techniques used for risk analysis require large amounts of quantitative data along with a great deal of qualitative information. Machine learning and other techniques related to Big Data can be useful in modeling and testing risk, particularly if firms use real-time data to monitor risk exposures.

Algorithmic trading refers to computerized securities trading based on a predetermined set of rules. For example, algorithms may be designed to enter the optimal execution instructions for any given trade based on real-time price and volume data. Algorithmic trading can also be useful for executing large orders by determining the best way to divide the orders across exchanges. Another application of algorithmic trading is **high-frequency trading** that identifies and takes advantage of intraday securities mispricings.

Robo-advisors are online platforms that provide automated investment advice based on a customer's answers to survey questions. The survey questions are designed to elicit an investor's financial position, return objectives, risk tolerance, and constraints such as time horizon and liquidity needs. Robo-advisor services may be fully automated or assisted by a human investment advisor.

Robo-advisory services tend to offer passively managed investments with low fees, low minimum account sizes, traditional asset classes, and conservative recommendations. The primary advantage of robo-advisors is their low cost to customers, which may make advice more accessible to a larger number of investors.

A disadvantage of robo-advisors is that the reasoning behind their recommendations might not be apparent. Without a human investment advisor to explain the reasoning, customers may hesitate to trust the appropriateness of a robo-advisor's recommendations, particularly in crisis periods.

Regulation of robo-advisors is still emerging. However, in many countries robo-advisory services are subject to the same regulations and registration requirements as any other investment advisor.

LOS 55.d: Describe financial applications of distributed ledger technology.

CFA® Program Curriculum, Volume 6, page 240

A **distributed ledger** is a database that is shared on a network so that each participant has an identical copy. A distributed ledger must have a consensus mechanism to validate new entries into the ledger. Distributed ledger technology uses cryptography to ensure only authorized network participants can use the data.

A **blockchain** is a distributed ledger that records transactions sequentially in blocks and links these blocks in a chain. Each block has a cryptographically secured "hash" that links it to the previous block. The consensus mechanism in a blockchain requires some of the computers on the network to solve a cryptographic problem. These computers are referred to as **miners**. Mining requires vast resources of computing power and electricity. This imposes substantial costs on any attempt to manipulate a blockchain's historical record. To do so would also require one party to control a majority of the network. For this reason, a blockchain is more likely to succeed with a large number of participants in its network.

Distributed ledgers can take the form of permissionless or permissioned networks. In **permissionless networks**, all network participants can view all transactions. These networks have no central authority, which gives them the advantage of having no single point of failure. The ledger becomes a permanent record visible to all, and its history cannot be altered (short of the manipulation described previously). This removes the need for trust between the parties to a transaction.

In **permissioned networks**, users have different levels of access. For example, a permissioned network might allow network participants to enter transactions while giving government regulators permission to view the transaction history. A distributed ledger that allowed regulators to view records that firms are required to make available would increase transparency and decrease compliance costs.

Financial Applications of Distributed Ledger Technology

Cryptocurrencies are a current example of distributed ledger technology in finance. A cryptocurrency is an electronic medium of exchange that allows participants to engage in real-time transactions without a financial intermediary. Cryptocurrencies typically reside on permissionless networks.

Demonstrating the impact cryptocurrencies are already having in finance, companies have raised capital through **initial coin offerings**, in which they sell cryptocurrency for money or another cryptocurrency. This reduces the cost and time frame compared to carrying out a regulated IPO, and initial coin offerings typically do not come with voting rights. Investors should note that fraud has occurred with initial coin offerings and they may become subject to securities regulations.

Post-trade clearing and settlement is an area of finance to which distributed ledger technology might be applied productively. Distributed ledgers could automate many of the processes currently carried out by custodians and other third parties. The technology has the potential to bring about real-time trade verification and settlement, which (as we will see in Equity Investments) currently takes one or more days for many securities. This would reduce trading costs and counterparty risk. On the other hand, the inability to alter past transactions on a distributed ledger is problematic when cancelling a trade is required.

Other potential applications of distributed ledger technology in finance include smart contracts and tokenization. **Smart contracts** are electronic contracts that could be programmed to self-execute based on terms agreed to by the counterparties. For example, an options contract could be set up to be exercised automatically if certain defined conditions exist in the market. **Tokenization** refers to electronic proof of ownership of physical assets, which could be maintained on a distributed ledger. For example, such a ledger could potentially replace the paper real estate deeds currently filed at government offices.

MODULE QUIZ 55.1

To best evaluate your performance, enter your quiz answers online.

1. Fintech is *most accurately* described as:
   A. the application of technology to the financial services industry.
   B. the replacement of government-issued money with electronic currencies.
   C. the clearing and settling securities trades through distributed ledger technology.
2. Which of the following technological developments is *most likely* to be useful for analyzing Big Data?
   A. Machine learning.
   B. High-latency capture.
   C. The Internet of Things.
3. A key criticism of robo-advisory services is that:
   A. they are costly for investors to use.
   B. the reasoning behind their recommendations can be unclear.
   C. they tend to produce overly aggressive investment recommendations.
4. Which of the following statements about distributed ledger technology is *most accurate?*
   A. A disadvantage of blockchain is that past records are vulnerable to manipulation.
   B. Tokenization can potentially streamline transactions involving high-value physical assets.
   C. Only parties who trust each other should carry out transactions on a permissionless network.

KEY CONCEPTS

LOS 55.a

Fintech refers to developments in technology that can be applied to the financial services industry. Companies that develop technologies for the finance industry are referred to as fintech companies.

LOS 55.b

Big Data refers to the potentially useful information that is generated in the economy, including data from traditional and non-traditional sources. Characteristics of Big Data include its volume, velocity, and variety.

Artificial intelligence refers to computer systems that can be programmed to simulate human cognition. Neural networks are an example of artificial intelligence.

Machine learning is programming that gives a computer system the ability to improve its performance of a task over time and is often used to detect patterns in large sets of data.

LOS 55.c

Applications of fintech to investment management include text analytics, natural language processing, risk analysis, algorithmic trading, and robo-advisory services.

Text analytics refers to analyzing unstructured data in text or voice forms. Natural language processing is the use of computers and artificial intelligence to interpret human language. Algorithmic trading refers to computerized securities trading based on predetermined rules.

Robo-advisors are online platforms that provide automated investment advice based on a customer's answers to survey questions. The primary advantage of robo-advisors is their low cost to customers. A disadvantage is that the reasoning behind their recommendations might not be apparent.

LOS 55.d

A distributed ledger is a database that is shared on a network, with a consensus mechanism so that each participant has an identical copy of the ledger.

A cryptocurrency is an electronic medium of exchange that allows network participants in a distributed ledger to engage in real-time transactions without a financial intermediary.

Potential financial applications of distributed ledger technology include smart contracts, tokenization, and more efficient post-trade clearing and settlement.

ANSWER KEY FOR MODULE QUIZZES

Module Quiz 55.1

1. **A** Fintech refers to the application of technology to the financial services industry and to companies that are involved in developing and applying technology for financial services. Cryptocurrencies and distributed ledger technology are examples of fintech-related developments. (LOS 55.a)

2. **A** Machine learning is a computer programming technique useful for identifying and modeling patterns in large volumes of data. The Internet of Things refers to the network of devices that is one of the sources of Big Data. Capture is one aspect of processing data. Latency refers to the lag between when data is generated and when it is needed. (LOS 55.b)

3. **B** One criticism of robo-advisory services is that the reasoning behind their recommendations might not be readily apparent to customers. Recommendations from robo-advisors tend to be conservative rather than aggressive. Low cost is a primary advantage of robo-advisors. (LOS 55.c)

4. **B** By enabling electronic proof of ownership, tokenization has the potential to streamline transfers of physical assets such as real estate. The high cost and difficulty of manipulating past records is a strength of blockchain technology. Permissionless networks do not require trust between the parties to a transaction because the record of a transaction is unchangeable and visible to all network participants. (LOS 55.d)

TOPIC QUIZ: PORTFOLIO MANAGEMENT

You have now finished the Portfolio Management topic section. Please log into your Schweser online dashboard and take the Topic Quiz on Portfolio Management. The Topic Quiz provides immediate feedback on how effective your study has been for this material. The number of questions on this quiz is approximately the number of questions for the topic on one-half of the actual Level I CFA exam. Questions are more exam-like than typical Module Quiz or QBank questions; a score of less than 70% indicates that your study likely needs improvement. These tests are best taken timed; allow 1.5 minutes per question.

After you've completed this Topic Quiz, select "Performance Tracker" to view a breakdown of your score. Select "Compare with Others" to display how your score on the Topic Quiz compares to the scores of others who entered their answers.

The following is a review of the Ethical and Professional Standards principles designed to address the learning outcome statements set forth by CFA Institute. Cross-Reference to CFA Institute Assigned Reading #56.

READING 56

Ethics and Trust in the Investment Profession

Study Session 19

EXAM FOCUS

From this reading, candidates should learn the definitions of ethics and ethical behavior presented by the authors and the arguments presented for having a code of ethics and following ethical principles. Additionally, the arguments for integrating ethics into the decision-making process include testable material.

MODULE 56.1: ETHICS AND TRUST

Video covering this content is available online.

LOS 56.a: Explain ethics.

CFA® Program Curriculum, Volume 6, page 257

Ethics can be described as a set of shared beliefs about what is good or acceptable behavior and what is bad or unacceptable behavior. Ethical conduct has been described as behavior that follows moral principles and is consistent with society's ethical expectations.

Ethical conduct has also been described as conduct that improves outcomes for **stakeholders**, who are people directly or indirectly affected by the conduct. Examples of stakeholders in the case of investment professionals include their clients, coworkers, employers, and the investment profession as a whole. Some decisions may bring positive results for you, but negative consequences for a stakeholder, such as a coworker. Ethical conduct is behavior that balances your self-interest with the impact on others.

LOS 56.b: Describe the role of a code of ethics in defining a profession.

CFA® Program Curriculum, Volume 6, page 259

A **code of ethics** is a written set of moral principles that can guide behavior by describing what is considered acceptable behavior. Having a code of ethics is a way to communicate the values, principles, and expectations of an organization or other group of people and provides a general guide to what constitutes acceptable behavior. Some codes of ethics include a set of rules or standards that require some minimum level of ethical behavior.

A **profession** refers to a group of people with specialized skills and knowledge who serve others and agree to behave in accordance with a code of ethics. A professional code of ethics is a way for a profession to communicate to the public that its members will use their knowledge and skills to serve their clients in an honest and ethical manner.

LOS 56.c: Describe professions and how they establish trust.

CFA® Program Curriculum, Volume 6, page 259

A **profession** is an occupational group (e.g., doctors or lawyers) that has requirements of specialized expert knowledge, and often a focus on ethical behavior and service to the larger community or society. Additionally, a profession may have the following characteristics:

- A code and standards for professional behavior.
- A regulatory body to enforce rules concerning professional behavior and monitor the ethical behavior of members.
- A focus on the needs of their clients (e.g., students, patients).
- A focus on service to society.
- A requirement to put client interests first.
- A focus on or requirement for continuing education.

Ways that professions establish trust include:

- Requiring high standards of expertise, knowledge, and skill.
- Establishing standards of ethical behavior.
- Monitoring professional conduct.
- Encouraging continuing education to maintain and increase competence.
- Being focused on clients' needs.
- Mentoring and inspiring others in the profession.

LOS 56.d: Describe the need for high ethical standards in investment management.

CFA® Program Curriculum, Volume 6, page 259

Investment professionals have a special responsibility because they arc entrusted with their clients' wealth. The responsibility to use their specialized knowledge and skills to both protect and grow client assets makes high ethical standards all the more important. Investment advice and management are intangible products, making quality and value received more difficult to evaluate than for tangible products such as a laptop computer or a restaurant meal. For this reason, trust in investment professionals takes on an even greater importance than in many other businesses.

Failure to act in a highly ethical manner can damage not only client wealth but also impede the success of investment firms and investment professionals because potential investors will be less likely to use their services.

Unethical behavior by financial services professionals can have negative effects for society as a whole. The financial services industry serves as an intermediary between savers and those seeking financing for their business activities. A lack of trust in financial advisors will reduce the funds entrusted to them and increase the cost of raising capital for business investment and growth. When investors cannot rely on the information they receive from financial services professionals, this adds another layer of risk on top of the investment risks that investors face. Even the perception of additional risk will reduce the amounts invested and increase the returns required to attract investor capital.

In addition to reducing the amount of investment overall, unethical behavior—such as providing incomplete, misleading, or false information to investors—can affect the allocation of the capital that is raised. Misallocation of capital to businesses other than those with the most potential for growth and societal benefit reduces the growth of an economy and the well-being of its people. When the allocation of investment capital is constrained or inefficient, the negative consequences extend to all the participants in an economy.

LOS 56.e: Explain professionalism in investment management.

CFA® Program Curriculum, Volume 6, page 262

Because clients of investment professionals rely on their expertise, judgment, and ethical principles, many of the characteristics of a profession we have described apply.

Ethical principles are of great importance because clients often do not have significant knowledge about financial securities, fee structures, or sources of potential bias in investment recommendations. Currently, some financial professionals are held to a **suitability standard**, while others are held to a **fiduciary standard**. *Suitability* refers to the match between client return requirements and risk tolerances and the characteristics of the securities recommended. A fiduciary standard is stronger, requiring professionals to use their knowledge and expertise to act in the best interests of the client.

LOS 56.f: Identify challenges to ethical behavior.

CFA® Program Curriculum, Volume 6, page 265

One challenge to ethical behavior is that individuals tend to overrate the ethical quality of their behavior on a relative basis and overemphasize the importance of their own personal traits in determining the ethical quality of their behavior.

It is claimed that external or **situational influences** are a more important determinant of the ethical quality of behavior than internal (personal) traits that influence behavior. One situational influence is social pressure from others. Loyalty to an employer, supervisor, organization, or coworkers can cause individuals to act in unethical ways as they place more importance on their self-interest and short-term results than on longer-term results and the ethical quality of their decisions and behavior. The prospect of acquiring more money or greater prestige can cause individuals to engage in unethical behavior.

Firms with strict rules-based compliance procedures run the risk of fostering a culture that is so focused on adhering to compliance rules that individuals only ask themselves what they *can* do. The question of what behavior they *should* engage in, based on ethical principles and longer-term results, is often not addressed in such situations.

LOS 56.g: Compare and contrast ethical standards with legal standards.

CFA® Program Curriculum, Volume 6, page 267

Not all unethical actions are illegal, and not all illegal actions are unethical. In some places it may be illegal to report one's employer's actions against the best interests of clients by sharing what is considered private company information with authorities, but doing so may be considered ethical "whistle-blowing" behavior by some. Acts of civil disobedience that are illegal are also considered by many to be ethical behavior. On the other hand, recommending investment in a relative's firm without disclosure may not be illegal, but would be considered unethical by many.

Ethical principles often set a higher standard of behavior than laws and regulations. New laws and regulations often result from recent instances of what is perceived to be unethical behavior. Just as the Securities Act of 1933, the Glass-Steagall Act, and the Securities Exchange Act of 1934 followed the perceived bad behavior by investment professionals and bankers leading to the 1929 market crash, the Sarbanes-Oxley laws followed the accounting scandals at Enron and Worldcom, and the Dodd-Frank Act followed the 2008 financial crisis. New laws and regulations can create opportunities for different unethical behavior. In general, ethical decisions require more judgment and consideration of the impact of behavior on many stakeholders compared to legal decisions.

LOS 56.h: Describe and apply a framework for ethical decision making.

CFA® Program Curriculum, Volume 6, page 270

Ethical decisions will be improved when ethics are integrated into a firm's decision-making process. This will allow decision makers and teams to consider alternative actions as well as shorter- and longer-term consequences from various perspectives, improving the ethical aspects of their decisions. To do this it is first necessary that the firm adopt a code of ethics to guide the process.

Such integration provides an opportunity to teach, practice, and reinforce ethical decision-making. This is an important part of developing an ethical culture. The support of senior management for integrating ethics into the decision-making process is also very important in developing a culture and processes that will result in ethical decision-making.

Using a framework for ethical decision-making helps individuals identify the important issues involved, examine these issues from multiple perspectives, develop the necessary judgment and decision-making skills required, and avoid unanticipated ethical consequences.

The following ethical decision-making framework is presented in the Level I CFA curriculum:[1]

- Identify: Relevant facts, stakeholders and duties owed, ethical principles, conflicts of interest.
- Consider: Situational influences, additional guidance, alternative actions.
- Decide and act.
- Reflect: Was the outcome as anticipated? Why or why not?

In the first step, decision makers need to identify the facts they have to work with, and the facts they would like to have, before making a decision. Stakeholders—those affected by the decision—must be identified. These stakeholders may include the employer, clients, coworkers, self, family, and others in the industry, and the duties to each stakeholder should be identified. This part of the process will also help in explicitly identifying potential conflicts of interest among the various stakeholders. At this point the decision makers should be able to identify the ethical principles involved in the decision, although greater clarity about those may also be gained throughout the process.

In the second step, the framework suggests situational factors that may influence decision makers should be identified and considered along with any personal biases that may come into play. At this point, decision makers may seek outside guidance which can come from a mentor, colleagues, or friends who have shown good judgment in the past. Guidance may also be sought from the firm's legal and compliance departments. This guidance from alternative sources will help to provide a variety of perspectives from which the decision under consideration can be viewed, as well as help in developing alternatives that should be considered.

1. "Ethics and Trust in the Investment Profession," Bidhan L Parmar, PhD, Dorothy C. Kelly, CFA, and David B. Stevens, CFA, in CFA Program 2022 Level I Curriculum, Volume 1 (CFA Institute, 2021).

Finally, the alternative actions that have been identified are all considered, taking into account both the short-term and long-term effects of each alternative action and any potential but unanticipated ethical implications.

In the final step, decision makers should evaluate the outcomes of the actions that were taken. In particular, they should consider whether the decisions had their intended results and whether appropriate consideration was given to ethical principles, situational influences, and duties to clients and other stakeholders.

MODULE QUIZ 56.1

To best evaluate your performance, enter your quiz answers online.

1. Professional standards of practice:
   A. are a personal view of acceptable behavior.
   B. encompass current "best practices."
   C. specify a minimum level of acceptable conduct.
2. A professional code of conduct:
   A. can increase public trust in the profession.
   B. guarantees that members will adhere to a minimum level of ethical conduct.
   C. includes standards that provide guidance for specific behaviors.
3. Situational factors that influence ethical behavior are *least likely* to include:
   A. social pressure.
   B. large financial rewards.
   C. a lack of ethical principles.
4. Compared to complying with laws and regulations, complying with a code of ethics:
   A. is considered a lower standard.
   B. often involves more judgment.
   C. includes compliance with all laws and regulations.
5. Employing a framework for decision-making that includes the ethical aspects of the decision is *most likely* to:
   A. lead to higher profits.
   B. avoid any unintended ethical consequences of decisions.
   C. balance the interests of various stakeholders.

KEY CONCEPTS

LOS 56.a

Ethical behavior is that which conforms to a set of rules and moral principles based on shared beliefs about what behavior is acceptable and what behavior is unacceptable.

LOS 56.b

A professional code of ethics is a way for a profession to communicate to the public that its members will use their knowledge and skills to serve their clients in an honest and ethical manner, and can increase public confidence and trust that members will act ethically.

LOS 56.c

A profession is an occupational group that has requirements of specialized expert knowledge. Professions establish trust by requiring high standards of expertise, setting standards for ethical behavior, and monitoring professional conduct.

LOS 56.d

Investment professionals have a special responsibility to use their specialized knowledge and skills to both protect and grow client assets. The fact that investment management is an intangible product makes high ethical standards all the more important in the financial services profession.

LOS 56.e

Some financial professionals are held to a suitability standard, while others are held to a fiduciary standard. Suitability refers to the match between client return requirements and risk tolerances and the characteristics of the securities recommended. A fiduciary standard requires professionals to act in the best interests of the client.

LOS 56.f

Challenges to ethical behavior include overestimating one's own ethical character, considering only near-term consequences and not longer-term consequences of behavior, and letting situational (external) influences, such as peer pressure, unduly affect one's decisions and behavior.

LOS 56.g

Not all unethical actions are illegal, and not all illegal actions are unethical. Laws are more specific than ethical principles and often address prior unethical behavior. Ethical behavior requires more judgment; acts such as civil disobedience may be considered ethical even when they are illegal.

LOS 56.h

A framework for ethical decision-making is designed to lead to better decisions by identifying the stakeholders affected and the conflicts of interest among them, considering alternative actions and the relevant situational influences on decision makers, seeking out different perspectives, and evaluating decisions to see if they had unintended consequences.

ANSWER KEY FOR MODULE QUIZZES

Module Quiz 56.1

1. **C** Professional standards of practice specify a minimum level of acceptable conduct for a group or organization, whereas "best practices" are suggested behavior, not a minimum acceptable level. (LOS 56.b)

2. **A** A professional code of conduct communicates to the public that members have promised to uphold a minimum level of ethical conduct when acting for clients. This is no guarantee that all members will follow the code at all times. A code of conduct may include specific standards of behavior or only state principles of conduct without specific standards or guidance. (LOS 56.b)

3. **C** Situational factors are those external to the decision makers, such as financial rewards and desire to please coworkers or others. Researchers have found that external factors are often more likely than a lack of personal ethics to lead to poor ethical decisions. (LOS 56.f)

4. **B** A code of ethics is considered a higher standard of behavior as it goes beyond simply legality of behavior. Compliance with the ethical principles of a code of ethics often requires judgment in balancing the interests of various stakeholders and consideration of short-term effects with longer-term effects of decisions. Some behavior that is illegal, such as civil disobedience or "whistle-blowing," is considered to be ethical behavior by many. (LOS 56.g)

5. **C** A decision-making framework that includes the ethical aspects of the decision should consider the conflicts among the interests of various stakeholders so that decision makers can use the company's stated ethical principles and their judgment to balance these interests in an ethical manner. Profit maximization, at least in the short term, does not necessarily follow from sound ethical judgment. While integrating ethics into the decision-making process can consider and reduce unintended ethical consequences of a decision, avoiding them altogether can never be assured. (LOS 56.h)

The following is a review of the Ethical and Professional Standards principles designed to address the learning outcome statements set forth by CFA Institute. Cross-Reference to CFA Institute Assigned Reading #57.

READING 57

Code of Ethics and Standards of Professional Conduct

Study Session 19

EXAM FOCUS

In addition to reading this review of the ethics material, we strongly recommend that all candidates for the CFA® examination read the *Standards of Practice Handbook 11th Edition* (2014) multiple times. As a Level I CFA candidate, it is your responsibility to comply with the *Code and Standards*. The complete *Code and Standards* are reprinted in Volume 1 of the CFA Program Curriculum.

MODULE 57.1: CODE AND STANDARDS

Video covering this content is available online.

LOS 57.a: Describe the structure of the CFA Institute Professional Conduct Program and the process for the enforcement of the Code and Standards.

CFA® Program Curriculum, Volume 6, page 285

The CFA Institute Professional Conduct Program is covered by the CFA Institute Bylaws and the Rules of Procedure for Proceedings Related to Professional Conduct. The Program is based on the principles of fairness of the process to members and candidates and maintaining the confidentiality of the proceedings. The CFA Institute Board of Governors has overall responsibility for the Professional Conduct Program and its Disciplinary Review Committee is responsible for enforcing of the Code and Standards.

The CFA Institute Professional Conduct staff conducts inquiries related to professional conduct. Several circumstances can prompt such an inquiry:

1. Self-disclosure by members or candidates on their annual Professional Conduct Statements of involvement in civil litigation or a criminal investigation, or that the member or candidate is the subject of a written complaint.
2. Written complaints about a member or candidate's professional conduct that are received by the Professional Conduct staff.

3. Evidence of misconduct by a member or candidate that the Professional Conduct staff received through public sources, such as a media article or broadcast.
4. A report by a CFA exam proctor of a possible violation during the examination.
5. Analysis of exam materials and monitoring of social media by CFA Institute.

Once an inquiry has begun, the Professional Conduct staff may request (in writing) an explanation from the subject member or candidate and may: (1) interview the subject member or candidate, (2) interview the complainant or other third parties, and/or (3) collect documents and records relevant to the investigation.

The Professional Conduct staff may decide: (1) that no disciplinary sanctions are appropriate, (2) to issue a cautionary letter, or (3) to discipline the member or candidate. In a case where the Professional Conduct staff finds a violation has occurred and proposes a disciplinary sanction, the member or candidate may accept or reject the sanction. If the member or candidate chooses to reject the sanction, the matter will be referred to a disciplinary review panel of CFA Institute members for a hearing. Sanctions imposed may include condemnation by the member's peers or suspension of candidate's continued participation in the CFA Program.

LOS 57.b: Identify the six components of the Code of Ethics and the seven Standards of Professional Conduct.

CFA® Program Curriculum, Volume 6, page 285

Code of Ethics

Members of CFA Institute [including Chartered Financial Analyst® (CFA®) charterholders] and candidates for the CFA designation ("Members and Candidates") must:[1]

- Act with integrity, competence, diligence, respect, and in an ethical manner with the public, clients, prospective clients, employers, employees, colleagues in the investment profession, and other participants in the global capital markets.
- Place the integrity of the investment profession and the interests of clients above their own personal interests.
- Use reasonable care and exercise independent professional judgment when conducting investment analysis, making investment recommendations, taking investment actions, and engaging in other professional activities.
- Practice and encourage others to practice in a professional and ethical manner that will reflect credit on themselves and the profession.
- Promote the integrity and viability of the global capital markets for the ultimate benefit of society.
- Maintain and improve their professional competence and strive to maintain and improve the competence of other investment professionals.

---

1. Copyright 2014, CFA Institute. Reproduced and republished from "The Code of Ethics," from *Standards of Practice Handbook, 11th Ed.*, 2014, with permission from CFA Institute. All rights reserved.

The Standards of Professional Conduct

I. Professionalism

II. Integrity of Capital Markets

III. Duties to Clients

IV. Duties to Employers

V. Investment Analysis, Recommendations, and Actions

VI. Conflicts of Interest

VII. Responsibilities as a CFA Institute Member or CFA Candidate

---

LOS 57.c: Explain the ethical responsibilities required by the Code and Standards, including the sub-sections of each Standard.

CFA® Program Curriculum, Volume 6, page 285

Standards of Professional Conduct[2]

I. PROFESSIONALISM

A. Knowledge of the Law. Members and Candidates must understand and comply with all applicable laws, rules, and regulations (including the CFA Institute *Code of Ethics* and *Standards of Professional Conduct*) of any government, regulatory organization, licensing agency, or professional association governing their professional activities. In the event of conflict, Members and Candidates must comply with the more strict law, rule, or regulation. Members and Candidates must not knowingly participate or assist in any violation of laws, rules, or regulations and must dissociate themselves from any such violation.

B. Independence and Objectivity. Members and Candidates must use reasonable care and judgment to achieve and maintain independence and objectivity in their professional activities. Members and Candidates must not offer, solicit, or accept any gift, benefit, compensation, or consideration that reasonably could be expected to compromise their own or another's independence and objectivity.

C. Misrepresentation. Members and Candidates must not knowingly make any misrepresentations relating to investment analysis, recommendations, actions, or other professional activities.

D. Misconduct. Members and Candidates must not engage in any professional conduct involving dishonesty, fraud, or deceit or commit any act that reflects adversely on their professional reputation, integrity, or competence.

2. Ibid.

II. INTEGRITY OF CAPITAL MARKETS

A. **Material Nonpublic Information.** Members and Candidates who possess material nonpublic information that could affect the value of an investment must not act or cause others to act on the information.

B. **Market Manipulation.** Members and Candidates must not engage in practices that distort prices or artificially inflate trading volume with the intent to mislead market participants.

III. DUTIES TO CLIENTS

A. **Loyalty, Prudence, and Care.** Members and Candidates have a duty of loyalty to their clients and must act with reasonable care and exercise prudent judgment. Members and Candidates must act for the benefit of their clients and place their clients' interests before their employer's or their own interests.

B. **Fair Dealing.** Members and Candidates must deal fairly and objectively with all clients when providing investment analysis, making investment recommendations, taking investment action, or engaging in other professional activities.

C. **Suitability.**

1. When Members and Candidates are in an advisory relationship with a client, they must:

    a) Make a reasonable inquiry into a client's or prospective clients' investment experience, risk and return objectives, and financial constraints prior to making any investment recommendation or taking investment action and must reassess and update this information regularly.

    b) Determine that an investment is suitable to the client's financial situation and consistent with the client's written objectives, mandates, and constraints before making an investment recommendation or taking investment action.

    c) Judge the suitability of investments in the context of the client's total portfolio.

2. When Members and Candidates are responsible for managing a portfolio to a specific mandate, strategy, or style, they must make only investment recommendations or take only investment actions that are consistent with the stated objectives and constraints of the portfolio.

D. **Performance Presentation.** When communicating investment performance information, Members or Candidates must make reasonable efforts to ensure that it is fair, accurate, and complete.

E. **Preservation of Confidentiality.** Members and Candidates must keep information about current, former, and prospective clients confidential unless:

1. The information concerns illegal activities on the part of the client or prospective client,
2. Disclosure is required by law, or
3. The client or prospective client permits disclosure of the information.

IV. DUTIES TO EMPLOYERS

A. **Loyalty.** In matters related to their employment, Members and Candidates must act for the benefit of their employer and not deprive their employer of the advantage of their skills and abilities, divulge confidential information, or otherwise cause harm to their employer.

B. **Additional Compensation Arrangements.** Members and Candidates must not accept gifts, benefits, compensation, or consideration that competes with or might reasonably be expected to create a conflict of interest with their employer's interest unless they obtain written consent from all parties involved.

C. **Responsibilities of Supervisors.** Members and Candidates must make reasonable efforts to ensure that anyone subject to their supervision or authority complies with applicable laws, rules, regulations, and the Code and Standards.

V. INVESTMENT ANALYSIS, RECOMMENDATIONS, AND ACTIONS

A. **Diligence and Reasonable Basis.** Members and Candidates must:

1. Exercise diligence, independence, and thoroughness in analyzing investments, making investment recommendations, and taking investment actions.
2. Have a reasonable and adequate basis, supported by appropriate research and investigation, for any investment analysis, recommendation, or action.

B. **Communication with Clients and Prospective Clients.** Members and Candidates must:

1. Disclose to clients and prospective clients the basic format and general principles of the investment processes they use to analyze investments, select securities, and construct portfolios and must promptly disclose any changes that might materially affect those processes.

2. Disclose to clients and prospective clients significant limitations and risks associated with the investment process.

3. Use reasonable judgment in identifying which factors are important to their investment analyses, recommendations, or actions and include those factors in communications with clients and prospective clients.

4. Distinguish between fact and opinion in the presentation of investment analysis and recommendations.

C. **Record Retention.** Members and Candidates must develop and maintain appropriate records to support their investment analysis, recommendations, actions, and other investment-related communications with clients and prospective clients.

VI. CONFLICTS OF INTEREST

A. **Disclosure of Conflicts.** Members and Candidates must make full and fair disclosure of all matters that could reasonably be expected to impair their independence and objectivity or interfere with respective duties to their clients, prospective clients, and employer. Members and Candidates must ensure that such disclosures are prominent, are delivered in plain language, and communicate the relevant information effectively.

B. **Priority of Transactions.** Investment transactions for clients and employers must have priority over investment transactions in which a Member or Candidate is the beneficial owner.

C. **Referral Fees.** Members and Candidates must disclose to their employer, clients, and prospective clients, as appropriate, any compensation, consideration, or benefit received by, or paid to, others for the recommendation of products or services.

VII. RESPONSIBILITIES AS A CFA INSTITUTE MEMBER OR CFA CANDIDATE

A. **Conduct as Participants in CFA Institute Programs.** Members and Candidates must not engage in any conduct that compromises the reputation or integrity of CFA Institute or the CFA designation or the integrity, validity, or security of CFA Institute programs.

B. Reference to CFA Institute, the CFA Designation, and the CFA Program. When referring to CFA Institute, CFA Institute membership, the CFA designation, or candidacy in the CFA Program, Members and Candidates must not misrepresent or exaggerate the meaning or implications of membership in CFA Institute, holding the CFA designation, or candidacy in the CFA Program.

MODULE QUIZ 57.1

To best evaluate your performance, enter your quiz answers online.

1. In the case of a complaint about a member's professional conduct, CFA Institute Professional Conduct Program staff are *least likely* to:
   A. review documents and records related to the complaint.
   B. request an interview with the member or with the party making the complaint.
   C. suspend the member's right to use the CFA designation while an investigation is in progress.
2. Which of the following requirements for members and candidates is one of the six components of the Code of Ethics?
   A. Maintain and improve their professional competence.
   B. Do not act or cause others to act on material nonpublic information.
   C. Distinguish between fact and opinion when presenting investment analysis.
3. If a member or candidate is offered an additional compensation arrangement by a client, which of the seven Standards of Professional Conduct states the requirements the member or candidate must follow?
   A. Duties to Clients.
   B. Conflicts of Interest.
   C. Duties to Employers.

ANSWER KEY FOR MODULE QUIZZES

Module Quiz 57.1

1. **C** The process for enforcing the Code and Standards does not include suspending a member or candidate while an inquiry is in progress. If CFA Institute Professional Conduct staff receive information that prompts an inquiry, the staff may request information from the member or candidate, interview parties who initiated a complaint, or review relevant records and documents. (LOS 57.a)

2. **A** One of the six components of the Code of Ethics requires members and candidates to "maintain and improve their professional competence and strive to maintain and improve the competence of other investment professionals." The other two answer choices are required by the Standards of Professional Conduct but are not components of the Code of Ethics. (LOS 57.b)

3. **C** The standard related to additional compensation arrangements is a subsection of Standard IV Duties to Employers. (LOS 57.c)

The following is a review of the Ethical and Professional Standards principles designed to address the learning outcome statements set forth by CFA Institute. Cross-Reference to CFA Institute Assigned Reading #58.

READING 58 Guidance for Standards I–VII

Study Session 19

EXAM FOCUS

The Standards of Professional Conduct comprise seven Standards (I–VII) and a total of 22 subsections. These Standards and their application are described in the *Standards of Practice Handbook, 11th Edition, 2014,* published by CFA Institute. We recommend carefully reading the *Standards of Practice Handbook* multiple times in preparation for your Level I exam (yes, the whole thing, including all examples). Fifteen percent of your exam questions will be based on this book and the two relatively short readings concerning Global Investment Performance Standards (GIPS). Given that much of this material must simply be memorized, we also suggest that your final reading of the *Standards of Practice Handbook* be on the Friday prior to your exam. You probably don't need to read all the examples that day, but if you highlighted some points during an earlier reading, you can revisit those as you go through all the Standards, the guidance, and the recommended best practices.

MODULE 58.1: GUIDANCE FOR STANDARDS I(A) AND I(B)

Video covering this content is available online.

LOS 58.a: Demonstrate the application of the Code of Ethics and Standards of Professional Conduct to situations involving issues of professional integrity.

LOS 58.b: Identify conduct that conforms to the Code and Standards and conduct that violates the Code and Standards.

LOS 58.c: Recommend practices and procedures designed to prevent violations of the Code of Ethics and Standards of Professional Conduct.

CFA® Program Curriculum, Volume 6, page 305

The *Standards of Practice Handbook* is included in its entirety in the CFA curriculum as Readings 2 and 3 of Volume 1. You can also download a PDF of the *Standards of Practice Handbook* at the website for CFA Institute, www.cfainstitute.org. A third alternative is to purchase the *Standards of Practice Handbook* through Amazon (make sure you get the 11th edition) for about $30 or get the Kindle edition for $0.99.

In our summary of the Standards of Practice, we focus on describing three things: (1) actions that clearly violate the subsection, (2) the behaviors that each subsection is intended to either encourage or discourage, and (3) recommended best practices for members and their firms.

In many cases the actions that members and candidates must not take are explained using terms open to interpretation, such as "reasonable," "adequate," and "token."

Some examples from the Standards themselves are:

...use reasonable care and judgment to achieve...

...accept any gift, that reasonably could be expected to compromise...

...act with reasonable care and exercise prudent judgment...

...deal fairly and objectively with all clients...

...make a reasonable inquiry into...

...make reasonable efforts to ensure...

...might reasonably be expected to create a conflict of interest with...

...Have a reasonable and adequate basis...

...Use reasonable judgment in...

...matters that could be reasonably expected to impair...

The requirement of the LOS is that you know what constitutes a violation, not that you draw a distinction between what is "reasonable" and what is not in a given situation. We believe the exam writers take this into account and that if they intend, for example, to test whether a recommendation has been given without reasonable care and judgment, it will likely be clear either that the care and judgment exhibited by the analyst did not rise to the level of "reasonable," or that it did.

No monetary value for a "token" gift is given in the Standards, although it is recommended that a firm establish such a monetary value for its employees. Here, again, the correct answer to a question will not likely hinge on candidate's determination of what is a token gift and what is not. Questions should be clear in this regard. A business dinner is likely a token gift, but a week at a condominium in Aspen or tickets to the Super Bowl are likely not. Always look for clues in the questions that lead you to the question-writer's preferred answer choice, such as "lavish" entertainment and "luxury" accommodations.

Next, we present a summary of each subsection of the Standards of Professional Conduct. For each one, we first detail actions that violate the Standard and then list actions and behaviors that are recommended within the Standards. We suggest you learn the violations especially well so you understand that the other items are recommended. For the exam, it is not necessary to memorize the Standard number and subsection letter. Knowing that an action violates, for example, Professionalism, rather than Duties to Employers or Duties to Clients, should be sufficient in this regard. Note that some actions may violate more than one Standard.

One way to write questions for this material is to offer a reason that might make one believe a Standard does not apply in a particular situation. In most, if not all, cases the "reason" does not change the requirement of the Standard. If you are prohibited from some action, the motivations for the action or other circumstances simply do not matter. If the Standard says it's a violation, it's a violation. An exception is when intent is key to the Standard, such as intending to mislead clients or market participants in general.

STANDARD I: PROFESSIONALISM[1]

Standard I(A) Knowledge of the Law

Members and Candidates must understand and comply with all applicable laws, rules, and regulations (including the CFA Institute Code of Ethics and Standards of Professional Conduct) of any government, regulatory organization, licensing agency, or professional association governing their professional activities. In the event of conflict, Members and Candidates must comply with the more strict law, rule, or regulation. Members and Candidates must not knowingly participate or assist in and must dissociate from any violation of such laws, rules, or regulations.

The Standards begin with a straightforward statement: Don't violate any laws, rules, or regulations that apply to your professional activities. This includes the Code and Standards, so any violation of the Code and Standards will also violate this subsection.

A member may be governed by different rules and regulations among the Standards, the country in which the member resides, and the country where the member is doing business. Follow the most strict of these, or, put another way, do not violate any of the three sets of rules and regulations.

If you know that violations of applicable rules or laws are taking place, either by coworkers or clients, CFA Institute strongly encourages members and candidates to report potential violations.[2] One way to do so is to approach your supervisor or compliance department to remedy the situation. If they will not or cannot, then you must dissociate from the activity (e.g., not working with a trading group you know is not allocating client trades properly according to the Standard on Fair Dealing, or not using marketing materials that you know or should know are misleading or erroneous). If this cannot be accomplished, you may, in an extreme case, have to resign from the firm to be in compliance with this Standard.

Recommendations for Members

- Establish, or encourage employer to establish, procedures to keep employees informed of changes in relevant laws, rules, and regulations.

---

1. Copyright 2014, CFA Institute. Reproduced and republished from *Standards of Practice Handbook, 11th Ed.*, 2014, with permission from CFA Institute. All rights reserved.
2. Ibid.

- Review, or encourage employer to review, the firm's written compliance procedures on a regular basis.
- Maintain, or encourage employer to maintain, copies of current laws, rules, and regulations.
- When in doubt about legality, consult supervisor, compliance personnel, or a lawyer.
- When dissociating from violations, keep records documenting the violations, encourage employer to bring an end to the violations.
- There is no requirement in the Standards to report wrongdoers, but local law may require it; members are "strongly encouraged" to report violations to CFA Institute Professional Conduct Program.

Recommendations for Firms

- Have a code of ethics.
- Provide employees with information on laws, rules, and regulations governing professional activities.
- Have procedures for reporting suspected violations.

Standard I(B) Independence and Objectivity

Members and Candidates must use reasonable care and judgment to achieve and maintain independence and objectivity in their professional activities. Members and Candidates must not offer, solicit, or accept any gift, benefit, compensation, or consideration that reasonably could be expected to compromise their own or another's independence and objectivity.

Analysts may face pressure or receive inducements to give a security a specific rating, to select certain outside managers or vendors, or to produce favorable or unfavorable research and conclusions. Members who allow their investment recommendations or analysis to be influenced by such pressure or inducements will have violated the requirement to use reasonable care and to maintain independence and objectivity in their professional activities. Allocating shares in oversubscribed IPOs to personal accounts is a violation.

Normal business entertainment is permitted. Members who accept, solicit, or offer things of value that could be expected to influence the member's or others' independence or objectivity are violating the Standard. Gifts from clients are considered less likely to compromise independence and objectivity than gifts from other parties. Client gifts must be disclosed to the member's employer prior to acceptance, if possible, but after acceptance, if not.

Members may prepare reports paid for by the subject firm if compensation is a flat rate not tied to the conclusions of the report (and if the fact that the research is issuer-paid is disclosed). Accepting compensation that is dependent on the conclusions, recommendations, or market impact of the report, and failure to disclose that research is issuer-paid, are violations of this Standard.

Recommendations for Members

Members or their firms should pay for their own travel to company events or tours when practicable and limit use of corporate aircraft to trips for which commercial travel is not an alternative.

Recommendations for Firms

- Restrict employee participation in IPOs and private placements, require pre-approval for participation.
- Appoint a compliance officer, have written policies on independence and objectivity and clear procedures for reporting violations.
- Limit gifts, other than from clients, to token items only.

MODULE 58.2: GUIDANCE FOR STANDARDS I(C) AND I(D)

Video covering this content is available online.

Standard I(C) Misrepresentation

Members and Candidates must not knowingly make any misrepresentations relating to investment analysis, recommendations, actions, or other professional activities.

Misrepresentation includes knowingly misleading investors, omitting relevant information, presenting selective data to mislead investors, and plagiarism. Plagiarism is using reports, forecasts, models, ideas, charts, graphs, or spreadsheets created by others without crediting the source. Crediting the source is not required when using projections, statistics, and tables from recognized financial and statistical reporting services. When using models developed or research done by other members of the firm, it is permitted to omit the names of those who are no longer with the firm as long as the member does not represent work previously done by others as his alone.

Actions that would violate the Standard include:

- Presenting third-party research as your own, without attribution to the source.
- Guaranteeing a specific return on securities that do not have an explicit guarantee from a government body or financial institution.
- Selecting a valuation service because it puts the highest value on untraded security holdings.
- Selecting a performance benchmark that is not comparable to the investment strategy employed.
- Presenting performance data or attribution analysis that omits accounts or relevant variables.
- Offering false or misleading information about the analyst's or firm's capabilities, expertise, or experience.
- Using marketing materials from a third party (outside advisor) that are misleading.

Recommendations for Members

- Prepare a summary of experience, qualifications, and services a member is able to perform.
- Encourage employers to develop procedures for verifying marketing materials provided by third parties concerning their capabilities, products, and services.
- Cite the source of any summaries of materials provided by others.
- Keep copies of all reports, articles, or other materials used in the preparation of research reports.
- Provide a list, in writing, of the firm's available services and qualifications.
- Periodically review documents and communications of members for any misrepresentation of employee or firm qualifications and capabilities.

Standard I(D) Misconduct

Members and Candidates must not engage in any professional conduct involving dishonesty, fraud, or deceit or commit any act that reflects adversely on their professional reputation, integrity, or competence.

The first part here regarding professional conduct is clear: no dishonesty, fraud, or deceit. The second part, while it applies to all conduct by the member, specifically requires that the act, "reflects adversely on their professional reputation, integrity, or competence." The guidance states, in fact, that members must not try to use enforcement of this Standard against another member to settle personal, political, or other disputes that are not related to professional ethics or competence.

Recommendations for Firms

- Develop and adopt a code of ethics and make clear that unethical behavior will not be tolerated.
- Give employees a list of potential violations and sanctions, including dismissal.
- Check references of potential employees.

Video covering this content is available online.

MODULE 58.3: GUIDANCE FOR STANDARD II

STANDARD II: INTEGRITY OF CAPITAL MARKETS

Standard II(A) Material Nonpublic Information

Members and Candidates who possess material nonpublic information that could affect the value of an investment must not act or cause others to act on the information.

Information is "material" if its disclosure would affect the price of a security or if a reasonable investor would want the information before making an investment decision. Information that is ambiguous as to its likely effect on price may not be considered material.

Information is "nonpublic" until it has been made available to the marketplace. An analyst conference call is not public disclosure. Selective disclosure of information by corporations creates the potential for insider-trading violations.

The prohibition against acting on material nonpublic information extends to mutual funds containing the subject securities as well as related swaps and options contracts. It is the member's responsibility to determine if information she receives has been publicly disseminated prior acting or causing others to act on it.

Some members and candidates may be involved in transactions during which they are provided with material nonpublic information by firms (e.g., investment banking transactions). Members and candidates may use this information for its intended purpose, but must not use the information for any other purpose unless it becomes public information.

Under the so-called **mosaic theory**, reaching an investment conclusion through perceptive analysis of public information combined with non-material nonpublic information is not a violation of the Standard.

Recommendations for Members

- Make reasonable efforts to achieve public dissemination by the firm of information they possess.
- Encourage their firms to adopt procedures to prevent the misuse of material nonpublic information.

Recommendations for Firms

Use a firewall within the firm, with elements including:

- Exercise substantial control of relevant interdepartmental communications through a clearance area, such as the compliance or legal department.
- Review employee trades.
- Maintain "watch," "restricted," and "rumor" lists.

Monitor and restrict proprietary trading while a firm is in possession of material nonpublic information. However, prohibiting all proprietary trading while a firm is in possession of material nonpublic information may be inappropriate because it may send a signal to the market. In these cases, firms should only take the opposite side of unsolicited customer trades.

Standard II(B) Market Manipulation

Members and Candidates must not engage in practices that distort prices or artificially inflate trading volume with the intent to mislead market participants.

Member actions may affect security values and trading volumes without violating this Standard. The key point here is that if there is the *intent to mislead*, then the Standard is violated. Of course, spreading false information to affect prices or volume is a violation of this Standard as is making trades intended to mislead market participants.

MODULE QUIZ 58.1, 58.2, 58.3

To best evaluate your performance, enter your quiz answers online.

1. In situations where the laws of a member or candidate's country of residence, the local laws of regions where the member or candidate does business, and the Code and Standards specify different requirements, the member or candidate must abide by:
   A. local law or the Code and Standards, whichever is stricter.
   B. the Code and Standards or his country's laws, whichever are stricter.
   C. the strictest of local law, his country's laws, or the Code and Standards.
2. According to the Standard on independence and objectivity, members and candidates:
   A. may accept gifts or bonuses from clients.
   B. may not accept compensation from an issuer of securities in return for producing research on those securities.
   C. should consider credit ratings issued by recognized agencies to be objective measures of credit quality.
3. Bill Cooper finds a table of historical bond yields on the website of the U.S. Treasury that supports the work he has done in his analysis and includes the table as part of his report without citing the source. Has Cooper violated the Code and Standards?
   A. Yes, because he did not cite the source of the table.
   B. Yes, because he did not verify the accuracy of the information.
   C. No, because the table is from a recognized source of financial or statistical data.
4. Which of the following statements about the Standard on misconduct is *most accurate*?
   A. Misconduct applies only to a member or candidate's professional activities.
   B. Neglecting to perform due diligence when required is an example of misconduct.
   C. A member or candidate commits misconduct by engaging in any illegal activity.
5. Ed Ingus, CFA, visits the headquarters and main plant of Bullitt Company and observes that inventories of unsold goods appear unusually large. From the CFO, he learns that a recent increase in returned items may result in earnings for the current quarter that are below analysts' estimates. Based on his visit, Ingus changes his recommendation on Bullitt to "Sell." Has Ingus violated the Standard concerning material nonpublic information?
   A. Yes.
   B. No, because the information he used is not material.
   C. No, because his actions are consistent with the mosaic theory.

6. Green Brothers, an emerging market fund manager, has two of its subsidiaries simultaneously buy and sell emerging market stocks. In its marketing literature, Green Brothers cites the overall emerging market volume as evidence of the market's liquidity. As a result of its actions, more investors participate in the emerging markets fund. Green Brothers *most likely*:
   A. did not violate the Code and Standards.
   B. violated the Standard regarding market manipulation.
   C. violated the Standard regarding performance presentation.

MODULE 58.4: GUIDANCE FOR STANDARDS III(A) AND III(B)

Video covering this content is available online.

STANDARD III: DUTIES TO CLIENTS

Standard III(A) Loyalty, Prudence, and Care

Members and Candidates have a duty of loyalty to their clients and must act with reasonable care and exercise prudent judgment. Members and Candidates must act for the benefit of their clients and place their clients' interests before their employer's or their own interests.

Client interests always come first. Although this Standard does not impose a fiduciary duty on members or candidates where one did not already exist, it does require members and candidates to act in their clients' best interests and recommend products that are suitable given their clients' investment objectives and risk tolerances. Members and candidates must:

- Exercise the prudence, care, skill, and diligence under the circumstances that a person acting in a like capacity and familiar with such matters would use.
- Manage pools of client assets in accordance with the terms of the governing documents, such as trust documents or investment management agreements.
- Make investment decisions in the context of the total portfolio.
- Inform clients of any limitations in an advisory relationship (e.g., an advisor who may only recommend her own firm's products).
- Vote proxies in an informed and responsible manner. Due to cost-benefit considerations, it may not be necessary to vote all proxies.
- Client brokerage, or "soft dollars" or "soft commissions," must be used to benefit the client.
- The "client" may be the investing public as a whole rather than a specific entity or person.

Recommendations for Members

Submit to clients, at least quarterly, itemized statements showing all securities in custody and all debits, credits, and transactions.

Encourage firms to address these topics when drafting policies and procedures regarding fiduciary duty:

- Follow applicable rules and laws.

- Establish investment objectives of client.
- Consider suitability of a portfolio relative to the client's needs and circumstances, the investment's basic characteristics, or the basic characteristics of the total portfolio.
- Diversify.
- Deal fairly with all clients in regard to investment actions.
- Disclose conflicts.
- Disclose compensation arrangements.
- Vote proxies in the best interest of clients and ultimate beneficiaries.
- Maintain confidentiality.
- Seek best execution.

Standard III(B) Fair Dealing

Members and Candidates must deal fairly and objectively with all clients when providing investment analysis, making investment recommendations, taking investment action, or engaging in other professional activities.

Do not discriminate against any clients when disseminating recommendations or taking investment action. "Fairly" does not mean "equally." In the normal course of business, there will be differences in the time emails, faxes, and other communications are received by different clients.

Different service levels are acceptable, but they must not negatively affect or disadvantage any clients. Disclose the different service levels to all clients and prospects, and make premium levels of service available to all those willing to pay for them.

Give all clients a fair opportunity to act on every recommendation. Clients who are unaware of a change in the recommendation for a security should be advised of the change before an order for the security is accepted.

Treat clients fairly in light of their investment objectives and circumstances. Treat both individual and institutional clients in a fair and impartial manner. Members and candidates should not take advantage of their position in the industry to disadvantage clients (e.g., taking shares of an oversubscribed IPO).

Recommendations for Members

- Encourage firms to establish compliance procedures requiring proper dissemination of investment recommendations and fair treatment of all customers and clients.
- Maintain a list of clients and holdings—use to ensure that all holders are treated fairly.

Recommendations for Firms

- Limit the number of people who are aware that a change in recommendation will be made.
- Shorten the time frame between decision and dissemination.
- Publish personnel guidelines for pre-dissemination—have in place guidelines prohibiting personnel who have prior knowledge of a recommendation from discussing it or taking action on the pending recommendation.
- Disseminate new or changed recommendations simultaneously to all clients who have expressed an interest or for whom an investment is suitable.
- Develop written trade allocation procedures—ensure fairness to clients, timely and efficient order execution, and accuracy of client positions.
- Disclose trade allocation procedures.
- Establish systematic account review—ensure that no client is given preferred treatment and that investment actions are consistent with the account's objectives.
- Disclose available levels of service.

MODULE 58.5: GUIDANCE FOR STANDARDS III(C), III(D), AND III(E)

Video covering this content is available online.

Standard III(C) Suitability

1. When Members and Candidates are in an advisory relationship with a client, they must:
    a. Make a reasonable inquiry into a client's or prospective client's investment experience, risk and return objectives, and financial constraints prior to making any investment recommendation or taking investment action and must reassess and update this information regularly.
    b. Determine that an investment is suitable to the client's financial situation and consistent with the client's written objectives, mandates, and constraints before making an investment recommendation or taking investment action.
    c. Judge the suitability of investments in the context of the client's total portfolio.
2. When Members and Candidates are responsible for managing a portfolio to a specific mandate, strategy, or style, they must make only investment recommendations or take only investment actions that are consistent with the stated objectives and constraints of the portfolio.

In advisory relationships, members must gather client information at the beginning of the relationship, in the form of an investment policy statement (IPS). Consider clients' needs and circumstances and, thus, their risk tolerance. Consider whether or not the use of leverage is suitable for the client.

If a member is responsible for managing a fund to an index or other stated mandate, he must select only investments that are consistent with the stated mandate.

Unsolicited Trade Requests

An investment manager may receive a client request to purchase a security that the manager knows is unsuitable, given the client's investment policy statement. The trade may or may not have a material effect on the risk characteristics of the client's total portfolio and the requirements are different for each case. In either case, however, the manager should not make the trade until he has discussed with the client the reasons (based on the IPS) that the trade is unsuitable for the client's account.

If the manager determines that the *effect on the risk/return profile of the client's total portfolio is minimal*, the manager, after discussing with the client how the trade does not fit the IPS goals and constraints, may follow his firm's policy with regard to unsuitable trades. Regardless of firm policy, the client must acknowledge the discussion and an understanding of why the trade is unsuitable.

If the trade would have a *material impact on the risk/return profile of the client's total portfolio*, one option is to update the IPS so the client accepts a changed risk profile that would permit the trade. If the client will not accept a changed IPS, the manager may follow firm policy, which may allow the trade to be made in a separate client-directed account. In the absence of other options, the manager may need to reconsider whether to maintain the relationship with the client.

Recommendations for Members

- For each client, put the needs, circumstances, and investment objectives into a written IPS.
- Consider the type of client and whether there are separate beneficiaries, investor objectives (return and risk), investor constraints (liquidity needs, expected cash flows, time, tax, and regulatory and legal circumstances), and performance measurement benchmarks.
- Review the investor's objectives and constraints periodically to reflect any changes in client circumstances.

Standard III(D) Performance Presentation

When communicating investment performance information, Members and Candidates must make reasonable efforts to ensure that it is fair, accurate, and complete.

Members must not misstate performance or mislead clients or prospects about their investment performance or their firm's investment performance.

Members must not misrepresent past performance or reasonably expected performance, and must not state or imply the ability to achieve a rate of return similar to that achieved in the past.

For brief presentations, members must make detailed information available on request and indicate that the presentation has offered only limited information.

Recommendations for Members

- Encourage firms to adhere to Global Investment Performance Standards.
- Consider the sophistication of the audience to whom a performance presentation is addressed.
- Present the performance of a weighted composite of similar portfolios rather than the performance of a single account.
- Include terminated accounts as part of historical performance and clearly state when they were terminated.
- Include all appropriate disclosures to fully explain results (e.g., model results included, gross or net of fees, etc.).
- Maintain data and records used to calculate the performance being presented.

Standard III(E) Preservation of Confidentiality

Members and Candidates must keep information about current, former, and prospective clients confidential unless:

1. The information concerns illegal activities on the part of the client;
2. Disclosure is required by law; or
3. The client or prospective client permits disclosure of the information.

If illegal activities by a client are involved, members may have an obligation to report the activities to authorities.

The confidentiality Standard extends to former clients as well.

The requirements of this Standard are not intended to prevent members and candidates from cooperating with a CFA Institute Professional Conduct Program (PCP) investigation.

Recommendations for Members

- Members should avoid disclosing information received from a client except to authorized coworkers who are also working for the client.
- Members should follow firm procedures for storage of electronic data and recommend adoption of such procedures if they are not in place.

MODULE QUIZ 58.4, 58.5

To best evaluate your performance, enter your quiz answers online.

1. Cobb, Inc., has hired Jude Kasten, CFA, to manage its pension fund. The client(s) to whom Kasten owes a duty of loyalty are:
   A. Cobb's management.
   B. the shareholders of Cobb, Inc.
   C. the beneficiaries of the pension fund.

2. Which of the following actions is *most likely* a violation of the Standard on fair dealing?
   A. A portfolio manager allocates IPO shares to all client accounts, including her brother's fee-based retirement account.
   B. An investment firm routinely begins trading for its own account immediately after announcing recommendation changes to clients.
   C. After releasing a general recommendation to all clients, an analyst calls the firm's largest institutional clients to discuss the recommendation in more detail.
3. The Standard regarding suitability *most likely* requires that:
   A. an advisor must analyze an investment's suitability for the client prior to recommending or acting on the investment.
   B. a member or candidate must decline to carry out an unsolicited transaction that she believes is unsuitable for the client.
   C. when managing a fund to an index, a manager who is evaluating potential investments must consider their suitability for the fund's shareholders.
4. Which of the following is *most likely* a recommended procedure for complying with the Standard on performance presentation?
   A. Exclude terminated accounts from past performance history.
   B. Present the performance of a representative account to show how a composite has performed.
   C. Consider the level of financial knowledge of the audience to whom the performance is presented.
5. The CFA Institute Professional Conduct Program (PCP) has begun an investigation into Chris Jones, a Level II CFA candidate, and a number of his CFA charterholder colleagues. Jones has access to confidential client records that could be useful in clearing his name and wishes to share this information with the PCP. Which of the following *most accurately* describes Jones's duties with regard to preservation of confidentiality?
   A. Sharing the confidential information with the PCP would violate the Standards.
   B. The Standards encourage, but do not require, that Jones support the PCP investigation into his colleagues.
   C. Jones may share confidential information about former clients with the PCP but may not share confidential information about current clients.

Video covering this content is available online.

MODULE 58.6: GUIDANCE FOR STANDARD IV

STANDARD IV: DUTIES TO EMPLOYERS

Standard IV(A) Loyalty

In matters related to their employment, Members and Candidates must act for the benefit of their employer and not deprive their employer of the advantage of their skills and abilities, divulge confidential information, or otherwise cause harm to their employer.

This Standard is applicable to employees. If members are independent contractors, rather than employees, they have a duty to abide by the terms of their agreements.

Members must not engage in any activities that would injure the firm, deprive it of profit, or deprive it of the advantage of employees' skills and abilities.

Members should always place client interests above interests of their employer, but consider the effects of their actions on firm integrity and sustainability.

There is no requirement that the employee put employer interests ahead of family and other personal obligations; it is expected that employers and employees will discuss such matters and balance these obligations with work obligations.

There may be isolated cases where a duty to one's employer may be violated in order to protect clients or the integrity of the market, when the actions are not for personal gain.

Independent practice for compensation is allowed if a notification is provided to the employer fully describing all aspects of the services, including compensation, duration, and the nature of the activities and the employer consents to all terms of the proposed independent practice before it begins.

When leaving an employer, members must continue to act in their employer's best interests until their resignation is effective. Activities that may constitute a violation include:

- Misappropriation of trade secrets.
- Misuse of confidential information.
- Soliciting employer's clients prior to leaving.
- Self-dealing.
- Misappropriation of client lists.

Employer records on any medium (e.g., home computer, tablet, cell phone) are the property of the firm.

When an employee has left a firm, simple knowledge of names and existence of former clients is generally not confidential. There is also no prohibition on the use of experience or knowledge gained while with a former employer. If an agreement exists among employers (e.g., the U.S. "Protocol for Broker Recruiting") that permits brokers to take certain client information when leaving a firm, a member may act within the terms of the agreement without violating the Standard.

Members and candidates must adhere to their employers' policies concerning social media. When planning to leave an employer, members and candidates must ensure that their social media use complies with their employers' policies for notifying clients about employee separations.

Recommendations for Members

Members are encouraged to give their employer a copy of the Code and Standards.

Best practice is to use separate social media accounts for personal and professional communications.

Recommendations for Firms

Employers should not have incentive and compensation systems that encourage unethical behavior.

Standard IV(B) Additional Compensation Arrangements

Members and Candidates must not accept gifts, benefits, compensation, or consideration that competes with or might reasonably be expected to create a conflict of interest with their employer's interest unless they obtain written consent from all parties involved.

Compensation includes direct and indirect compensation from a client and other benefits received from third parties.

Written consent from a member's employer includes email communication.

Understand the difference between an additional compensation arrangement and a gift from a client:

- If a client offers a bonus that depends on the *future performance* of her account, this is an additional compensation arrangement that requires written consent in advance.
- If a client offers a bonus to reward a member for her account's *past performance*, this is a gift that requires disclosure to the member's employer to comply with Standard I(B) Independence and Objectivity.

Recommendations for Members

Make an immediate written report to the employer detailing any proposed compensation and services, if additional to that provided by the employer.

Members and candidates who are hired to work part time should discuss any arrangements that may compete with their employer's interest at the time they are hired and abide by any limitations their employer identifies.

Recommendations for Firms

Details of additional compensation, including any performance incentives, should be verified by the offering party.

Standard IV(C) Responsibilities of Supervisors

Members and Candidates must make reasonable efforts to ensure that anyone subject to their supervision or authority complies with applicable laws, rules, regulations, and the Code and Standards.

Members must make reasonable efforts to prevent employees from violating laws, rules, regulations, or the Code and Standards, as well as make reasonable efforts to detect violations.

An adequate compliance system must meet industry standards, regulatory requirements, and the requirements of the Code and Standards.

Members with supervisory responsibilities have an obligation to bring an inadequate compliance system to the attention of firm's management and recommend corrective action.

A member or candidate faced with no compliance procedures or with procedures he believes are inadequate must decline supervisory responsibility in writing until adequate procedures are adopted by the firm.

If there is a violation, respond promptly and conduct a thorough investigation while increasing supervision or placing limitations on the wrongdoer's activities.

Recommendations for Members

A member should recommend that his employer adopt a code of ethics. Members should encourage employers to provide their codes of ethics to clients.

Once the compliance program is instituted, the supervisor should:

- Distribute it to the proper personnel.
- Update it as needed.
- Continually educate staff regarding procedures.
- Issue reminders as necessary.
- Require professional conduct evaluations.
- Review employee actions to monitor compliance and identify violations.

Recommendations for Firms

Employers should not commingle compliance procedures with the firm's code of ethics—this can dilute the goal of reinforcing one's ethical obligations.

While investigating a possible breach of compliance procedures, it is appropriate to limit the suspected employee's activities.

Adequate compliance procedures should:

- Be clearly written.
- Be easy to understand.
- Designate a compliance officer with authority clearly defined.
- Have a system of checks and balances.
- Outline the scope of procedures.
- Outline what conduct is permitted.
- Contain procedures for reporting violations and sanctions.
- Structure incentives so unethical behavior is not rewarded.

Video covering this content is available online.

MODULE 58.7: GUIDANCE FOR STANDARD V

STANDARD V: INVESTMENT ANALYSIS, RECOMMENDATIONS, AND ACTIONS

Standard V(A) Diligence and Reasonable Basis

Members and Candidates must:

1. Exercise diligence, independence, and thoroughness in analyzing investments, making investment recommendations, and taking investment actions.
2. Have a reasonable and adequate basis, supported by appropriate research and investigation, for any investment analysis, recommendation, or action.

The application of this Standard depends on the investment philosophy adhered to, members' and candidates' roles in the investment decision-making process, and the resources and support provided by employers. These factors dictate the degree of diligence, thoroughness of research, and the proper level of investigation required.

The level of research needed to satisfy the requirement for due diligence will differ depending on the product or service offered. A list of things that should be considered prior to making a recommendation or taking investment action includes:

- Global and national economic conditions.
- A firm's financial results and operating history, and the business cycle stage.
- Fees and historical results for a mutual fund.
- Limitations of any quantitative models used.
- A determination of whether peer group comparisons for valuation are appropriate.

Recommendations for Members

Members should encourage their firms to adopt a policy for periodic review of the quality of third-party research, if they have not. Examples of criteria to use in judging quality are:

- Review assumptions used.
- Determine how rigorous the analysis was.
- Identify how timely the research is.
- Evaluate objectivity and independence of the recommendations.

Members should *encourage their firms to consider* these policies and procedures supporting this Standard:

- Have a policy requiring that research reports and recommendations have a basis that can be substantiated as reasonable and adequate.
- Have detailed, written guidance for proper research and due diligence.
- Have measurable criteria for judging the quality of research, and base analyst compensation on such criteria.
- Have written procedures that provide a minimum acceptable level of scenario testing for computer-based models and include standards for the range of

scenarios, model accuracy over time, and a measure of the sensitivity of cash flows to model assumptions and inputs.

- Have a policy for evaluating outside providers of information that addresses the reasonableness and accuracy of the information provided and establishes how often the evaluations should be repeated.
- Adopt a set of standards that provides criteria for evaluating external advisers and states how often a review of external advisers will be performed.

Standard V(B) Communication With Clients and Prospective Clients

Members and Candidates must:

1. Disclose to clients and prospective clients the basic format and general principles of the investment processes they use to analyze investments, select securities, and construct portfolios and must promptly disclose any changes that might materially affect those processes.
2. Disclose to clients and prospective clients significant limitations and risks associated with the investment process.
3. Use reasonable judgment in identifying which factors are important to their investment analyses, recommendations, or actions and include those factors in communications with clients and prospective clients.
4. Distinguish between fact and opinion in the presentation of investment analyses and recommendations.

All means and types of communication with clients are covered by this Standard, not just research reports or other written communications.

Members must distinguish between opinions and facts and always include the basic characteristics of the security being analyzed in a research report. Expectations based on statistical modeling and analysis are not facts.

Members must explain to clients and prospects the investment decision-making process used.

In preparing recommendations for structured securities, allocation strategies, or any other nontraditional investment, members must communicate those risk factors specific to such investments. In all cases, members should communicate the potential gains and losses on the investment clearly in terms of total returns.

Members must communicate significant changes in the risk characteristics of an investment or investment strategy.

Members must update clients regularly about any changes in the investment process, including any risks and limitations that have been newly identified.

When using projections from quantitative models and analysis, members may violate the Standard by not explaining the limitations of the model and the assumptions it uses, which provides a context for judging the uncertainty regarding the estimated investment result.

Members and candidates must inform clients about limitations inherent to an investment. Two examples of such limitations are liquidity and capacity. Liquidity refers to the ability to exit an investment readily without experiencing a significant extra cost from doing so. Capacity refers to an investment vehicle's ability to absorb additional investment without reducing the returns it is able to achieve.

Recommendations for Members

Selection of relevant factors in a report can be a judgment call so members should maintain records indicating the nature of the research, and be able to supply additional information if it is requested by the client or other users of the report.

Standard V(C) Record Retention

Members and Candidates must develop and maintain appropriate records to support their investment analyses, recommendations, actions, and other investment-related communications with clients and prospective clients.

Members must maintain research records that support the reasons for the analyst's conclusions and any investment actions taken. Such records are the property of the firm. All communications with clients through any medium, including emails and text messages, are records that must be retained.

A member who changes firms must re-create the analysis documentation supporting her recommendation using publicly available information or information obtained from the company and must not rely on memory or materials created at her previous firm.

Recommendations for Members

If no regulatory standards or firm policies are in place, the Standard recommends a seven-year minimum holding period.

Recommendations for Firms

This recordkeeping requirement generally is the firm's responsibility.

MODULE QUIZ 58.6, 58.7

To best evaluate your performance, enter your quiz answers online.

1. Connie Fletcher, CFA, works for a small money management firm that specializes in pension accounts. Recently, a friend asked her to act as an unpaid volunteer manager for the city's street sweep pension fund. As part of the position, the city would grant Fletcher a free parking space in front of her downtown office. Before Fletcher accepts, she should *most appropriately*:
   A. do nothing because this is a volunteer position.
   B. inform her current clients in writing and discuss the offer with her employer.
   C. disclose the details of the volunteer position to her employer and obtain written permission from her employer.

2. Sarah Johnson, a portfolio manager, is offered a bonus directly by a client if Johnson meets certain performance goals. To comply with the Standard that governs additional compensation arrangements, Johnson should:
   A. decline to accept a bonus outside of her compensation from her employer.
   B. disclose this arrangement to her employer in writing and obtain her employer's permission.
   C. disclose this arrangement to her employer only if she actually meets the performance goals and receives the bonus.
3. A member or candidate who has supervisory responsibility:
   A. should place particular emphasis on enforcing investment-related compliance policies.
   B. is responsible for instructing those to whom he has delegated authority about methods to detect and prevent violations of the law and the Code and Standards.
   C. has complied with the Standards if she reports employee violations to upper management and provides a written warning to the employee to cease such activities.
4. Which of the following actions is a *required*, rather than *recommended*, action under the Standard regarding diligence and a reasonable basis for a firm's research recommendations?
   A. Compensate analysts based on a measure of the quality of their research.
   B. Review the assumptions used and evaluate the objectivity of third-party research reports.
   C. Have a policy requiring that research reports and recommendations have a basis that can be substantiated as reasonable and adequate.
5. Claire Marlin, CFA, manages an investment fund specializing in foreign currency trading. Marlin writes a report to investors that describes the basic characteristics of her strategy, which is based on an expected appreciation of the euro relative to other major currencies. Marlin shows the projected returns from the strategy if the euro appreciates less than 5%, between 5% and 10%, or more than 10%, while clearly stating that these forecasts are her opinion. Has Marlin violated the Standard related to communication with clients?
   A. Yes, because she did not include a scenario in which the euro depreciates.
   B. No, because she disclosed the basic characteristics of the investment.
   C. No, because she distinguished fact from opinion and discussed how the strategy may perform under a range of scenarios.
6. If regulations do not specify how long to retain the documents that support an analyst's conclusions, the Code and Standards recommend a period of at least:
   A. 5 years.
   B. 7 years.
   C. 10 years.

Video covering this content is available online.

MODULE 58.8: GUIDANCE FOR STANDARD VI

STANDARD VI: CONFLICTS OF INTEREST

Standard VI(A) Disclosure of Conflicts

Members and Candidates must make full and fair disclosure of all matters that could reasonably be expected to impair their independence and objectivity or interfere with respective duties to their clients, prospective clients, and employer. Members and Candidates must ensure that such disclosures are prominent, are delivered in plain language, and communicate the relevant information effectively.

Members must fully disclose to clients, prospects, and their employers all actual and potential conflicts of interest in order to protect investors and employers. These disclosures must be clearly stated.

The requirement that all potential areas of conflict be disclosed allows clients and prospects to judge motives and potential biases for themselves. Disclosure of broker-dealer market-making activities would be included here. Board service is another area of potential conflict.

The most common conflict that requires disclosure is actual ownership of stock in companies that the member recommends or that clients hold.

Another common source of conflicts of interest is a member's compensation/bonus structure, which can potentially create incentives to take actions that produce immediate gains for the member with little or no concern for longer-term returns for the client. Such conflicts must be disclosed when the member is acting in an advisory capacity and must be updated in the case of significant change in compensation structure.

Members must give their employers enough information to judge the impact of a conflict, take reasonable steps to avoid conflicts, and report them promptly if they occur.

Recommendations for Members

Any special compensation arrangements, bonus programs, commissions, and incentives should be disclosed.

Standard VI(B) Priority of Transactions

Investment transactions for clients and employers must have priority over investment transactions in which a Member or Candidate is the beneficial owner.

Client transactions take priority over personal transactions and over transactions made on behalf of the member's firm. Personal transactions include situations where the member is a beneficial owner.

Personal transactions may be undertaken only after clients and the member's employer have had an adequate opportunity to act on a recommendation. Note that family member accounts that are client accounts should be treated just like any client account; they should not be disadvantaged.

Members must not act on information about pending trades for personal gain. The overriding considerations with respect to personal trades are that they do not disadvantage any clients.

When requested, members must fully disclose to investors their firm's personal trading policies.

Recommendations for Members

Members can avoid conflicts that arise with IPOs by not participating in them.

Members should encourage their firms to adopt the procedures listed in the following recommendations for firms if they have not done so.

Recommendations for Firms

All firms should have basic procedures in place that address conflicts created by personal investing. The following areas should be included:

- Establish limitations on employee participation in equity IPOs.
- Establish restrictions on participation in private placements. Strict limits should be placed on employee acquisition of these securities and proper supervisory procedures should be in place. Participation in these investments raises conflict of interest issues similar to those of IPOs.
- Establish blackout/restricted periods. Employees involved in investment decision-making should have blackout periods prior to trading for clients—no front running (i.e., purchase or sale of securities in advance of anticipated client or employer purchases and sales). The size of the firm and the type of security should help dictate how severe the blackout requirement should be.
- Establish reporting procedures, including duplicate trade confirmations, disclosure of personal holdings and beneficial ownership positions, and preclearance procedures.

Standard VI(C) Referral Fees

Members and Candidates must disclose to their employer, clients, and prospective clients, as appropriate, any compensation, consideration, or benefit received from or paid to others for the recommendation of products or services.

Members must inform employers, clients, and prospects of any benefit received for referrals of customers and clients, allowing them to evaluate the full cost of the service as well as any potential partiality. All types of consideration must be disclosed.

Recommendations for Members

Members should encourage their firms to adopt clear procedures regarding compensation for referrals.

Members should provide their employers with updates at least quarterly.

Recommendations for Firms

Firms that do not prohibit referral fees should have clear procedures for approval and policies regarding the nature and value of referral compensation received.

Video covering this content is available online.

MODULE 58.9: GUIDANCE FOR STANDARD VII

STANDARD VII: RESPONSIBILITIES AS A CFA INSTITUTE MEMBER OR CFA CANDIDATE

Standard VII(A) Conduct as Participants in CFA Institute Programs

Members and Candidates must not engage in any conduct that compromises the reputation or integrity of CFA Institute or the CFA designation or the integrity, validity, or security of CFA Institute programs.

Members must not engage in any activity that undermines the integrity of the CFA charter. This Standard applies to conduct that includes:

- Cheating on the CFA exam or any exam.
- Revealing anything about either broad or specific topics tested, content of exam questions, or formulas required or not required on the exam.
- Not following rules and policies of the CFA Program.
- Giving confidential information on the CFA Program to candidates or the public.
- Improperly using the designation to further personal and professional goals.
- Misrepresenting information on the Professional Conduct Statement (PCS) or the CFA Institute Professional Development Program.

Members and candidates are not precluded from expressing their opinions regarding the exam program or CFA Institute but must not reveal confidential information about the CFA Program.

Candidates who violate any of the CFA exam policies (e.g., calculator, personal belongings, Candidate Pledge) have violated Standard VII(A).

Members who volunteer in the CFA Program may not solicit or reveal information about questions considered for or included on a CFA exam, about the grading process, or about scoring of questions.

Standard VII(B) Reference to CFA Institute, the CFA Designation, and the CFA Program

When referring to CFA Institute, CFA Institute membership, the CFA designation, or candidacy in the CFA Program, Members and Candidates must not misrepresent or exaggerate the meaning or implications of membership in CFA Institute, holding the CFA designation, or candidacy in the CFA Program.

Members must not make promotional promises or guarantees tied to the CFA designation, such as over-promising individual competence or over-promising investment results in the future (i.e., higher performance, less risk, etc.).

Members must satisfy these requirements to maintain membership:

- Sign the PCS annually.
- Pay CFA Institute membership dues annually.

If they fail to do this, they are no longer active members.

Do not misrepresent or exaggerate the meaning of the CFA designation.

There is no partial CFA designation. It is acceptable to state that a candidate successfully completed the program in three years if, in fact, he did, but claiming superior ability because of this is not permitted.

Recommendations for Members

Members should be sure that their firms are aware of the proper references to a member's CFA designation or candidacy, as errors in these references are common.

MODULE QUIZ 58.8, 58.9

To best evaluate your performance, enter your quiz answers online.

1. Daniel Lyons, CFA, is an analyst who covers several stocks including Horizon Company. Lyons's aunt owns 30,000 shares of Horizon. She informs Lyons that she has created a trust in his name into which she has placed 2,000 shares of Horizon. The trust is structured so that Lyons will not be able to sell the shares until his aunt dies, but may vote the shares. Lyons is due to update his research coverage of Horizon next week. Lyons should *most appropriately*:
   A. update the report as usual because he is not a beneficial owner of the stock.
   B. advise his superiors that he is no longer able to issue research recommendations on Horizon.
   C. disclose the situation to his employer and, if then asked to prepare a report, also disclose his beneficial ownership of the shares in his report.
2. Kate Wilson, CFA, is an equity analyst. Wilson enters two transactions for her personal account. Wilson sells 500 shares of Tibon, Inc., a stock on which her firm currently has a "Buy" recommendation. Wilson buys 200 shares of Hayfield Co. and the following day issues a research report on Hayfield with a "Buy" recommendation. Has Wilson violated the Code and Standards?
   A. No.
   B. Yes, both of her actions violate the Code and Standards.
   C. Yes, but only one of her actions violates the Code and Standards.

3. Hern Investments provides monthly emerging market research to Baker Brokerage in exchange for prospective client referrals and European equity research from Baker. Clients and prospects of Hern are not made aware of the agreement, but clients unanimously rave about the high quality of the research provided by Baker. As a result of the research, many clients with nondiscretionary accounts have earned substantial returns on their portfolios. Managers at Hern have also used the research to earn outstanding returns for the firm's discretionary accounts. Hern has *most likely*:
   A. not violated the Code and Standards.
   B. violated the Code and Standards by using third-party research in discretionary accounts.
   C. violated the Code and Standards by failing to disclose the referral agreement with Baker.
4. After writing the Level I CFA exam, Cynthia White goes to internet discussion site *CFA Haven* to express her frustration. White writes, "CFA Institute is not doing a competent job of evaluating candidates because none of the questions in the June exam touched on Alternative Investments." White *most likely* violated the Standard related to conduct as a candidate in the CFA program by:
   A. publicly disputing CFA Institute policies and procedures.
   B. disclosing subject matter covered or not covered on a CFA exam.
   C. participating in an internet forum that is directed toward CFA Program participants.
5. After passing all three levels of the CFA exams on her first attempts and being awarded her CFA charter, Paula Osgood is promoting her new money management firm by issuing an advertisement. Which of these statements would *most likely* violate the Standard related to use of the CFA designation?
   A. "To earn the right to use the CFA designation, Paula passed three exams covering ethics, financial statement analysis, asset valuation, and portfolio management."
   B. "Paula passed three 6-hour exams on her first attempts and is a member of her local investment analyst society."
   C. "Because of her extensive training, Paula will be able to achieve better investment results than managers who have not been awarded the CFA designation."

ANSWER KEY FOR MODULE QUIZZES

Module Quiz 58.1, 58.2, 58.3

1. **C** To comply with Standard I(A) Knowledge of the Law, a member must always abide by the strictest applicable law, regulation, or standard. (Module 58.1, LOS 58.a, 58.b, 58.c)

2. **A** Gifts from clients are acceptable under Standard I(B) Independence and Objectivity, but the Standard requires members and candidates to disclose such gifts to their employers. Standard I(B) allows issuer-paid research as long as the analysis is thorough, independent, unbiased, and has a reasonable and adequate basis for its conclusions, and the compensation from the issuer is disclosed. Members and candidates should consider the potential for conflicts of interest inherent in credit ratings and may need to do independent research to evaluate the soundness of these ratings. (Module 58.1, LOS 58.a, 58.b, 58.c)

3. **C** According to Standard I(C) Misrepresentation, members and candidates must cite the sources of the information they use in their analysis, unless the information is factual data (as opposed to analysis or opinion) from a recognized financial or statistical reporting service. The U.S. Treasury is one example of a recognized source of factual data. (Module 58.2, LOS 58.a, 58.b, 58.c)

4. **B** Failing to act when required by one's professional obligations, such as neglecting to perform due diligence related to an investment recommendation, violates Standard I(D) Misconduct. Acts a member commits outside his professional capacity are misconduct if they reflect poorly on the member or candidate's honesty, integrity, or competence (e.g., theft or fraud).Violations of the law that do not reflect on the member or candidate's honesty, integrity, or competence (e.g., an act related to civil disobedience) are not necessarily regarded as misconduct. (Module 58.2, LOS 58.a, 58.b, 58.c)

5. **A** The statement from the CFO about the current quarter's earnings is material nonpublic information. Ingus violated Standard II(A) Material Nonpublic Information by acting or causing others to act on it. (Module 58.3, LOS 58.a, 58.b, 58.c)

6. **B** The intent of Green Brothers' actions is to manipulate the appearance of market liquidity in order to attract investment to its own funds. The increased trading activity was not based on market fundamentals or an actual trading strategy to benefit investors. It was merely an attempt to mislead market participants in order to increase assets under Green Brothers' management. The action violates Standard II(B) Market Manipulation. (Module 58.3, LOS 58.a, 58.b, 58.c)

Module Quiz 58.4, 58.5

1. **C** Standard III(A) Loyalty, Prudence, and Care specifies that for the manager of a pension or trust, the duty of loyalty is owed to the beneficiaries, not to the individuals who hired the manager. (Module 58.4, LOS 58.a, 58.b, 58.c)

2. **B** The firm must give its clients an opportunity to act on recommendation changes. Firms can offer different levels of service to clients as long as this is disclosed to all clients. The largest institutional clients would likely be paying higher fees for a greater level of service. The portfolio manager's brother's account should be treated the same as any other client account. (Module 58.4, LOS 58.a, 58.b, 58.c)

3. **A** According to Standard III(C) Suitability, a member or candidate who is in an advisory relationship with a client is responsible for analyzing the suitability of an investment for the client before taking investment action or making a recommendation. If a member or candidate believes an unsolicited trade is unsuitable for a client, the appropriate action is to discuss the trade with the client. The advisor may follow her firm's policies for obtaining client approval if the requested trade would not affect the risk and return of the client's portfolio materially. If the trade would have a material effect, the advisor should discuss with the client whether the IPS needs to be updated. When managing a fund to an index or stated mandate, the manager is responsible for ensuring that potential investments are consistent with the fund's mandate. Suitability for individuals would be a concern for an advisor who recommends the fund to clients, but not for the manager of the fund. (Module 58.5, LOS 58.a, 58.b, 58.c)

4. **C** Recommendations stated in Standard III(D) Performance Presentation include considering the sophistication and knowledge of the audience when presenting performance data. Other recommendations are to include terminated accounts in past performance history; to present the performance of a composite as a weighted average of the performance of similar portfolios, rather than using a single representative account; and to maintain the records and data that were used to calculate performance. (Module 58.5, LOS 58.a, 58.b, 58.c)

5. **B** Members and candidates are required to cooperate with PCP investigations into their own conduct and encouraged to cooperate with PCP investigations into the conduct of others. Sharing confidential information with the PCP is not a violation of Standard III(E) Preservation of Confidentiality. Any client information shared with the PCP will be kept in strict confidence. Standard III(E) states that members and candidates are required to maintain confidentiality of client records even after the end of the client relationship. (Module 58.5, LOS 58.a, 58.b, 58.c)

Module Quiz 58.6, 58.7

1. **C** According to Standard IV(A) Loyalty, members and candidates are expected to act for the benefit of their employer and not deprive the employer of their skills. Fletcher is performing work similar to the services that her employer provides. Although the position is a volunteer position, Fletcher will receive compensation in the form of a free parking space. In light of the circumstances, Fletcher must disclose the details of the position to her employer and get written permission before accepting the volunteer position. (Module 58.6, LOS 58.a, 58.b, 58.c)

2. **B** Johnson should disclose her additional compensation arrangement in writing to her employer and obtain her employer's written consent before accepting this offer, in accordance with Standard IV(B) Additional Compensation Arrangements. (Module 58.6, LOS 58.a, 58.b, 58.c)

3. **B** Members or candidates may delegate supervisory duties to subordinates but remain responsible for instructing them about how to detect and prevent violations. Reporting the violation and warning the employee are not sufficient to comply with Standard IV(C) Responsibilities of Supervisors. The supervisor must also take steps to prevent further violations while she conducts an investigation, such as limiting the employee's activity or increasing her monitoring of the employee. Supervisors should enforce investment-related and non-investment-related policies equally. (Module 58.6, LOS 58.a, 58.b, 58.c)

4. **B** Standard V(A) Diligence and Reasonable Basis requires analysts who use third-party research to review its assumptions and evaluate the independence and objectivity of the research. The other choices are recommended procedures for compliance with the Standard. (Module 58.7, LOS 58.a, 58.b, 58.c)

5. **A** Standard V(B) Communication with Clients and Prospective Clients requires that members and candidates communicate the risk associated with the investment strategy used and how the strategy is expected to perform in a range of scenarios. These scenarios should include those different from the current trend. Marlin should have discussed how her strategy would perform if the euro depreciates instead of appreciating as she expects. (Module 58.7, LOS 58.a, 58.b, 58.c)

6. **B** When no other regulatory guidance applies, Standard V(C) Record Retention recommends that records be maintained for a minimum of seven years. (Module 58.7, LOS 58.a, 58.b, 58.c)

Module Quiz 58.8, 58.9

1. **C** Even though the shares are held in trust, Lyons is considered a beneficial owner under Standard VI(A) Disclosure of Conflicts because he has a pecuniary interest in the shares and because has the power to vote the shares. Lyons is obligated to inform his employer of the potential conflict. If Lyons's employer permits him to continue issuing investment recommendations on the company, Lyons must disclose the existence of a potential conflict in his reports. (Module 58.8, LOS 58.a, 58.b, 58.c)

2. **C** Only one of these transactions is a violation. Standard VI(B) Priority of Transactions requires members and candidates to give clients an adequate opportunity to act on a recommendation before trading for accounts in which the member or candidate has a beneficial ownership interest. Members and candidates may trade for their own accounts as long as they do not disadvantage clients, benefit personally from client trades, or violate any regulations that apply. The Standard does not prohibit members and candidates from entering personal transactions that are contrary to what their firms are recommending for clients, as long as the transaction does not violate any of these criteria. (Module 58.8, LOS 58.a, 58.b, 58.c)

3. **C** According to Standard VI(C) Referral Fees, Hern must disclose the referral arrangement between itself and Baker so that potential clients can judge the true cost of Hern's services and assess whether there is any partiality inherent in the recommendation of services. (Module 58.8, LOS 58.a, 58.b, 58.c)

4. **B** Standard VII(A) Conduct as Participants in CFA Institute Programs prohibits candidates from revealing which portions of the Candidate Body of Knowledge were or were not covered on an exam. Members and candidates are free to disagree with the policies, procedures, or positions taken by the CFA Institute. The Standard does not prohibit participating in CFA Program-related internet blogs, forums, or social networks. (Module 58.9, LOS 58.a, 58.b, 58.c)

5. **C** Standard VII(B) Reference to CFA Institute, the CFA Designation, and the CFA Program prohibits members and candidates from implying superior performance as a result of being a CFA charterholder. Concise factual descriptions of the requirements to obtain the CFA charter are acceptable. Osgood's statement that she passed the exams on her first attempts is acceptable because it states a fact. (Module 58.9, LOS 58.a, 58.b, 58.c)

The following is a review of the Ethical and Professional Standards principles designed to address the learning outcome statements set forth by CFA Institute. Cross-Reference to CFA Institute Assigned Reading #59.

READING 59

Introduction to the Global Investment Performance Standards (GIPS)

Study Session 19

EXAM FOCUS

This topic review covers the key features of the Global Investment Performance Standards (GIPS) as adopted by CFA Institute in 1999 and subsequently updated. Compliance with GIPS is voluntary. For the Level I exam, you are responsible for the GIPS material included in the book of candidate readings for Level I and also for sections of the GIPS standards for firms that are referenced in the Level I material. The GIPS standards for firms are available on the CFA Institute website.

MODULE 59.1: INTRODUCTION TO GIPS

Video covering this content is available online.

LOS 59.a: Explain why the GIPS standards were created, what parties the GIPS standards apply to, and who is benefitted by the standards.

CFA® Program Curriculum, Volume 6, page 492

When firms choose their own methodologies for reporting investment performance, the results are not comparable across firms, and firms have a tendency to choose a methodology that makes their performance look good. Some choices that tend to bias results are:

- Choosing a top-performing portfolio and claiming it represents a firm's overall results for all assets managed.
- Excluding terminated accounts, which may tend to be accounts closed by investors due to sub-par performance.
- Selecting time periods to report that put firm performance in the best possible light.

GIPS present a standardized methodology for performance reporting that makes comparison of performance across firms meaningful, provides specific information that is useful to both current and prospective clients, and avoids misrepresentation of performance. Widespread usage of GIPS can also give oversight bodies a clearer understanding of the returns achieved and the risks taken by the firms they supervise.

GIPS only apply to firms that actually manage assets. Presenting performance information compliant with GIPS is voluntary for such firms, and they may only claim compliance with GIPS if they comply fully and on a firmwide basis. Other firms related to the asset management business, such as software developers, may state that they endorse GIPS but may not claim compliance with GIPS.

LOS 59.b: Describe the key concepts of the GIPS standards for firms.

CFA® Program Curriculum, Volume 6, page 492

The GIPS standards for firms consist of eight sections:

1. *Fundamentals of Compliance.* The fundamental issues involved in complying with GIPS are (a) defining the firm, (b) providing GIPS-compliant reports to all clients and prospects, (c) complying with applicable regulations and laws, and (d) presenting information that is neither false nor misleading.
2. *Input Data and Calculation Methodology.* Input data should be consistent in order to establish full, fair, and comparable investment performance presentations. Certain methodologies are required for portfolio return calculations, and certain other methodologies are required for composite return calculations. Uniformity in methods across firms is required so that their results are comparable.
3. *Composite and Pooled Fund Maintenance*. Creation of meaningful, asset-weighted composites is important to achieve a fair presentation. Composite performance is based on the performance of one or more portfolios that have the same investment strategy or investment objective. Composite returns are the asset-weighted average (not a simple average) of the returns on the portfolios that are included in each composite. Pooled funds must be included in a composite if they fit its definition.
4. *Composite Time-Weighted Return Report.*
5. *Composite Money-Weighted Return Report.*
6. *Pooled Fund Time-Weighted Return Report.*
7. *Pooled Fund Money-Weighted Return Report.*

   Sections 4 through 7 contain required and recommended procedures for reporting the performance of composites and pooled funds, as well as the necessary disclosures. There are some disclosures that all firms must make, but some disclosures may not apply to all firms. If a disclosure is not applicable to a specific firm, the firm is not required to include any statement regarding it. A firm that has met all the requirements of GIPS may include an appropriate claim of compliance.

8. *GIPS Advertising Guidelines*. If an advertisement includes a claim of compliance with GIPS, the advertisement must comply with these guidelines. The guidelines do not apply to advertisements that do not reference the firm's GIPS compliance.

LOS 59.c: Explain the purpose of composites in performance reporting.

CFA® Program Curriculum, Volume 6, page 494

A **composite** is a grouping of individual discretionary portfolios representing a similar investment strategy, objective, or mandate. Examples of possible composites are large capitalization stocks, investment-grade domestic bonds, and accounts managed to match the performance of a specific securities index. Reporting on the performance of composites gives clients and prospects information about the firm's success in managing various types of securities and results for various investment styles.

A composite, such as international equities, must include all fee-paying, discretionary portfolios (current and past) that the firm has managed in accordance with a particular strategy. The firm should identify which composite each managed portfolio is to be included in before the portfolio's performance is known. This prevents firms from choosing portfolios to include in a composite in order to create composites with superior returns. All discretionary portfolios must be included in one, and only one, composite.

LOS 59.d: Describe the fundamentals of compliance, including the recommendations of the GIPS standards with respect to the definition of the firm and the firm's definition of discretion.

CFA® Program Curriculum, Volume 6, page 494

The definition of the firm, for purposes of GIPS compliance, must be the corporation, subsidiary, or division that is held out to clients as a business entity. If a firm has different geographic locations (e.g., all doing business under the name of Bluestone Advisers), then the definition of the firm should include all the various geographic locations and their clients.

The definition of **discretion** refers to how a firm determines which of the portfolios it manages should be included in a composite. A firm may determine that a portfolio is nondiscretionary—and therefore not include it in a composite—if the client places restrictions on it that prevent the manager from carrying out the intended strategy.

LOS 59.e: Describe the concept of independent verification.

CFA® Program Curriculum, Volume 6, page 495

Firms are *encouraged* to pursue independent verification of their compliance with GIPS. Verification applies to the entire firm's performance measurement practices and methods, not a selected composite.

Reading 59

If a firm chooses to pursue verification, it must be performed by a third party, not by the firm itself, on a firmwide basis. This third-party verifier must attest that (1) the firm has complied with all GIPS requirements for composite construction on a firmwide basis and (2) the firm's processes and procedures are established to present performance in accordance with the calculation methodology required by GIPS, the data requirements of GIPS, and in the format required by GIPS.

Verified firms should include the following disclosure language:

> [Insert name of firm] has been verified for the periods [insert dates] by [name of verifier]. A copy of the verification report is available upon request.

MODULE QUIZ 59.1

To best evaluate your performance, enter your quiz answers online.

1. Which of the following statements *most accurately* describes the parties that GIPS are intended to apply to and serve?
   A. GIPS apply to consultants who serve their existing and prospective clients.
   B. GIPS apply to firms that issue securities and serve investment management firms.
   C. GIPS apply to investment management firms and serve their existing and prospective clients.
2. For a composite to be constructed in compliance with GIPS, the portfolios included in the composite must:
   A. have been managed by the firm for the full performance-reporting period.
   B. be selected immediately after the last business day of the period for which the composite's performance will be presented.
   C. include all fee-paying, discretionary portfolios that are managed according to the same strategy, mandate, or investment objective.
3. Verification of compliance with GIPS:
   A. may be performed on single composites.
   B. is required for a firm to claim GIPS compliance.
   C. requires the verification report to be issued for the entire firm.

KEY CONCEPTS

LOS 59.a

GIPS are principles that investment firms can voluntarily follow. They are designed to avoid misrepresentations of historical investment results to clients and prospects. GIPS allow clients to more easily compare investment performance among investment firms and have more confidence in reported performance.

LOS 59.b

The eight sections of the GIPS standards for firms are:

1. Fundamentals of Compliance.
2. Input Data and Calculation Methodology.
3. Composite and Pooled Fund Maintenance.
4. Composite Time-Weighted Return Report.
5. Composite Money-Weighted Return Report.
6. Pooled Fund Time-Weighted Return Report.
7. Pooled Fund Money-Weighted Return Report.
8. GIPS Advertising Guidelines.

LOS 59.c

A composite is a grouping of discretionary portfolios representing a similar investment strategy, objective, or mandate. A composite must include all portfolios (current and past) that the firm has managed in accordance with this particular strategy. The firm should identify which composite each managed portfolio is to be included in before the portfolio's performance is known.

LOS 59.d

GIPS compliance must be firmwide, where the *firm* is the distinct business entity that is held out to clients and prospects.

A firm must establish criteria to determine which of the portfolios it manages are discretionary or nondiscretionary.

LOS 59.e

Firms are encouraged to pursue independent verification of GIPS compliance. If they seek verification, it must be performed by a third party, not by the firm itself. The third-party verifier must attest that (1) the firm has complied with all GIPS requirements for composite construction on a firmwide basis and (2) the firm's processes and procedures are established to present performance in accordance with the calculation methodology required by GIPS, the data requirements of GIPS, and in the format required by GIPS.

ANSWER KEY FOR MODULE QUIZZES

Module Quiz 59.1

1. **C** GIPS apply to investment management firms. They are intended to serve prospective and existing clients of investment management firms and consultants who advise these clients. (LOS 59.a)

2. **C** To comply with GIPS, a composite must include all fee-paying, discretionary portfolios managed according to the same investment objective, strategy, or mandate. The composite or composites in which a portfolio will be included must be determined on an ex ante basis (i.e., before the period for which the composite's performance will be calculated). A GIPS-compliant composite must include terminated accounts. (LOS 59.c)

3. **C** Verification of GIPS compliance is optional, but if a firm chooses to seek third-party verification, the report must be issued with respect to the whole firm. GIPS verification cannot be carried out for a single composite. (LOS 59.e)

The following is a review of the Ethical and Professional Standards principles designed to address the learning outcome statements set forth by CFA Institute. Cross-Reference to CFA Institute Assigned Reading #60.

READING 60

Ethics Application

Study Session 19

EXAM FOCUS

In this topic review, we cover key points about applying the Standards, drawn from cases illustrating their application included in the *Ethics in Investment Management Casebook* (CFA Institute, 2019). While this provides a suitable review, just as we do for the *Standards of Practice Handbook*, we strongly suggest that you read the complete coverage of these cases in the Level I CFA Curriculum, Volume 6 (at least once). Studying the full cases will help candidates understand how irrelevant points and unfounded justifications for a member's actions can be used to distract from the essence of violations of the Standards.

MODULE 60.1: ETHICS APPLICATION

Video covering this content is available online.

LOS 60.a: Evaluate practices, policies, and conduct relative to the CFA Institute Code of Ethics and Standards of Professional Conduct.

LOS 60.b: Explain how the practices, policies, and conduct do or do not violate the CFA Institute Code of Ethics and Standards of Professional Conduct.

CFA® Program Curriculum, Volume 6, page 499

Standard I: Professionalism

Standard I(A) Knowledge of the Law

Case 1: A member reports to his supervisor that their firm is overcharging clients by seeking to recover the cost of expenses that are actually reimbursable. The actions taken only remedy the situation for some clients but not for others. The member must disassociate from the activity and not work with any clients who are still being overcharged.

Case 2: A member violates the Standard by failing to investigate transactions in an account that appear to be at high risk of violating money-laundering laws (because it was a long-standing client who has relationships with board members).

Case 3: A member violates the Standards (and the law) by forging customer signatures for expediency.

Standard I(B) Independence and Objectivity

Case 1: A member violates the Standard by contributing to a politician's campaign, believing that it may lead to preferential treatment with regard to receiving management contracts for government pension fund money.

Standard I(C) Misrepresentation

Case 1: A member violates the Standard by assuring a client that returns on a fund will outweigh the penalties incurred from shifting funds from an existing investment, essentially guaranteeing a specific rate of return on an investment that has no actual guarantee of returns.

Case 2: A proposal to manage pension assets lists all personnel and their qualifications, but while the proposal is under consideration, one of the key personnel leaves the firm. The member is required to inform the potential client of this personnel change (misrepresentation by omission).

Case 3: A member who is the CEO of an electric car company posts on social media that private financing has been secured to take the company private at $420 per share when that is untrue and the member admits the price "was a joke." This is clearly a violation of the Standard regarding misrepresentation.

Standard I(D) Misconduct

Case 1: A member is arrested for minor criminal offenses that are part of civil disobedience related to protesting and expressing her personal beliefs. This is not necessarily a violation of the Standard regarding misconduct, which states in part that members are prohibited from "engaging in any professional conduct involving dishonesty, fraud, or deceit" or committing an act that "reflects adversely on their professional reputation, integrity, or competence."

Case 2: A member violates the Standard by using his firm's error-correction policy to effectively give his own money to a client account in order to make his management of the account look better.

Standard II: Integrity of Capital Markets

Standard II(A) Material Nonpublic Information

Case 1: A member violates the Standard by using material nonpublic information he acquired by overhearing a friend's phone conversation and inferring that a takeover offer for a specific company was imminent.

Case 2: A member violates the Standard by sharing information with clients about a regulator's positive response to trials of a company's new drug that he learned of during a meeting of analysts with company management. The information is considered nonpublic because sharing it with a specific group of analysts was "selective sharing" of the information and cannot be considered public disclosure.

Standard II(B) Market Manipulation

Case 1: A member violates the Standard by fraudulently including the names of people who do not actually own shares to meet the minimum required number of shareholders for a firm to be listed on an exchange, misleading market participants about the potential liquidity of the shares.

Standard III: Duties to Clients

Standard III(A) Loyalty, Prudence, and Care

Case 1: A member violates the Standard by putting a policy into an investment firm's client agreements that indicates that their representatives are excused in some cases from acting in a client's best interest or failing to adequately investigate suitability of recommendations to clients, and that clients' rights to make claims for violating securities laws are restricted. Members and candidates cannot "opt out" of the Standards.

Case 2: A member executes trades for a client who self-directs their own account and has received the firm's policies regarding margin requirements. In this case, the member's requirements to act in the client's best interests are limited, compared with a relationship in which the member is providing investment advice. There is no intent to limit the member's responsibilities to act in good faith and not misrepresent the services to be provided according to firm policies. The terms regarding the firm's actions in the event of a margin shortfall are open to negotiation at the inception of the relationship.

Case 3: A member allocates expenses to a client that arise from actions designed to reduce total expenses (staying over a weekend to reduce transportation costs but increasing lodging costs). This is not a violation, but charging a client for expenses that benefit other clients or that are for personal activities of the member is.

Standard III(B) Fair Dealing

Case 1: A member treats clients fairly by simultaneously sending emails regarding a change in investment recommendation. Providing individual clients with updates or clarifications regarding the change in recommendation is not a violation. Further, the member's firm offers some clients, for an additional fee, weekly updates about securities that may indicate a change in recommendation may be forthcoming. This is not a violation as long as clients are all informed about the availability of the weekly updates for a fee and as long as no change in recommendation is included in a weekly update that would disadvantage clients who do not subscribe to the additional service.

Standard III(C) Suitability

Case 1: A member violates the Standard by recommending investments that carry more risk than is suitable for some clients, even though there are tax advantages to the recommended portfolios.

Case 2: A member violates the Standard by making a client-requested change to their portfolio without investigating the client circumstances adequately to determine whether the requested investment is suitable for the clients.

Standard III(D) Performance Presentation

Case 1: A member violates the Standard by presenting performance data based on a composite of separately managed accounts the firm managed before creating the fund that is being reported, giving the impression that the fund has been in existence for many years when, in fact, it is relatively new.

Standard III(E) Preservation of Confidentiality

Case 1: Member A downloads clients' personally identifiable information to his personal server at home to make working from home easier and gets hacked. The member has violated the Standard by not taking adequate steps to protect client information. Member B, who is the firm's head of compliance, likely violated the Standard by not taking the proper steps to protect client information, as evidenced by the fact that Member A was able to download sensitive client information to his personal server.

Standard IV: Duties to Employers

Standard IV(A) Loyalty

Case 1: A member violates the Standard by making harmful statements about Firm A, her current employer, and promoting the firm that she intends to move to while she is still employed by Firm A.

Case 2: A member is pressured by his firm to sell the firm's proprietary investment products that are relatively expensive and haven't performed well. He has complained to management, and they have done nothing. He copies client records and he records conversations with his supervisor to document his conduct. He takes this information to securities regulators. His actions are not a violation of the Standard because he is acting in the interest of his clients.

Case 3: A member violates the Standard by taking client information with her when she leaves her firm; the client list is the property of her current firm. Although she only intends to send her clients thank-you notes, the client list she copied has personal information.

Standard IV(B) Additional Compensation Arrangements

Case 1: A member works for a firm that produces issuer-paid research reports and is involved with the decision of which companies her firm will cover. Some companies seeking coverage by the firm offer her a bonus payment if their firm is selected. Because this creates a possible conflict between her interests and her firm's interests, she must get approval in writing from her employer to accept the bonus arrangement.

Standard IV(C) Responsibilities of Supervisors

Case 1: A member with supervisory responsibility over a branch office violates the Standard by not making reasonable efforts to ensure that those under his supervision are not engaging in misconduct. He also violates the Standard by not having clear written compliance policies and procedures in place, along with employee training. If these are not in place, he must decline to take supervisory responsibility.

Case 2: A member violates the Standard by accepting the title of chief compliance officer even though she has no experience in compliance, is denied permission to contact clients or review client communications, and is not allowed to enforce company policies. She is in violation of the Standard because it requires her to make reasonable efforts to both detect and prevent violations of laws, rules, and regulations by those subject to her supervision. Knowing she could not do this, she should have declined to take on supervisory responsibilities.

Standard V: Investment Analysis, Recommendations, and Actions

Standard V(A) Diligence and Reasonable Basis

Case 1: A member violates the Standard by recommending the purchase of shares of a company for which he has not performed a diligent, thorough, and independent analysis. A second member bases her recommendation on the analysis of the first member and incorporates part of the first member's research report in her own and is thereby also in violation of the Standards.

Standard V(B) Communication With Clients and Prospective Clients

Case 1: A member's firm begins calculating client fees using different methods from those spelled out in the disclosures made to them when they opened their accounts. The member is required by the Standard to inform clients that the fee calculation methods have changed, prior to changing the methods, even if fees are not higher overall using the new processes.

Case 2: A credit rating agency changes its methodology of determining the ratings of commercial mortgage-backed securities without disclosing the change to potential users of the ratings. A member who is responsible for publishing the ratings violates the Standard by publishing ratings without disclosing the change in methodology.

Standard V(C) Record Retention

Case 1: A member violates the Standard by not updating client records in a timely manner. Although he keeps himself updated on changes in client circumstances and adjusts portfolios accordingly, he does not do a good job of keeping written client profiles up to date.

Standard VI: Conflicts of Interest

Standard VI(A) Disclosure of Conflicts

Case 1: A member receives payment from third-party subadvisors that she uses to manage client funds invested in some asset classes. To avoid violating the Standard, she must disclose these arrangements to clients because the payments may influence her choice of subadvisors.

Standard VI(B) Priority of Transactions

Case 1: A member violates the Standard by buying shares and call options in his personal account just prior to purchasing large blocks of the same stocks in client accounts (front-running the trades), in anticipation of an increase in the price of the stocks as a result of the large purchases.

Case 2: A member violates the Standard by telling friends and relatives about large buy orders he is to execute for clients of his employer prior to executing those orders, allowing them to front-run those trades for quick profits.

Case 3: A member enters client trades grouped as block orders and allocates them to specific client accounts after the market closes for the day. The member violates the Standard (and likely the Standard on fair dealing as well) by allocating profitable trades to personal accounts and allocating a disproportionate amount of losing trades to his largest client accounts where they will likely go unnoticed.

Standard VI(C) Referral Fees

Case 1: A member invites existing clients who have referred very profitable accounts to her to lavish parties, rewarding them with discounts on fees and gift cards as well. The member violates the Standard by not disclosing these "referral fees" to all existing clients and prospective clients.

Standard VII: Responsibilities as a CFA Institute Member or CFA Candidate

Standard VII(A) Conduct as Participants in CFA Institute Programs

Case 1: A member who teaches exam-prep classes hosts a post-exam party for candidates who took the exam. He solicits their general impressions about the difficulty of the exam and their opinions on the most difficult exam questions. He is permitted to share their opinions about the difficulty of the exam with future candidates in his exam-prep classes. However, he is not permitted to solicit or share any information about specific exam questions or about which topics were or were not tested on the exam.

Standard VII(B) Reference to CFA Institute, the CFA Designation, and the CFA Program

Case 1: A previous member who has not paid her dues to CFA Institute violates the Standard by using the CFA designation in marketing materials and on her business cards. Another member violates the Standard by claiming that all senior employees, which includes the member who has not paid her dues, are CFA charterholders.

MODULE QUIZ 60.1

To best evaluate your performance, enter your quiz answers online.

1. Karen Jones, CFA, is an outside director for Valley Manufacturing. At a director's meeting, Jones finds out that Valley Corp. has made several contributions to foreign politicians that she suspects were illegal. Jones checks with her firm's legal counsel and determines that the contributions were indeed illegal. At the next board meeting, Jones urges the board to disclose the contributions. The board, however, votes not to make a disclosure. Jones's *most appropriate* action would be to:
   A. protest the board's actions in writing to the executive officer of Valley.
   B. resign from the board and seek legal counsel as to her legal disclosure requirements.
   C. inform her supervisor of her discovery and cease attending meetings until the matter is resolved.

2. Beth Bixby, CFA, uses a quantitative model to actively manage a portfolio of stocks with an objective of earning a greater return than the market. Over the last three years, the returns to a portfolio constructed using the model have been greater than the returns to the S&P Index by between 2% and 4%. In promotional materials, Bixby states, "Through our complex quantitative approach, we select a portfolio that has similar risk to the S&P 500 Index but will receive a return between 2% and 4% greater than the index." This statement is:
   A. permissible because prior returns to the firm's model provide a reasonable and adequate basis for the promotional material.
   B. permissible because the statement describes the basic characteristics of the fund's risk and return objectives.
   C. not permissible because Bixby is misrepresenting the investment performance her firm can reasonably expect to achieve.
3. Over the past two days, Lorraine Quigley, CFA, manager of a hedge fund, has been purchasing large quantities of Craeger Industrial Products' common stock while at the same time shorting put options on the same stock. Quigley did not notify her clients of the trades, although they are aware of the fund's general strategy to generate returns. Which of the following statements is *most likely* correct?
   A. Quigley did not violate the Code and Standards.
   B. Quigley violated the Code and Standards by manipulating the prices of publicly traded securities.
   C. Quigley violated the Code and Standards by failing to disclose the transactions to clients before they occurred.
4. Julia Green, CFA, has friends from her previous employer who have suggested that she receive information from them via an internet chat room. In this way, she receives news about an exciting new product being developed by a firm in Singapore that has the potential to double the firm's revenue. The firm has not revealed any information regarding the product to the public. According to the Code and Standards, this information is:
   A. both material and nonpublic, and Green may not trade on it in Singapore but may trade on it elsewhere.
   B. both material and nonpublic and Green may not trade on it in any jurisdiction.
   C. public by virtue of its release in the chat room and Green may trade on it.

5. Melvin Byrne, CFA, manages a portfolio for James Martin, a very wealthy client. Martin's portfolio is well diversified with a slight tilt toward capital appreciation. Martin requires very little income from the portfolio. Recently, Martin's brother Cliff has become a client of Byrne. Byrne proceeds to invest Cliff's portfolio in a similar manner to James's portfolio based on the fact that both brothers have a similar lifestyle and are only two years apart in age. Which of the following statements is *most accurate*?
   A. Byrne violated the Code and Standards by knowingly creating a conflict between the interests of James's and Cliff's portfolios.
   B. Byrne violated the Code and Standards by failing to determine Cliff's objectives and constraints prior to investing his portfolio.
   C. Byrne violated the Code and Standards by failing to have a reasonable and adequate basis for Cliff's portfolio allocation.

6. Beth Anderson, CFA, is a portfolio manager for several wealthy clients, including Reuben Carlyle. Anderson manages Carlyle's personal portfolio of stock and bond investments. Carlyle recently told Anderson that he is under investigation by the IRS for tax evasion related to his business, Carlyle Concrete (CC). After learning about the investigation, Anderson proceeds to inform a friend at a local investment bank so that they may withdraw their proposal to take CC public. Which of the following is *most likely* correct?
   A. Anderson violated the Code and Standards by failing to maintain the confidentiality of her client's information.
   B. Anderson violated the Code and Standards by failing to detect and report the tax evasion to the proper authorities.
   C. Anderson did not violate the Code and Standards because the information she conveyed pertained to illegal activities on the part of her client.

7. Robert Blair, CFA, director of research, has had an ongoing battle with management about the adequacy of the firm's compliance system. Recently, it has come to Blair's attention that the firm's compliance procedures are inadequate in that they are not being monitored or carefully followed. What should Blair *most appropriately* do?
   A. Resign from the firm unless the compliance system is strengthened and followed.
   B. Send his superior a memo outlining the problem.
   C. Decline in writing to continue to accept supervisory responsibility until reasonable compliance procedures are adopted.

8. Eugene Nieder, CFA, has just accepted a new job as a quantitative analyst for Paschal Investments, LLP. Nieder developed a complex model while working for his previous employer and plans to recreate the model for Paschal. Nieder did not make copies of the model or any supporting documents because his employer refused to grant him permission to do so. Nieder will recreate the model from memory. Which of the following statements is *most likely* correct?
   A. Nieder can recreate the model without violating the Code and Standards as long as he also generates supporting documentation.
   B. Nieder can recreate the model without violating the Code and Standards without documentation if the model is modified from its original form.
   C. Nieder cannot recreate the model without violating the Code and Standards because it is the property of his former employer.

Reading 60

9. Fred Johnson, CFA, a financial analyst and avid windsurfer, has begun an investment survey of the water sports leisure industry. His brother sells windsurfing gear in Tampa and tells him that Swordfish9 is the "hottest windsurfing rig on the market and will be highly profitable for Swordfish Enterprises." Johnson had never heard of Swordfish9 previously, but after testing the board himself became very excited about the Swordfish9 and issued an investment recommendation of "buy" on Swordfish Enterprises. As a result of issuing the recommendation, Johnson has:
   A. not violated the Code and Standards.
   B. violated the Code and Standards by failing to establish a reasonable and adequate basis.
   C. violated the Code and Standards by failing to consider the suitability of the investment for his clients.

10. Neiman Investment Co. receives brokerage business from Pick Asset Management in exchange for referring prospective clients to Pick. Pick advises clients—in writing, at the time the relationship is established—of the nature of its arrangement with Neiman. With regard to this practice, Pick has:
   A. complied with the Code and Standards.
   B. violated the Code and Standards by failing to preserve the confidentiality of the agreement with Neiman.
   C. violated the Code and Standards by inappropriately negotiating an agreement that creates a conflict of interest.

11. After sitting for the Level I CFA exam, Cynthia White visits CFA Haven, an online forum, to express her frustration. White writes, "CFA Institute is not doing a competent job of evaluating candidates, because none of the questions in the June exam touched on Alternative Investments." Regarding the CFA Institute Standards of Professional Conduct, White *most likely*:
   A. did not violate any Standard, because she was exercising her right to freedom of speech.
   B. violated the Standards by discussing exam content.
   C. violated the Standards by impugning the reputation of CFA Institute.

ANSWER KEY FOR MODULE QUIZZES

Module Quiz 60.1

1. **B** According to Standard I(A) Knowledge of the Law, because she has taken steps to stop the illegal activities and the board has ignored her, Jones must dissociate from the board and seek legal advice as to what other actions would be appropriate in this instance. She may need to inform legal or regulatory authorities of the illegal activities. (LOS 60.a, 60.b)

2. **C** There can be no assurance that a premium of 2% to 4% will consistently be obtained. Bixby is in violation of Standard I(C) Misrepresentation, because she has made an implicit guarantee of the fund's expected performance. (LOS 60.a, 60.b)

3. **A** Quigley's trades are most likely an attempt to take advantage of an arbitrage opportunity that exists between Craeger's common stock and its put options. She is not manipulating the prices of securities in an attempt to mislead market participants, which would violate Standard II(B) Market Manipulation. She is pursuing a legitimate investment strategy. Participants in her hedge fund are aware of the fund's investment strategy, and thus, Quigley did not violate the Code and Standards by not disclosing this specific set of trades in advance of trading. (LOS 60.a, 60.b)

4. **B** The release of such information to a limited circle via an internet chat room does not cause the information to be public. The information is also clearly material. Therefore, Green is not allowed to trade on the information under Standard II(A) Material Nonpublic Information. (LOS 60.a, 60.b)

5. **B** Standard III(C) Suitability requires that before taking investment action, members and candidates must make a reasonable inquiry into a client's or prospect's investment objectives and constraints, as well as their prior investment experience. Byrne cannot assume that because the brothers have similar lifestyles and are close in age that they should have similarly managed portfolios. Byrne should have interviewed Cliff directly before investing his portfolio. (LOS 60.a, 60.b)

6. **A** Standard III(E) Preservation of Confidentiality requires Anderson to maintain the confidentiality of client information. Confidentiality may be broken in instances involving illegal activities on the part of the client, but the client's information may only be relayed to proper authorities. Anderson did not have the right to inform the investment bank of her client's investigation. (LOS 60.a, 60.b)

7. **C** According to Standard IV(C) Responsibilities of Supervisors, because he is aware that the firm's compliance procedures are not being monitored and followed and because he has repeatedly tried to get company management to correct the situation, Blair should decline supervisory responsibility until adequate procedures to detect and prevent violations of laws, regulations, and the Code and Standards are adopted and followed. If he does not do so, he will be in violation of the Code and Standards. (LOS 60.a, 60.b)

8. **A** Nieder must not take models or documents from his previous employer without explicit permission to do so, or he would violate Standard IV(A) Loyalty. He is allowed to reproduce the model from memory but must recreate the supporting documentation to maintain compliance with Standard V(C) Record Retention. (LOS 60.a, 60.b)

9. **B** Johnson has apparently let his recreational passion cloud his judgment. This is not to say that Swordfish Enterprises is not or will not be an excellent investment. However, if he had never heard of the firm previously, issuing an investment recommendation without conducting a thorough financial investigation indicates a failure to exercise diligence and also indicates that he lacks a reasonable and adequate basis for his recommendation. He is in violation of Standard V(A) Diligence and Reasonable Basis. (LOS 60.a, 60.b)

10. **A** There is no violation of the Standards regarding this matter. The referral arrangement is fully disclosed to clients before they agree to do business with Pick. Therefore, clients can fully assess the effect of the agreement on the referral and how the agreement may affect their accounts before hiring Pick as their asset manager. (LOS 60.a, 60.b)

11. **B** Standard VII(A) Conduct as Participants in the CFA Programs prohibits candidates from revealing which portions of the Candidate Body of Knowledge were or were not covered on an exam. Members and candidates are free to disagree with the policies, procedures, or positions taken by the CFA Institute and express their opinion on such policies, procedures, and positions. (LOS 60.a, 60.b)

TOPIC QUIZ: ETHICAL AND PROFESSIONAL STANDARDS

You have now finished the Ethical and Professional Standards topic section. Please log into your Schweser online dashboard and take the Topic Quiz on Ethical and Professional Standards. The Topic Quiz provides immediate feedback on how effective your study has been for this material. The number of questions on this quiz is approximately the number of questions for the topic on one-half of the actual Level I CFA exam. Questions are more exam-like than typical Module Quiz or QBank questions; a score of less than 70% indicates that your study likely needs improvement. These tests are best taken timed; allow 1.5 minutes per question.

After you've completed this Topic Quiz, select "Performance Tracker" to view a breakdown of your score. Select "Compare with Others" to display how your score on the Topic Quiz compares with the scores of others who entered their answers.

FORMULAS

$$\text{holding period return} = \frac{\text{end-of-period value}}{\text{beginning-of-period value}} - 1$$

$$= \frac{P_t + Div_t}{P_0} - 1 = \frac{P_t - P_0 + Div_t}{P_0}$$

$$\text{arithmetic mean return} = \frac{(R_1 + R_2 + R_3 + \ldots + R_n)}{n}$$

$$\text{geometric mean return} = \sqrt[n]{(1 + R_1) \times (1 + R_2) \times (1 + R_3) \times \ldots \times (1 + R_n)} - 1$$

$$\text{correlation: } \rho_{1,2} = \frac{Cov_{1,2}}{\sigma_1 \times \sigma_2}$$

standard deviation for a two-asset portfolio:

$$\sigma_p = \sqrt{w_1^2\sigma_1^2 + w_2^2\sigma_2^2 + 2w_1w_2\sigma_1\sigma_2\rho_{1,2}} \text{ or } \sqrt{w_1^2\sigma_1^2 + w_2^2\sigma_2^2 + 2w_1w_2Cov_{1,2}}$$

$$\text{equation of the CML: } E(R_P) = R_f + \left(\frac{E(R_M) - R_f}{\sigma_M}\right)\sigma_P$$

$$E(R_P) = R_f + \left(E(R_M) - R_f\right)\left(\frac{\sigma_P}{\sigma_M}\right)$$

total risk = systematic risk + unsystematic risk

$$\beta_i = \frac{Cov_{i,mkt}}{\sigma_{mkt}^2} = \rho_{i,mkt}\frac{\sigma_i}{\sigma_{mkt}}$$

capital asset pricing model (CAPM): $E(R_i) = R_f + \beta_i[E(R_{mkt}) - R_f]$

$$\text{Sharpe ratio} = \left(\frac{R_P - R_f}{\sigma_P}\right)$$

$$\text{M-squared} = (R_P - R_f)\frac{\sigma_M}{\sigma_P} - (R_M - R_f)$$

$$\text{Treynor measure} = \frac{R_P - R_f}{\beta_P}$$

Jensen's alpha = $\alpha_P = R_P - [R_f + \beta_P(R_M - R_f)]$

INDEX

Notes

Notes